CONTEMPORARY POLITICAL STUDIES

Race and Politics in Britain

by

Shamit Saggar

New York London Toronto Sydney Tokyo Singapore

To my uncle, Braham Dev Saggar

First published 1992 by
Campus 400, Marylands Avenue
Hemel Hempstead
Hertfordshire, HP2 7EZ
A division of
Simon & Schuster International Group

© 1992 Shamit Saggar

All rights reserved. No part of this publication may be reproduced, stored in a retrieval system, or transmitted, in any form or by any means, electronic, mechanical, photocopying, recording or otherwise, without the prior permission, in writing, from the publisher.

Typeset in 10/12pt Times by
Inforum Typesetting, Portsmouth

Printed and bound in Great Britain by
Biddles Ltd, Guildford and King's Lynn

British Library Cataloguing in Publication Data

Saggar, Shamit
Race and politics in Britain. – (Contemporary political studies)
I. Title II. Series
305.800941

ISBN 0–7450–1205–1
ISBN 0–7450–1206–X pbk

2 3 4 5 96 95 94 93 92

The C… ter Library

…ice …nd Politics in Britain

LEEDS BECKETT UNIVERSITY
LIBRARY
…DED

CONTEMPORARY POLITICAL STUDIES

Series Editor: John Benyon, *Director, Centre for the Study of Public Order, University of Leicester*

A series which provides authorative, yet concise introductory accounts of key topics in contemporary political studies.

Other titles in the series include:

Elections and Voting Behaviour in Britain
DAVID DENVER, *University of Lancaster*

Pressure Groups, Politics and Democracy in Britain
WYN GRANT, *University of Warwick*

UK Political Parties since 1945
Edited by ANTHONY SELDON, *Institute of Contemporary British History*

Politics and Policy Making in Northern Ireland
MICHAEL CONNOLLY, *University of Ulster*

British Political Ideologies
ROBERT LEACH, *Leeds Polytechnic*

Local Government and Politics in Britain
JOHN KINGDOM, *Sheffield Polytechnic*

British Government: The Central Executive Territory
PETER MADGWICK, Professor Emeritus, *Oxford Polytechnic*

Contents

List of Tables

Preface and Acknowledgements

This book seeks to bring the political aspects of Britain's multiracial society into the heart of the analysis of British politics. For far too long, Britain's multiracial character has either been left to the minor footnotes in leading studies of the British system of government and politics or else overlooked altogether. While in some cases it is possible to justify the reasons behind writers' apparent racial myopia, on the whole the record of scholars on this front has been disappointing. The deficiency in these studies stems from their narrow conception of race and politics in Britain. The topics of black votes and candidates appear to dominate writing in this area, thereby relegating a number of other important and interesting issues to the periphery.

It is no longer tenable for political analyses of race and racism to be marginalised from mainstream research and writing on British politics in this way. If the study of British politics is really to expand its analytical frontiers, then this surely cannot be achieved at the price of overlooking the political implications of racial pluralism.

The preparation of this book has benefited greatly from the support of many people. I would like to thank a number of friends, colleagues and family members for their help. First and foremost, I am indebted to Rita Alfred for the valuable support and patience she provided; besides being a constant source of encouragement, she very carefully read and improved the various drafts of the manuscript. My students and colleagues in the Department of Political Studies at Queen Mary and Westfield College provided a stimulating environment in which to work on my ideas for this book. I am especially grateful for the friendly guidance and words of encouragement provided by Wayne Parsons whose own experiences in teaching public policy have indirectly shaped my thinking on the politics of race. In addition, those students who took my courses on 'The Politics of Race in Britain' and 'The Government and Politics of the United Kingdom' during the 1989–90 and 1990–91 sessions also played an important part in shaping the arguments of this book. Timely secretarial support was provided by Debbie Emory and Julia King, both of whom must, I am sure, continue to marvel at my determination to enliven undergraduate teaching. Ken Young, my Head of Department, supplied his usual steady encouragement to my scholarship. I was also the beneficiary of enormous patience shown by Clare Grist, my commissioning editor, with the many delays in finishing the book. Invaluable inspiration for my work continued to be provided by my uncle, Devinder K. Saggar. Finally, I have always been inspired by the constant encouragement provided by my father and it is unlikely that this project would ever have been undertaken without the great confidence he has shown in my work. This book is dedicated to him and to the treasured memory of my mother.

Shamit Saggar
London
August 1991

Notes on Terminology

Black

The term 'black' is used to denote people of non-white origin, principally Asian and Afro-Caribbean. Its use as a broad 'umbrella' label is deliberate, to signify reference to a wide variety of non-white minority ethnic groups. Where greater precision is required with reference to specific component groups within the black population, allowances and departures from this term are made in the text.

The reader should be aware that an important debate over race and nomenclature exists in contemporary British society. However, for the purposes of this volume no particular political or sociological inference should be drawn from the use of this label.

New Commonwealth

Chapter 3 makes use of the familiar term 'New Commonwealth' (NCW) as an expression for the common origin of immigrants and their offspring. In doing so, the chapter follows the custom of most demographic research in this field.

It should be noted that a number of publications make reference to 'New Commonwealth and Pakistan' (NCWP) in order to signal the long spell of Pakistan's exile from the Commonwealth between 1971 and 1990. However, following Pakistan's readmission in November 1990, many writers have begun to revert to the earlier term, NCW. This diplomatic development may have led to some confusion in the minds of readers of demographic writing on black people in Britain over a twenty-year period. For the purposes of this volume, the two terms are interchangeable.

1 Introduction

> I don't believe this is a multicultural society. England is England and always shall be, and I quite like it being England. I would like people who come here to accept its culture and its nostrums, and I think that if you come to an understanding, bit by bit you begin to work together.
>
> (Bob Geldof, 1991)

> [Integration is defined] . . . not [as] a flattening process of assimilation but as equal opportunity accompanied by cultural diversity, in an atmosphere of mutual tolerance.
>
> (Roy Jenkins, 1966)

> Racism is normally defined as prejudice plus power where prejudice is an unfavourable opinion or feeling formed beforehand or without knowledge, thought or reason, often unconsciously and on the grounds of race, colour, nationality, ethnic or national origins. Power is the ability to make things happen or prevent things from happening. Thus racism is having the power to put into effect one's prejudices to the detriment of particular racial groups.
>
> (GLC Ethnic Minorities Unit, 1985)

There are many competing views about race and racism in British politics. The above statements represent merely an indication of their contrasting characters and diverse origins. Traditionally, political scientists have looked to the formal arena of politics in order to study the significance of racial issues in British politics. But, as is so often the case, by spreading our analytical nets a little wider we may discover that many areas of British society have become or have long been racialised in one way or another.

This book has three principal objectives. The first aim is to examine the process by which issues of race have affected British politics in the post-war era. In order to do this, the book looks both to the political history of race in Britain as well as to features of contemporary British politics. The second aim is to explore the political role of black[1] people in Britain. The book is thus concerned with *inter alia* aspects of black political participation including political socialisation, opinion formation, electoral behaviour and activism.

Finally, the book has a third aim, one which is both unusual and important to the study of the politics of race. The book attempts to provide a synthesis between the rather specialist understanding of the politics of race and the more mainstream understanding of the British political process. Too often it is the case that questions of race and racism are ringfenced for specialist consideration, thus overlooking the racialisation of British political life in general. The role of the major political parties in debates about non-white immigration is a good example of an area where greater synthesis is sorely needed. This book aims to fill that void and, in doing so, provide the reader with a more incisive and sagacious analysis of the politics of race in Britain.

Thinking about race in British politics

Britain is a multiracial society. The 1991 General Census reminded us all too clearly that we live in a multiracial society. Certainly as far as the most recent figures are concerned, around 2.5 million Britons – or 4.5 per cent of the population – are of one minority ethnic group or another. The term 'multiracial society' has become so over-used in recent years that few commentators have paused to consider the extent to which Britain is now made up of several distinctive racial and ethnic groups.

What does this simple piece of demographic information mean for British government and politics? The question can be approached from at least three perspectives, each of which has some relevance for the themes and arguments pursued in this book.

First, it must be stressed that, for the most part, textbook accounts of the British political process seem to have either overlooked or underestimated the sociological change that has taken place among the British population in the years following mass non-white immigration. With relatively few exceptions (Dearlove and Saunders, 1984), authors of such texts have merely surveyed the picture of British political participation and institutions with little or no regard to the social – let alone racial – make-up of contemporary Britain. Even where writers have deliberately sought to incorporate some form of race dimension into their work, sadly it has been at the price of tokenism, albeit in a form not easily recognised by many established scholars of British politics (see Kavanagh, 1990, for an illustration of such tokenism). The failure to bring together satisfactorily studies of British race relations and British politics is a theme that will be returned to throughout this book. At this stage, however, it is only necessary to note and acquaint ourselves with this general criticism. A critical perspective of the literature on British politics will be implicit in the chapters that follow and it is therefore important that the reader is aware of the general direction of the argument to be pursued.

Second, despite the rapid growth of sub-disciplines such as policy studies within the discipline in general, it is far from clear whether issues of race and ethnicity have been fully reflected in recent writing on the British policy process. This is a curious position since there can be little doubt that British policy-makers have been kept fairly busy with the task of trying to resolve numerous conflicts in this general area. For example, the street disorders (or 'race riots', depending on the level of sensationalism adopted by different writers) that afflicted many inner city areas during the early and mid-1980s yielded a series of fairly detailed and explicit policy responses both from central and sub-central government. These policies have certainly gained prominence within the writing on urban affairs, local government, central–local relations, and so on (Benyon, 1984). However, comparatively little has been written about their significance to students of the politics of public policy-making. Moreover, going back over thirty years, policy studies – as a distinctive aspect of the discipline in Britain – have remained largely silent on the lessons of forging and implementing public policy in a multiracial environment. The patchy record of even this aspect of the discipline is further emphasised when we take into account the well-developed and fruitful volume of comparative research that exists on ethnic pluralism and public policy in other industrial democracies (see for example, Glazer and Young, 1983).

Third, the apparent failure to incorporate the so-called race dimension into mainstream studies of British government and politics contrasts fairly sharply with the more innovative and self-critical record of the sociologists. Even the most casual observer of the sociology of contemporary Britain cannot have failed to notice the extent to which challenging questions regarding British multi-racial society have been taken on in many of the leading textbooks. Of course, even the sociologists' far-greater willingness to examine race and ethnicity issues is a long way from being an ideal picture, and the dominance of functionalism has been difficult to avoid. However, it is unmistakable that many of the major texts of the sociology of contemporary Britain have not shied away from the subject matter and, indeed, many have actively attempted to place these issues into the wider context of British society. Moreover, while such a dynamic and progressive approach has not always proved to be successful or intellectually watertight, its real significance lies in the determination to put forward to students a realistic and relevant account of modern British society. The multiracial character of British society has therefore become part and parcel of the account sketched by such textbooks (see, for example, Abercrombie and Warde, 1988).

From the perspective of political studies of contemporary Britain, the obvious contrast with the more active patterns of sociologists need not be all that significant. The disciplines can and do, after all, stand alone on a wide variety of topics with little direct cost to their intellectual integrity. The deficiency becomes more apparent, however, when account is taken of the trends in recent years in the political sociology of Britain. It has been in this area that many of the most significant theoretical developments in British government and politics have taken place, in particular the changing agenda of researchers away from traditional institutional and behavioural themes, and towards questions to do with the analysis of political power, issue formation and agenda-setting. This change has meant that British politics can no longer be satisfactorily described or explained using narrow participation-oriented terms of reference.

The analytical picture has opened up considerably in recent years, in part through the work of political sociologists unhappy with traditional pluralist views of political power. To that end, the work of academics interested in British politics has also slowly begun to broaden in terms of the salient questions to be raised and discussed, not least in textbooks on the subject. That said, the process has been slow and habitually shrouded in complex, stultifying theory at the expense of rich empirical data. Issues of race and ethnicity, and questions concerning political power in these areas, have yet to be fully reflected in mainstream writing on British politics. This deficiency afflicts both large parts of research work on British politics and policy-making as well as the bulk of textbooks on British politics.

Writers on British politics have therefore yet to develop a satisfactory political analysis of race. Given this endemic weakness, the average, textbook-reliant student of British politics may quite innocently overlook the multiracial character of British society. Moreover, even when these issues are *not* overlooked by textbook writer and reader alike, it is probably the case that the most interesting and challenging aspects of the politics of race in Britain remain to be discovered (Saggar, 1990).

One of the subsidiary purposes of this book, therefore, will be to shift greater descriptive and analytical emphasis towards plugging some of these shortcomings in the academic understanding of race and politics in Britain.

These three criticisms of the state of the present picture derive from an underlying dissatisfaction with the themes and questions pursued both in mainstream textbooks on British politics as well as more specialist studies of the politics of race in Britain. Certainly, textbook accounts of British politics have been published in recent years that make some attempt to refer to Britain's multiracial identity where previously such references were conspicuous by their absence (compare for example Moran, 1989, with Kavanagh, 1990).

All too often these textbooks fail even the most modest tests of tokenism and the reader is frequently left with an unquenched thirst to know more about issues of race and ethnicity in British politics. Moreover, even the few accounts that do not fall down on this basic test are nonetheless left wanting in their theoretical treatment of race and ethnicity. The reader is usually supplied with selections of important information regarding the political activity of certain black and ethnic minority groups, but little about how race and ethnicity affects the political process. That is, the emphasis is squarely upon minority groups as participants in the process rather than upon trying to characterise the process's response – or lack of it – to racial demands and conflicts. Numerous sociologists in contemporary Britain, one suspects, would not be content to leave standing such a heavily skewed analytical framework. And yet, this appears to be a current – and unchallenged – orthodoxy across the main approaches to the study of British politics.

Beyond the colourblindness of political studies

The picture is not much brighter when it comes to specialist works on race in British politics. Since the publication of Paul Foot's highly lucid *Immigration and Race in British Politics* in 1965, a number of accounts of race and politics in Britain have been written. Taken together, they have successfully carved out a specialist niche within the discipline and generated a trove of empirical research; however, they have not been so keen to develop a theoretical understanding of 'race politics'.

It is not the purpose of this chapter to furnish the reader with an exhaustive review of the literature on race and politics since this task is more than adequately undertaken in each of the substantive chapters. Instead, it is worth noting some of the highlights of the volume of specialist writing in this field.

Early studies, such as those of Rose (1969) and Deakin (1970), were concerned with surveying race relations and the changing social context of public policy. Based on the findings of a pioneering survey of British race relations, both publications were laced with more than a tinge of myopic paternalism about the prospects of (a) integrating black immigrants into the mainstream of British society, and (b) the possibilities for securing racial harmony. Crewe's (1975) collection of essays represented one of the earliest attempts to bring together the findings of scattered empirical research, and contained several important insights into black political participation, anti-immigrant politics and issue voting. Layton-Henry and Rich's (1986) much later edited volume made another similar contribution to the literature, including important new perspectives on the anatomy of race policy (Bulpitt, 1986), Conservative ideology (Rich, 1986a) and the political agenda (Studlar, 1986). In between, Layton-Henry's (1984) survey provided a scholarly, though now rather dated, first attempt at an introduction to the subject.

The works of Young and Connelly (1981) and Young and Glazer (1983) have been important milestones in the development of policy studies of racial and ethnic pluralism and have been preceded and followed by several other studies (for example, Bachrach and Baratz, 1970; Jenkins and Solomos, 1987; Saggar, 1991a). More recently, Messina's (1989) study has presented us with a more fundamental return to the political analysis of race using familiar, though not always satisfactory, political science concepts and approaches. Other useful specialist studies have been written, though they often pertain to selected case studies and/or outdated findings (for example, Beetham, 1970; Hill and Issacharoff, 1971; Katznelson, 1973; Lawrence, 1974). Finally, some of the most interesting contributions to the literature have been made by studies of the sociology and politics of black communities. The work of *inter alia* John (1969), Southall Rights/CARF (1981), Mukherjee (1982), Bhachu (1985) and Gilroy (1987) has been invaluable in this regard.

The structure of the book

The main body of the book is composed of six substantive chapters. Chapter 2 places our enquiry into a historical context and looks at the central role of race in British history and the history of the black presence in Britain. Chapter 3 sketches a profile of the social demography of race in Britain and contains important, though frequently under-reported, information about Britain's black population. Chapters 4 and 5 turn to matters of party politics. The former examines the politics of 'race policy' during the liberal hour of British race relations in the 1960s; the latter traces the development of post-war Labour and Conservative political strategies towards race and immigration. The question of black participation in the realm of formal politics – principally policy preferences, voting behaviour and candidate performance – is the subject of Chapter 6. The penultimate chapter is devoted to a discussion of the politics of nationhood and cultural pluralism; the chapter charts the political legacy of Powellism from the rise and fall of neo-fascism in the 1970s through to the emergence of neo-conservative critiques of a multiracial Britain in the 1980s. Finally, these six substantive chapters are followed by a short final chapter devoted to a discussion of several themes raised throughout the course of the book, which gives some thought to recent developments in the analysis of race and politics in contemporary Britain.

Note

1. See Notes on Terminology at the beginning of this text.

2

The Historical Context

Introduction

According to Ramdin (1987: 1), black people have been a part of British society since the days of the Roman Empire! Contrary to received wisdom, the black presence in Britain began neither in the recent post-colonial era nor in the nineteenth-century high-water mark of British imperialism. As the following chapter goes on to note, the scale of the black presence in Britain certainly multiplied greatly during the 1950s, 1960s and 1970s, rising through a combination of migration and generational replacement to more than 2 million people in 1981. However, the backdrop to mass post-war black immigration was not that of a snow-white, racially homogeneous Britain, but rather a receiving country that had a long, if selective, experience of black faces in its midst.

This observation then leads to questions concerning the construction of racialism as a systematic and coherent set of ideas – as an ideology. This is an important question for this chapter because present-day racial structures and value systems are more fully understood with reference to their historical context. There are a number of clear continuities with the past which help to explain racialist phenomena in contemporary Britain. As noted in the previous chapter, many of the recent additions to the literature on race and politics in Britain suffer from a general under-appreciation of the historical context of the phenomena they purport to describe and explain. Moreover, those that have attempted to place explanation within a historical framework have tended to adopt artificial demarcations between the historical processes underlying firstly, different racial phenomena and, secondly, the passage of different immigrant groups to Britain. For example, historical studies of black immigrant communities in Britain have frequently ignored the related histories of various non-black immigrant groups such as the Jews and Irish (Miles, 1982). Fortunately, in recent years several useful volumes have been published that have provided us with detailed examinations (Ramdin, 1987) and clear overviews (Holmes, 1988) of the history of migration to Britain. In addition, Fryer's *Staying Power* (1984) is a rich volume which traces the black presence in British history in some considerable detail.

This chapter will seek to redress the relative neglect of historical processes in the political analysis of race and racism in British society. Naturally it cannot claim to provide a comprehensive historical coverage of race and racism in Britain. Therefore the chapter deliberately confines itself to examining some of the most important features of British history and, in doing so, focuses attention on certain areas rather than others. It charts its historical overview from the rise of England as a world power in the sixteenth century, turns to examine several important legacies of this role, including the black presence within English society, and closes with some observations about black political activism in the first half of the twentieth century. Examination and discussion of the politics of race and immigration since 1945 is reserved for a later chapter.

This chapter is composed of six main sections which will aim to give an overview of the historical context of British race relations and to focus on the key issues that have been pursued in political discussions of race and immigration. First, starting with the era of the pre-capitalist English economy, the chapter looks at the development of European trading links with the African and North American continents and traces the role of African slavery in the emerging British Empire. The second section of the chapter examines the role played by the British in India in the development of other varieties of racial thinking and sentiment. The era of the Victorians and the rapid sophistication in quasi- and pseudo-scientific ideas concerning race at this time are the subject of the third section. The fourth section is devoted to the other (white) minorities, namely the Jews and Irish, in British history. The fifth section is concerned with early twentieth-century attitudes towards race and the presence of black minorities in Britain. The final section signals key developments in the development of autonomous black politics in Britain during the interwar period and pays particular attention to the case of the League of Coloured People.

British history, black people and British capitalism

It was the rise of early mercantilism and pre-capitalist economic forces across Europe during the sixteenth century that served to extend English trading links into Africa and North America. The voyages of discovery to the New World – precipitated by that of Cabot in 1497 – provided the major impetus to the dramatic growth in English trade that was to occur over the following four hundred years. Colonialism served both to expand trading links as well as to broaden the scale and level of contact with the peoples of Africa. The search among the English and their colonial rivals in France and Spain in particular for their 'place in the sun' became one of the guiding themes of European history at this time. This search would be eclipsed only by the rather different – that is, more literal and involuntary – place occupied by black slaves 'in the broiling sun of sugar, tobacco and cotton plantations' (Williams, 1944: 4).

The growth of trade during the sixteenth and seventeenth centuries was closely paralleled by the trade in indentured labour. The establishment of the Colonial Board in 1661 was at least partly brought about by the need to regulate this trade in some way. But, as the seventeenth century wore on, the focus of both traders and government shifted to the question of how 'best' to populate – and thus work – the colonies of the New World. The question was in part underscored by fears that white emigration to work the plantations was growing and would eventually drain the home country of suitable cheap labour. By 1680 the African slave trade had received the patronage of the Royal Family in the form of the Royal African Company (Ramdin, 1987: 3-4). In English trading circles this development signalled the new orthodoxy regarding the African's greater suitability to the toils of production.

In the final analysis, it was the simple economics of substituting poor white labourers with black slaves commanding no rights that proved to be decisive. 'Three blacks work better and cheaper than one white man', declared the Governor of Barbados. The emerging industrialisation in Britain was to be launched on the backs of African slaves. The central factor behind the establishment of the African slave trade appears then to have been economic rather than racial. Several writers have commented upon the historical context of slavery and observed that the wide range of rationalisations of the slave trade involving notions of racial and cultural inferiority tended to *follow* the actual practice of slavery and that these ideas were expressed in a non-systematic incremental manner (see, for example, James, 1938, and Williams, 1944). In fact, the role of Africans within the slave trade had been preceded by the black, brown, white and yellow unfree labour of the New World. Indigenous Indian slavery in particular had been popular on the plantations under the Spaniards, who had long complained of the native's alleged lack of physical strength and their shortage of numbers. Black Africans, in contrast, drew no such complaints from the planters. Furthermore, poor whites were also used extensively as servants, both as indentured labour and as convicts. Thus a thriving trade in white labour was established during the seventeenth century, commonly involving kidnapping in British cities, and resulting eventually in no less than a sixth of Virginia's population being composed of white servants by 1683! The part played by African slavery was to come later and only after the economical and logistical possibilities for exploiting non-African labour had been exhausted.

As already noted, black individuals and communities were already a feature of British society prior to the arrival of large numbers of black immigrants after the Second World War. From the seventeenth century onwards, small but significant pockets of black settlement could be identified in several British cities including London, Bristol, Southampton, Cardiff and Liverpool. Black seamen in particular, associated with the buoyant trade-related economies of many port towns, made up the larger part of the black presence. That said, writers such as Ramdin (1987) and Fryer (1984) have highlighted the much longer establishment of black communities in Britain, predating the port-related settlements and often connected with domestic service. From the 1600s onward, English society appeared increasingly struck by exotic tales of 'the African'. Walvin (1973: 1) for example describes the fascination of ruling elites with Africans at this time, resulting in the former's adoption of the latter as domestic servants and even as novelty 'pets'.

Slavery and abolition

The problem of isolating the factors comprising and responsible for racism in British history is further confounded by the example of slavery and its abolition. The campaign for abolition of slavery led by social reformers such as William Wilberforce finally resulted in a successful Parliamentary Bill passed in 1807. Much has been made of this key development by historians of British imperialism and the slave trade (Shyllon, 1974; Walvin, 1982), but the main question – that of the reasons for abolition – remains the subject of considerable debate.

The more prevalent and familiar view held that the humanitarian arguments put forward by Wilberforce and his colleagues and supporters lay behind the end of slavery. Several influential campaigners had lobbied elite opinion in the mother country throughout the latter part of the eighteenth century. Their efforts served to build a clearly identifiable abolitionist lobby, centred on leading social commentators, enlightened parliamentarians, voices in the press, and the Quakers. Substantial quantities of evidence were also collected on the human consequences of slavery, much of it from the traders themselves. In 1785, one of the future leaders of the abolition campaign, Thomas Clarkson, published his *Essay on the Slavery and Commerce of the Human Species* which immediately caused a wave of public horror at the details of suffering uncovered in the publication. However, ranged against this campaign were those opposed to slavery's legal termination. Opponents stressed rather different arguments, suggesting that the mind of the slave was both exclusively and best suited to labouring, and that the system of slavery merely reflected the more general racial superiority of white over black races. The counter-arguments did not stop there by any means. Indeed, a great outpouring of pseudo-scientific interest was shown in wide areas of black behaviour, ranging from the sexual to the artistic and cultural. In *History of the British Colonies in the West Indies* by Bryan Edwards, published in 1793, it was argued that the Negro had no meaningful capacity for romance nor caring relationships. The debate continued long after the 1807 Act, and in 1853 the much celebrated English essayist Thomas Carlyle published *The Nigger Question* which argued that, unlike poor whites, black West Indians were an innately happy and content people. 'How pleasant', he wrote, 'to have always this fact to fall back upon: our beautiful Black darlings are at least happy' (1853: 4).

A radically different view of the end of slavery was advanced by the Caribbean writer C.L.R. James in his 1938 prize-winning book *The Black Jacobins*. James suggested that economic reasons lay behind Britain's abolition of slavery. The impact of James' work, together with Eric William's seminal 1944 study, *Capitalism and Slavery*, was that the traditional view, centred on humanitarian justifications, appeared to be less credible. Since the publication of these two pioneering studies, the received view of abolition has shifted towards economic-centred explanations. It seems fairly clear then that, as with the original establishment of the slave trade, abolition also came about as a result of the changing requirements of the British economy. Moreover, the date of abolition also coincides approximately with the start of the rapid growth of British capitalism, penetrating into massive foreign sources of raw materials and new markets at home and abroad for the fruits of production.

The strong mood of indignation that had surrounded the original campaign appeared to swing the other way during the 1840s and 1850s when the issue turned to slavery in British colonial territories. The 'scientific' claims of anti-abolitionists were renewed with vigour and were largely based on the recounted observations of absentee planters from the West Indies. Periodic bursts of paranoia concerning black sexuality littered the arguments of numerous scholars. For example, Edward Long's volume entitled *History of Jamaica* (1774) saw no offence in proposing the idea of marriage between an ape male and a black female! Such contributions to the debate were not uncommon. Even the views of liberal philanthropists such as John Stuart Mill seemed to accept the logic of racial superiority, whilst denouncing British involvement in slavery in its colonies and in the United States as 'a true work of the devil' (1850: 31). Moreover, the debate could no longer be so easily limited to the morality of slavery since, in Britain at least, it had already been formally done away with. Instead, with the focus of the debate on the colonies and the rising conflict over slavery in the United States, political voices at home had to operate within a milieu bogged down with Irish famine and immigration, industrial change and an upsurge in workers' radicalism. As Walvin (1984: 40) writes, 'many became disillusioned with the altruism of the black cause . . . [and] there emerged a revived form of racism which was to characterise Victorian responses to non-white people throughout the rest of the nineteenth century.'

The black poor in English society

Despite the abolition of slavery in 1807, black settlement did not die out in Britain during the nineteenth century. The ending of the pulling forces of the slave trade certainly had the effect of dramatically reducing the black population in Britain. Their reduced absolute numbers were accentuated in relative terms at a time when there were massive leaps in the size of the indigenous population. Estimates of the black population at the beginning of the nineteenth century put the figure at around 10,000 (Ramdin, 1987: 18). The vast majority suffered endemic poverty and the daily fight for bare survival. Their high mortality rate, coupled with net negative replacement through fresh migration, served to push the black presence downwards and into reliance upon professional beggary and petty theft. The price of being apprehended was not limited to conventional punishment but extended to the very real threat of deportation to the West Indies, a threat which meant a return to slavery. This dilemma meant that

> On one hand, hunger and poverty forced them to beg and steal, while on the other, they were faced with the possibility of deportation and slavery. The position of the black poor in English society was a desperate one. Cornered like animals, they had to fight for the barest existence.
>
> (Ramdin, 1987: 17).

England during post-Elizabethan and pre-Victorian times was also a home to various other black communities not derived from the legacy of slavery. Although most of the research on the history of black people in Britain has tended to focus on African and Caribbean black descendants of slavery, it is important to note the presence of small yet vibrant Indian and Chinese communities. As with the African link, it was commerce and the launch of an imperial role that brought significant numbers of people from Asia and the Orient to what was orginally the hub of the trading network and later the 'mother country'. Writers such as Fryer (1984) and Ramdin (1987) have documented in some detail the Indian community which settled in London. For example, beginning in the early nineteenth century a group of Indian seamen, the Lascars, numbering around 1,500 individuals, were dependent on financial aid given by the East India Company, though this support did not prevent many of their number dying each year from the unfamiliar cold of the English winter. Again, the plight of those that protested was similiar to that meted out to black beggars caught thieving: the threat of deportation. A parliamentary investigation into their conditions revealed the extent of their wretched lot, but it did little to help transfer the question onto the political agenda. Indeed, political discussion of the problem was easily and routinely seen in terms that were less and less altruistic. As Walvin (1984: 40) reminds us, the attention of British politicians had, by the time of Queen Victoria's accession to the throne, moved towards the glories of empire and the rapid growth of capitalism at home and abroad. The social position of black Africans, Caribbeans and Asians living in Britain was far from the outward-looking, imperial minds of the Victorians. Consequently, awareness and portrayals of black individuals and communities were to be found in Victorian society, but usually at its fringes.

Yet the re-ordering of Victorian priorities did not mean that race declined in salience. On the contrary, the period from the 1850s until the early twentieth century witnessed a new and unprecedented interest in concepts of race and social structure. It is in this crucial era that many of the most important developments in the evolution of racism in British society took place.

The British Raj and aftermath

The British experience in India during the latter half of the nineteenth century was shrouded in mixed attitudes about race. As a purely foreign policy phenomenon, it undoubtedly marked the heyday of British subjugation of foreign lands and peoples. However, when the historical processes involved in the rise – and eventual fall – of the Raj are examined, we can see that the experience led to a further sharpening of peculiarly British forms of racism.

The approach of British colonialism towards the indigenous faiths and cultures of the subcontinent seemed to exemplify the civilising crusade underlying the Raj. The campaign to seek converts to Christianity was just one aspect of a collective attitude which saw the ancient religions of India as outdated and superstitious barriers to modernisation and advancement. So too was the view taken of a wide range of traditions and customs practised by different groups in India. For example, it is significant that the young Maharaja Dalip Singh, who had come to live in England as something of a 'pet' of Queen Victoria during the 1850s, was not only dispossessed of his land and riches but also of his Sikh faith. Whilst the mysticism of the east represented by the young ousted Maharaja and the Indian ruling classes may have captured the imagination of the Victorians, the relationship remained a highly paternalistic one. Indeed, several writers have commented on the parallels between the conversion and civilising impetus behind British imperial rule of India and the pressures faced by Asian and other immigrants in Britain to conform to the 'host' country's customs and traditions more than a century later (Banton, 1985; Foot, 1965; Walvin, 1984).

The British relationship with India during the early to mid-Victorian era appeared to undergo a significant change in terms of cross-cultural understanding. In earlier periods the relationship had been characterised by a strong cultural curiosity and a certain degree of mutual respect. Although they had not been widely written about nor publicised until the nineteenth century, the links based upon a common ancient Indo-European language served to enrich and solidify the relationship of the early explorers and their Indian hosts. The rapid expansion of British capitalism into India during the nineteenth century, searching for raw materials and new markets, placed new and heavy burdens on that relationship. The political control of the Raj in legal–territorial terms threw up enormous practical difficulties. Although the established policy of pragmatically blending direct rule with the indirect proxy authority of local princes achieved most of the aims of the British Raj, it was by no means without cost. Moreover, as the policy was designed to facilitate the growth of *both* political and economic power, it inevitably yielded occasional naked displays of imperial authority over the Indian people. Given the size and scope of the political task facing British governments' Indian foreign policies, the real wonder is not so much the number or severity of these displays of authority, but rather their remarkable scarcity.

The date of the 1857 Indian Mutiny is frequently cited as the point of the major sea change in Anglo-Indian relations. Robert Miles has argued that this episode altered dramatically the public perception of India and Indians in British society. Justifications for the British presence in India took on a revived slant of racism in which the image of 'a docile, industrious Hindu . . . was represented increasingly as deceptive, fanatical and cruel' (Miles, 1989: 83). There was nothing particularly new in this representation of the Oriental, but in the aftermath of the 1857 Mutiny it served to heighten fears about a people who had previously been warmly received in British imperial discourse. The thought of an uprising of several hundred million colonial subjects against a combined military presence of under 50,000 soldiers was the most immediate consequence of the rebellion. As Miles notes, the reaction in Britain and throughout Europe to these events demonstrated the flexibility and adaptability of racism as an ideological tool of explanation. Parallels were also witnessed elsewhere in the Empire including in 1865 a major rebellion in Jamaica which was also portrayed as an illustration of African barbarism.

These episodes transformed the character of mid-Victorian attitudes on race. The civilising influences of western Christian beliefs were held in stark comparison with widespread views of the unworthy and irrational ways of non-white imperial subjects. The periodic rejection of the British imperial presence by these subjects was interpreted in harsh terms as representative of the collective wishes of inferior races. Moreover, the lexicon of mid-Victorian imperialism was one which appeared to become more disparaging towards black imperial subjects, with the label of 'nigger' returning to common usage. Indians themselves, for the first time, began to be referred to as 'niggers'. The significance of this was that it laid the ground for future systematic verbal abuse of Indians and others and, according to Walvin, it was

> to become the most abusive epithet used by successive generations throughout the world. When, in later years, growing numbers of non-white people . . . settled in Britain, they entered a society where widespread racial attitudes had developed . . . which instantly relegated non-whites to an inferior status and rank.
>
> (Walvin, 1984: 44)

Later the first stirrings of an independence movement in India and elsewhere were managed by the British colonial authorities in a similar fashion. British military conflicts abroad such as the Boer War at the turn of the century were portrayed at home as a further extension of 'The White Man's burden' written about by Rudyard Kipling. Whilst on the one hand the popular culture of Britain at this time emphasised the harsh brutality of the Boers towards black Africans, on the other, doubts were raised as to the necessity and cost of waging such a campaign in such a remote quarter of the Empire. Following the setbacks of the seige of Mafeking in 1899 by the Boers, jingoistic mobs rampaged through the streets of several English towns calling for both the black and the white rebels to be taught a lesson (Mackenzie, 1984).

An important debate has developed among historians of the British Empire over the question of whether the patriotic jingoism of this period was merely a symptom of successful British capitalism. The ideological basis for the view that imperial developments were closely entwined in a system of racist beliefs has hitherto remained on the sidelines of major historical studies. Racism certainly transcended all aspects of British society towards the end of the Victorian age and left an unmistakable legacy. Attempts to absolve the working class from the ideas and impact of Victorian racism are neither new nor restricted to the Victorian era. Starting with Hobson's *The Psychology of Jingoism* (1900), the debate has proceeded to the analysis of white working-class racism towards black immigrants since the late 1950s (Phizacklea and Miles, 1979). We shall return to the specific question of the role of the working class in British racism in Chapter 5.

The Victorians and scientific racism

The history of the British Empire stretches from the voyages of discovery and consolidation in the fifteenth and sixteenth centuries, through the race for colonies with her European rivals in the nineteenth century, to the eventual dismantling in stages during the middle part of this century. It undoubtedly reached its zenith in 1854 with the declaration of Queen Victoria as Empress of India. The incorporation of the subcontinent into the Empire was more than another mere colonial possession as its commonly used label, 'the jewel in the crown', vividly suggests.

However, the Victorian age was also one in which significant interest was shown in different concepts of race, not least in the putatively scientific claims of several leading commentators and politicians of the time. The debate to which they contributed served to lay the foundations of a near codified set of beliefs and assumptions regarding issues of racial and biological determinism. Aspects of these views can be seen reflected in more contemporary, post-war political debates concerning multiracial Britain in general and the hostile anti-immigrant reaction of far-right groups in particular (Thurlow, 1975).

Perhaps the most significant development during this era was the close interest shown in matters of racial ordering and classification. The heyday of British imperialism had yielded vast new territories and subjects, all brought under a single sovereign flag. It also fed the view of an abstract natural order among human beings as reflected in different civilisations and empires. The resounding theme of much of this thought seemed to be a notion of white racial and/or cultural supremacy, expressed both implicitly as well as explicitly. An early – and perhaps unexpected – illustration of the former was reflected in the remarks of Disraeli when he said to his parliamentary colleagues in 1849: 'Race implies difference and difference implies superiority, and superiority leads to predominance' (quoted in Walvin, 1984: 40). These words may have merely reflected the received view of British political elites at this time but beneath them lay a far deeper and arguably sophisticated set of propositions on the matter.

The iceberg, of which Disraeli's comments were the tip, extended through many liberal enlightened circles It concealed a growing obsession among many leading voices – both within Britain and in continental Europe – all trying to explain imperial gains in terms of human destiny. Most notoriously this process eventually came to a head in the writings of the German philosopher Nietzsche and others concerned about the future of Euro-Aryan civilisations (see for example Nietzsche, 1973). The first fully stated claim that a Nordic 'race' existed with undisputed superior creative skills was advanced in *The Racial Elements of European History* in the 1920s by Günther (1970). During the middle to late nineteenth century in particular, a number of social and political thinkers were turning their attention to questions of the 'Human Will' and its supposed triumph over the force of reason and logic espoused by leading liberal thinkers since the Enlightenment. 'The revolt against reason' as this movement became known, was prominent in the interplay of essentially Hegelian-derived ideas concerning the 'destiny' of discrete groups of people (Lúkas, 1980). In the case of several German philosophers, the notion of collective destiny was quickly applied to broader and related debates concerning German nationhood and national unification. Such a notion, as the experience of the heirs to Nietzsche's writings was to demonstrate, was centred on claims of racial and ethnic exclusivity and ordering.

The real significance of this movement, contemporary political philosophers have argued, was the challenge it laid down to liberal thinkers who had been so long and so closely attached to explanations of social and political behaviour based on abstract, unalienable principles and then shaped by rationality and reason. Moreover, the impact continues to be felt in contemporary debates between liberal political philosophers and their New Right critics. According to one commentator on this battle of ideas, the supremacy of the collective myths of liberalism suddenly

> changed in the late nineteenth century with the advent of a new kind of right-wing thinking, non-religious, sceptical, spurred on by Darwinism to draw attention to some of the less palatable human inclinations. Under the pitiless gaze of Nietzsche, Pareto, Michels . . . and other spiritual fathers of fascism, the liberal doctrine of equality, human rights and government by consent shrank from myths into childish delusions . . . . Liberal principles, notably the principle that human rights are universal and unrelated to membership of ethnic groups, are extremely vulnerable to movements that play on ubiquitous feelings of in-group loyalty and hostility to outsiders . . .
>
> (Canovan, 1990: 14–15)

Debates about human will and destiny were by no means conducted in a vacuum unrelated to intellectual interest in the creation and motivation of societies. Indeed, the search was very much on to look for and advance general theories to explain social action and behaviour, and, in doing so, leading thinkers of the late nineteenth century borrowed heavily from the work of natural scientists. Darwin's work in particular was quickly translated into a much wider endorsement for biologically determinist views of society (Jones, 1980).

A form of scientific racism – first codified and then laundered via the respectable quest for intellectual discovery and explanation – was born. Moreover, the debate was far from limited to the search for nationhood among continental philosophers; rather it permeated and was partially fed by the close interest in grand theory displayed by the Victorians. The close preoccupation with defining society in racial terms is illustrated in the claims of Robert Knox, a leading Scottish scientist of the Victorian age: 'That race is in human affairs everything is simply a fact, the most remarkable, the most comprehensive, which philosophy has ever announced. Race is everything: literature, science, art . . . depends on it' (quoted in Walvin: 1984: 41). Views such as this all served to convince both elite and mass opinion of the divine righteousness of their physical and cultural domination of non-whites. In political terms this changing perception of Britain and the British in the world meant that the debates of the mid-nineteenth century concerning slavery in the colonies were rather different from those that had surrounded the original abolition of its practice in 1807. The US civil war in particular fuelled a new mood in Britain which had the strongest of doubts as to the wisdom of waging war on behalf of the suppressed rights of black slave labour. Indeed, proponents of this argument held that lessons could and should be drawn from the historical failure of black people to produce engineers, artists and poets.

Further, by basing the argument on the supposition that racial ordering lay behind such an observation, it was suggested that, short of permanent enslavement of black people, the best that could be hoped for would be to raise the black capacity for understanding and achievement through inter-racial mixing. The suggestion was even discussed as a progressive move, designed at least partly to answer lingering questions about the post-slavery position of black people. The era of British and colonial slavery may have come to an end during the mid-nineteenth century, but the moral imperatives for its termination were no longer centre stage to the debate on race. Instead, attention had turned to underlying questions of domination and superiority, and, in doing so, towards power relationships between firstly, the 'mother country' and the colonial periphery, and secondly, the white masters and the black subjects of the British Empire.

Walvin (1984: 42) lays great emphasis on the development of sophisticated attitudes on racial matters by the Victorians at a time when Britain did not contain large black communities. The significance of this point has relevance for the development of racism in British society during the twentieth century, the second half of which can reasonably be described as a period when a sizable black population has been located in the United Kingdom. It is interesting that narrow, yet highly influential, ideas on race and racial determinism gained the most ground during a historical period when the black presence in Britain had, if anything, declined sharply to a tiny and fairly remote core. The Victorians, whilst thinking, writing and debating about black–white relations, *cannot* have done so on the basis of experience. Inter-racial contact within Britain was minimal and certainly not the basis of the vast outpouring of scientific racism at this time. As Walvin writes:

> The English, when talking or writing about the black, were normally dealing with an abstraction, even a stereotype. Those stereotypes undoubtedly had their roots in reality, however geographically or historically distant: the West Indian slave, the 'musical black' or the US cotton slave. But it had little substance in domestic experience.
> (Walvin, 1984: 42)

The other white minorities

The historical experience of the other ethnic minority communities has frequently been overlooked by scholars of race and racism in Britain. In recent years, however, writers such as Miles (1982) and Holmes (1979) have been at pains to draw a number of necessary and important links between the politics of the Irish and Jewish presence in Britain and the contemporary analysis of race in British politics and society. By examining these two experiences – as well as those of other migrant groups such as the Huguenots – we can see the way in which the British state has regulated entry into British society at different times and with varying degrees of flexibility. The exclusionary role of the state has undoubtedly ebbed and flowed at different times, making the comparison with post-war immigration policy towards non-white potential settlers more worthwhile. Additionally, examination of these other minorities reveals important clues regarding the development of

British racism and the dynamics of race-related issues in British politics.

The Jewish diaspora in British society

Few perspectives of the historcal context of immigration to Britain would be complete without consideration of the tradition of Jewish settlement. In the 1970s, estimates of the size of the Anglo-Jewish population suggested that they numbered just over 408,000 persons (Kosmin and Grizzard, 1974), although given the absence of firm census data on religious affiliation, it has always been difficult to provide precise measures of this population. Almost 260,000 of these were London-based Jews, the vast majority of whom were located in just five outer-London boroughs (Barnet, Redbridge, Brent, Harrow and Enfield, in order of scale). Moreover, as several social demographers have noted, the issue of the exact size of the Jewish population may be less significant than its internal composition and distribution across lines of religious affiliation (liberal as opposed to orthodox), place of origin (eastern as opposed to central European), period of settlement (pre-1914 as opposed to post-1914), and so on.

The origins of the Jewish presence within Britain stretch back far beyond nineteenth- and twentieth-century migration. Indeed, the Norman invasion of 1066 is widely credited with the first large wave of Jewish settlement alongside that of a variety of other communities. The Norman invasion also provides historians with a rich source of material for enquiries into the population of England since it was the Domesday Book compiled in 1086 which left a legacy of society at this time. Initially permitted to settle in England because of their renowned talent in commerce and finance, the Jews prospered under the successive English monarchs, all of whom were keen to exploit their vocation when it came to raising funds for military adventures.

However, the special protection and close association with the monarchy did not prevent the community from being singled out as targets for envy and hatred. 'Jew-baiting', as the practice of periodic attacks on the persons and property of Jews came to be known, was not only tolerated but occasionally encouraged by monarchs and their courtiers. For example, following the coronation of Richard I in 1189, some thirty Jews were killed in rioting in

London. The following year, York was the location of some of the fiercest pogroms ever witnessed in England. Even the Magna Carta settlement of 1215 contained two specific clauses aimed at reducing the scope and returns of Jewish financiers. The onslaught against Jewish wealth intensified during the thirteenth century, culminating in their eventual formal expulsion by Edward I in 1290. The attack on the Jewish community was particularly significant since, as Walvin (1984: 21) points out, they did not by any means hold a usury monopoly (Italians and the Flemish also featured heavily in this area of the economy). Moreover, from the early medieval era onward Jews were the subject of organised mythology which viewed their traditions as symbols of evil 'unleashing on the heads of medieval English Jewry destructive forces from which Jewish society was not able to recover' (Walvin, 1984: 21). Following expulsion, Jews did not return to English society in significant numbers until the seventeenth century, pursuing once again their familiar financial and commercial trades to the antipathy of others.

This picture of hostility, hatred and expulsion was the backdrop to the much larger-scale Jewish immigration which took place during the nineteenth and twentieth centuries. Moreover, with the rise of ideas of 'scientific racism' during the nineteenth century, older portrayals of the Jews as alien strangers to be feared were given new credence. Indeed, Miles (1989: 58–9) argues that the then newly-created notion of 'race' meant that earlier historical suspicions and myths concerning the Jews were transformed into a form of explanation in itself. According to Mosse's study of the history of European racism:

> The mystery of race transformed the Jew into an evil principle. This was nothing new for the Jew . . . . But in the last decades of the nineteenth century and the first half of the twentieth, the traditional legends which had swirled about the Jews in the past were revived as foils for racial mysticism and as instruments of political mobilisation.
>
> (Mosse, 1978)

The large bulk of Jewish settlement in Britain occurred between 1881–1945. Large-scale, New Commonwealth black settlement, in contrast, has been a largely post-war phenomenon. This rough historic demarcation has consequently lent itself to comparisons between the political responses to the two waves of immigration. Late-Victorian and Edwardian Britain became the destination of Jews both from eastern Europe and from Russia. The latter began fleeing tsarist Russia in the aftermath of the attacks made on them following the assassination of Alexander II in March 1881. They fled all over Europe, and the most populous group migrated to the United States, passing through Britain *en route*. Many also sought new lives in Britain and by 1901 their numbers stood at almost 83,000. The pressures pushing Jews out of Russia greatly escalated after 1899, with the effects of famine and war being felt most harshly. By 1905 the situation for virtually all remaining Russian Jews (still more than 5 million strong at the end of the nineteenth century) had become desperate in the wake of anti-Jewish violence which accompanied the first Russian Revolution. The rapid upswing in the numbers of Jewish refugees in Britain produced a political response during 1902–6 which focused on the most recent arrivals, thereby ignoring the longer tradition of Russian and east European *non*-Jewish settlement. Moreover, it is interesting to note that the flight west from Russia was not by Jews alone but also comprised large numbers of non-Jewish Russians, Poles and Germans.

At this time the term 'Jew' became more or less interchangable with 'immigrant'. The general response to the influx was one of a growing anti-Semitism which sought explanations for society's problems in terms of the influence of the spatially concentrated Jewish minority (Holmes, 1979). Significantly, the issue of the absolute size of the community appeared to be largely irrelevant to the scale of opposition to it: Gartner (1973) reports that some 120,000 Jews settled in Britain between 1870–1914, and according to Pollins (1982) the 1914 total stood no higher than 300,000. Further, this population was remarkably concentrated in a handful of cities, particularly in urban areas of Manchester, Leeds, and Glasgow, as well as in London's East End (Alderman, 1989: 27–53).

The campaign to restrict the inflow first gained currency during the late 1880s, but it was not until the Conservatives were returned to office in 1895 that there was any real prospect of passing new legislation on the issue. The popular campaign against further Jewish immigration was characterised by sloganeering and half-truths, all factors exacerbated greatly by the lack of reliable or plausible figures. Since 1836 an Aliens List had been kept by the Board of Trade based on the rather haphazard practice of requiring shipping captains to submit lists of all aliens arriving aboard their vessels. But because of the inadequacies of this system – a Select Committee criticised the procedure during the 1890s – it was not possible to arrive at an agreement on the rate of Jewish immigration. All that could be done was to press the operators of the existing machinery to implement it more diligently.

The political response to the perceived crisis was the 1905 Aliens Act. This piece of legislation constituted a major change in immigration control and also formed the basis of future post-war controls on immigration. In the short term the legislation had its desired affect: in the eleven years after the Act just 30,000 Jews settled in Britain as compared with over 67,000 in the five years immediately preceding it (Walvin, 1984: 64). The mechanism by which this dramatic reduction was attained was, firstly, by refusing entry to all those who did not have, nor had the means to obtain, the basis of subsistence, and secondly by automatically expelling any immigrants who, within a year of entry, either received poor relief or were convicted of vagrancy or living in insanitary or overcrowded conditions.

These measures reflected the common belief that immigrants were necessarily a drain on public resources. However, as Walvin (1984: 65) reports, the grounds for this belief were spurious: according to figures from 1901, some 15.2 per 1,000 of the non-immigrant population were in the workhouse whilst just 1.7 per 1,000 of the European immigrant population were similarly placed. Instead, the vast bulk of these early Jewish immigrants were found working in or alongside commercial activity of one form or another, with the garment trade in London's East End providing substantial employment for many. The new law also embodied a long-running line of *dual thinking* about immigrants in general which sought to limit their access and use of public resources whilst simultaneously pandering to common beliefs concerning their economic success and accumulation of wealth. Needless to say, such a contradiction has continued to characterise subsequent political debates relating to later cohorts of immigrants from the New Commonwealth.

The 1905 Act was important for two further reasons. First, the legislation established the principle of relatively free entry to refugees who could demonstrate that they were persecuted on either religious or political grounds (Macdonald, 1983). This principle would, of course, prove to have even greater resonance in the context of Jews fleeing the Third Reich in the 1930s. Second, the Act established the right of the Home Secretary to keep out or expel so-called 'undesirable' immigrants, albeit subject to appeal before the newly created Immigration Board. The effect of this device was to keep a close check not only on the *numbers* entering Britain but also on the *nature* of would-be immigrants.

It had taken a resolute Conservative government to bring in the new legal regime, but no sooner had the ink dried on the new Act than the government was replaced by a radical Liberal administration in 1906. Whilst the Act remained on the statute book, the new administration ensured that its implementation would not lead to a draconian policy of keeping out all potential immigrants. That said, from 1906 until the outbreak of war in 1914, 'the Aliens Act proved highly effective in the task for which it was designed: keeping immigrants out' (Walvin, 1984: 66–7). Control of immigration had been achieved, but virtually no attention was paid to the problems of Jewish and other immigrants already settled in the country.

With the Act firmly in place, the immigration question moved to the backburner until the outbreak of war in 1914. The heated, jingoistic atmosphere surrounding the descent into war had dramatically altered public fears about newcomers. Further, elite political opinion was chiefly motivated by the supposed imperatives of national security. The fear of spies, in short, enabled Parliament to pass the Aliens Restriction Act 1914 in just one day, giving immigration authorities wide powers to stop the entry of unsuitable would-be immigrants, to repatriate or intern foreign nationals seen as threats to national security, and to impose considerable limitations on the movement of other aliens within Britain. The new law also required a comprehensive register of aliens to be set up, a practice which continued after the war ended through the use of Orders in Council. Furthermore, after the war a number of additional Acts were passed, culminating in the Aliens Order 1920 which gave the Home Secretary extensive authority to regulate and bar aliens' entry into the country.

The second substantial wave of Jewish immigration occurred during the interwar period and trailed off in the immediate post-1945 years. Between 1933–45, around 65,000 Jews are estimated to have settled in Britain (Sharf, 1964: 155). The rise of European fascism – and particularly the Nazis in Germany – lay behind the massive movement in peoples from central Europe westwards at this time. However, despite the overwhelming threat and reality of persecution faced by Jews and others, the legal framework governing British immigration control remained unchanged since the 1920 Order. This meant that those refugees lacking the obvious means to support themselves and their dependants were subject to refusal by the immigration authorities. Furthermore, as Sherman (1973) has stressed, the response of British governments during the 1930s to the refugee tide was to claim that overcrowding and economic dislocation at home made Britain an unsuitable destination.

The campaign to limit refugee settlement as far as possible was on. But notable sharp comparisons were evident between the 1930s' influx and that of the pre-1914 era. To begin with, the former was largely composed of prosperous middle-class Jews who had previously formed the heart of successful German society (Walvin, 1984: 85). Few were poor or destitute, which effectively made earlier official responses to their immigration rather inappropriate. Second, the domestic climate within Britain during the 1930s was influenced by the emergence of Oswald Mosley's brand of British fascism. Opinion remains deeply divided among political historians as to the extent to which pro-fascist sympathies clouded the views of British elites at this time. The British Cabinet, reports Walvin (1984: 87), even received advice from MI5 in 1938 that German policy was to flood Britain with Jews in order to manufacture a 'Jewish problem in the UK'. Suffice to say, the issue of German Jewish refugees was not handled in a foreign-policy vacuum and was closely interlocked with Britain's rather nervous responses to the rise of German National Socialism and German foreign policy between 1933-39.

Lastly, the backdrop to the 1930s' debate was increasingly shaped by the issue of Palestine which, as a result of the British mandate since the end of the First World War, had put a new complexion on the question of Britain's relations with world Jewry. Despite these important contrasts between the two cohorts, the common thread behind both was that of anti-Semitism in British society (Kushner, 1986). The British Union of Fascists may have been the most vivid example of organised anti-Semitism during the second wave of Jewish settlement, but its roots went back to the same feelings of hostility and suspicion shown to the rather poorer and socially distinct Jews who had fled Russia at the turn of the century.

The 'special case' of the Irish

The presence of the Irish in Britain has tended to be analysed separately from that of other immigrant groups, thereby perhaps warranting the 'special case' label. While there have been important variations in Irish and non-Irish immigration, certain parallels can be observed and the experience of Irish settlement can be important to our wider understanding of migration. In addition, a historical survey of British political responses to immigration reveals certain forms of sentiment geared specifically to the Irish case.

The primary factor underlying the large-scale displacement of Irish people from Ireland was the famine of the middle part of the nineteenth century. But this well-documented emigration was preceded by an earlier movement during the eighteenth century when, largely as a result of the social turmoil caused by a doubling in the population between 1780–1840, significant numbers of Irish left their homeland for England, Scotland, Wales and the New World (Walvin, 1984). The rather uneven pace of economic development on either side of the Irish Sea ensured that the great bulk of the exodus took advantage of the geographic proximity of England and went eastwards. Walvin also notes that a dramatic fall in the cost of transportation to landings in various English ports also encouraged Irish immigration. The rapid industrially based growth witnessed at this time in the British economy created an upturn in the demand for labour which the Irish immigrants were able to satisfy (Miles, 1982).

But it was the potato famine that began in 1845 that fuelled the already established migration route across the Irish Sea. Estimates of the size of the Irish-origin population at the 1841 General Census put the number at around 415,000 people (across England, Wales and Scotland). This total rose by a colossal 311,000 in the ten years to 1851, putting the total just short of 750,000 persons. The 1861 Census recorded a total Irish population of over 805,000, after which subsequent censuses revealed a steady decline. From the 1851 peak of 2.9 per cent of the population of England and Wales, by 1891 the Irish origin population had declined to 1.6 per cent. On top of this massive immigration, many thousands more had left for promised better lives in the United States (between 1874–1921, a staggering 84 per cent of Irish emigrants took this route compared with just 8 per cent who settled in Britain!). Finally, the political turmoil surrounding the republican rising of 1916 and the birth of the Irish Free State in 1923 added a further impetus to migration to Britain. The route westwards to the United States had been sharply narrowed in 1924 when a quota of under 29,000 immigrants per annum was introduced, which was further cut back to under 18,000 per annum in 1929. This restriction meant that any remaining waves of immigrants turned in larger numbers than before to seeking a new life in Britain as opposed to the New World.

The 1840s saw large pockets of Irish minorities develop in many towns and regions, with the principal points of concentration in London, Birmingham and Liverpool (Gilley, 1978; Lees, 1978). Forty years later, many had drifted further afield and settled in towns with minimal previous contact with the Irish. Some fairly detailed accounts of the scale and nature of Irish settlement in different parts of Britain have been produced (see Jackson, 1963; Lees, 1978; Gilley, 1978; Finnigan, 1985).

Throughout the bulk of the period of mass Irish immigration, the British state adopted a more or less *laissez-faire* open-door policy to the regulation of the new arrivals. Perhaps one key factor in this approach was the Act of Union of 1800 which served to incorporate Ireland into the United Kingdom, thereby conferring a common citizenship upon the Irish masses (Miles, 1982). This factor surely placed great constraints upon any British politicians who may have wished to resort to legal controls over Irish immigration. Indeed, even following the establishment of Irish self-government after 1922, the people of Ireland continued to be afforded unique rights to enter and leave Britain at will. A largely intact derivative of that policy still survives to the present, allowing Irish citizens wide rights of movement, settlement and political enfranchisement.

Anti-Irish sentiment has been a feature of British society for several hundred years. That such sentiment extended into a series of well-developed caricatures and prejudices has not been questioned by many scholars of the Irish–British nexus. However, considerable disagreement does seem to exist on the question of whether such sentiments and attitudes were based on racial – rather than national or merely cultural – terms of reference. Aspects of Irish economic problems, rural environment, poverty, and Roman Catholicism have all featured in the English stereotypes of Ireland and the Irish people. Yet it is the case that observers of the Irish influx in eighteenth- and nineteenth-century Britain rarely turned to overt racial categories to explain the hardship and suffering of many Irish immigrants. Walvin (1984: 52) suggests that this was because

> the Irish invariably had the worst of everything: they were unquestionably the poorest, the worst-paid, most badly-housed and most alien of all urban groups. Merely to describe their social rank and suffering was to speak of the lowest orders of urban people, all without imputing to them the vices of and shortcomings of their 'nation' or their 'race'.
>
> (Walvin, 1984: 52)

Furthermore, the engine of Victorian attitudes towards race was largely fuelled by a fascination in the non-white races' social and cultural development. This curiosity served to create a 'gap' between an understanding of relations between white ethnic groups on one hand (for example, Saxon and Celt mixing which was seen as beneficial) and black–white relations on the other (for example, black–white racial mixing which was seen as harmful and to be regretted). However, the English Victorians were concerned to place a degree of distance between themselves and the Irish newcomers, choosing to think of the latter in socially, culturally and economically inferior terms. Miles (1989: 58) has argued that the Irish in nineteenth-century Britain were seen in terms that amounted to racial distinctiveness based on a deterministic understanding of what it meant to be Irish. Curtis (1971) has also stressed the tendency of the Victorians to adopt discrete racial categories to describe and explain the Irish presence in Britain.

In all of this, the determination to preserve notions of English 'purity' that had been ideologically constructed were crucial to Victorian and later attempts to locate the 'other' in white Anglo-Saxon society (Rich, 1986b). The use of such an ideological construction in the development of racial categories and arguments returned to shape the reaction of white British people to the arrival of black immigrants after 1945.

Early twentieth-century attitudes towards race

The development of British racial attitudes appears to owe less to the direct face-to-face contact between white Britons and black people and more to an underlying system of values and assumptions about Britain in a period of unique economic expansion. The racism of Empire therefore took its cue from the requirements of an imperial foreign and trade policy. Consequently, once the Empire began to decline and was dismantled during the first half of the twentieth century, Britain had developed a long tradition of viewing black people from the vantage point of superiority. The end of Empire was also coupled from the 1950s onwards with the migration of significant numbers of black people from former colonies to the 'mother country'. The new direct contact that this process led to – bringing many white Britons into face-to-face competition for scarce resources such as housing and employment with black immigrants – took place against the backdrop of an engrained racism. The contemporary politics of race in Britain have been further shaped by the social, economic and cultural implications of post-war mass immigration which occurred *after* the formal withdrawal of the British state from its imperial role.

Although large-scale black immigration to Britain only took root after the end of the Second World War, the black presence in British society continued to be significant throughout the first half of the century. During this period the underlying terms of the contemporary political debate about black migrants were forged. Significantly, fairly sophisticated ideas about racial ordering seemed to permeate across a largely white society with minimal experience of daily contact with black people.

The interwar period was one in which political discourse about race was mainly concerned with the alleged social problems associated with black settlers. The emphasis in such discourse was placed upon social decay, criminality and economic decline. Public images of the small yet relatively concentrated black communities of Bristol, Cardiff, Liverpool, Southampton and elsewhere were common and climaxed around the 1919 street disturbances in several of these port towns. Political historians of this period such as Ramdin (1987) have traced the origins of the 1919 race riots back to longer-standing tensions between local black and white communities. In Cardiff in particular, simmering tensions between local white working-class mobs and the city's small Chinese community had erupted into open conflict in 1911. Job prospects, housing, rates of pay, and personal security were all points of resentment among the city's white community, anxious to seek out scapegoats for the various social ills they suffered. Ramdin's description of the 1911 violence in Cardiff is particularly telling about the impossible corner in which black seamen and their families found themselves:

> Black men were hunted and beaten by the mobs. In general, the mood was kill and/or lynch black people. The bogey-man was always black; the scapegoat who was rooted out and rushed upon by the mob . . . . There was no doubt that [the racist attacks] caused the maximum physical and psychological damage to the black community.
>
> (Ramdin, 1987: 73)

The result in Cardiff and other towns was that the black community now faced a harsh choice between racist oppression and economic destitution on one hand and the possibility of voluntary repatriation on the other. Indeed, it was not uncommon for black families to seek official government assistance to return to their perceived 'homelands'. Before long a debate of sorts had begun on the long-term future of black communities such as those of Cardiff and Liverpool. Ports such as these shared a great deal in common, including significant black settlements. With the gradual decline of the local shipping industries, coupled with a more general structural decline in their local economies, the pressures of economic competition between black and white grew even greater.

In this context every conceivable advantage possessed by white workers over their black counterparts was pressed, not least through the role of the trade union movement in seeking to protect jobs for white members. The message conveyed to the black population was both short and clear: entry into the ranks of the British labour movement – notwithstanding the parallel struggles of black and white workers – was inconceivable. According to Kenneth Little's now somewhat dated historical study, *Negroes in Britain*, the black worker was viewed

> not as a section of the same labouring class striving for a livelihood on exactly the same basis as any other union member, but as the representative of an altogether different and competitive category, which directly or indirectly was responsible for keeping white seamen out of work, and forcing down their standard of living.
> (Little, 1947: 34–5)

The distinction between the interests of black and white workers that had been drawn was to underscore the historical development of labourism throughout the twentieth century. The relationship between race and racial issues and the politics of social class has been complex and characterised by unease and regular conflict. Moreover, following the arrival of large numbers of black workers in British society after 1945, the relationship became increasingly tenuous and strained, prompting several important academic debates concerning the race–class nexus. These events and debates will be returned to in later chapters.

The disturbances of 1919 in Liverpool and Cardiff merely represented a much wider rise in local racial conflicts throughout the country. A number of factors have been cited by writers to explain this abrupt outburst of anti-black sentiment, including rising unemployment caused by the declining shipping industry, the heavy-handedness of the police authorities, and the animosities caused by both the fact and fiction of black–white sexual relations. In addition, the role of the trades unions was crucial in the development of a common workers' racism centred on the competition for jobs.

The shipping industry presented a clear example of the early attempt to exclude black workers from the British working-class movement. The passage of the 1920 Aliens Order and the 1925 Special Restriction Order placed further pressure on black seamen and their families. Both pieces of legislation sought the restriction of alien immigration by clamping down on immigrants who were unable to show evidence that they could support themselves. The effect of this move was to create a clear opportunity to single out immigrants who were seen as a drain on the public purse. While many white workers also endured a similar regime later during the 1930s, the scope of the moral problem of the black unemployed was unparalleled at this time. The 1920 Order forced black seamen in Cardiff, Liverpool and elsewhere to register as aliens; the 1925 Order went further and extended black registration by ignoring altogether questions of nationality or residence. Those unable to demonstrate their identity or origin before the 1925 date were now placed in a very weak position, subject to immediate deportation without appeal at any time.

Another factor in the dramatic spiralling of racial tension at this time was the impact of mass demobilisation of troops following the end of the First World War. With local unemployment levels already extremely high, the return of large numbers of soldiers once the armistice had been agreed, meant that black workers who had previously been working in these port towns were suddenly under renewed pressure to stay one step ahead of the Public Assistance Committees and the police. Pressure was mounting on black seamen seeking to stay in jobs and in the country. Ramdin (1987: 78-79) reports that during the late 1920s several bodies began to lobby government to tackle the 'problem of coloured seamen'. For example, the 1929 report of the Cardiff Special Watch Committee adopted a resolution calling for new legislation to address these 'grave social evils', and in the same year the British Social Hygiene Council and the British Council for the Welfare of the Marine Merchant followed suit with similar pleas. Pitted against these calls however were a few voices which tried to highlight the plight of the black community as the consequence of racial discrimination. For example, the 1929 report of Cardiff's Juvenile Employment Committee stated that the problem was 'a very sad commentary on the Christian spirit . . . and indicates that the colour Bar is still very strong . . . ' (quoted in Little, 1947: 70).

The First World War had also seen large numbers of black colonial subjects join the war effort, both directly as enlisted armed servicemen and indirectly through the imperial manpower utilised to keep the British forces at war. At the outset of the bloody conflict in August 1914, the Liberal Prime Minister, Asquith, received 'comforting' news in a telegram from a colonial administration: 'Do not worry England, Barbados is behind you', it declared valiantly. The military contribution made by Britain's black colonial subjects was significant and by 1918 more than two and a half million colonials had fought for the British cause, including no less than 62,000 Indian casualties. The loyalty of the Empire proved to be a crucial assumption in the war effort leading to several historians taking the view that this factor was ultimately pivotal in securing victory (Walvin, 1984: 77-78).

Significant numbers of black colonials also found their way into British industries, resulting in many settling in existing black communities after the end of hostilities. From the 1920s onwards, it seems, the British Empire was changing in terms of the physical contacts it facilitated between the white metropolitan society on one hand and the non-white societies of its components on the other. Black settlement occurred and swelled because it provided black colonial workers the opportunity to try to improve their material conditions in Britain rather than return to the economically weak Caribbean or Indian subcontinent. The same basic rational calculations concerning improved life chances were to govern the much larger-scale immigration that was to occur a generation later after the 1945 victory.

Early black political activism

The interwar period saw an important development and extension of public awareness regarding the black presence in British society. This process was particularly fuelled by the activities of a number of national black figures in Britain and several prominent black organisations.

In 1931 the influential League of Coloured People was founded in London by a Dr Harold Moody, a revered Jamaican physician who had been strongly and publicly committed to fighting for equal rights for all black people in Britain. The organisation represented an early attempt at creating a national body committed to eliminating racial discrimination and it is interesting to note that even though mass non-white immigration did not take place until after 1945, many of its concerns and campaigns resembled those that were later taken up by organisations such as the better-known Campaign Against Racial Discrimination in the 1960s. The League became an important organisation in black political, social and cultural life during the 1930s and it even organised holidays for London's black schoolchildren (Walvin, 1984: 80). But its main focus remained political in the sense of campaigning for the rights of blacks in Britain in a pressure group role. For example, prior to 1948 many pre-National Health Service (NHS) hospitals placed a bar on the employment of black nurses and the League's activists were at the head of lobbies against this codified form of overt discrimination.

Whilst several other organisations and individuals also came to prominence within the ranks of the black community during this period, the League and Moody were by far and away the most significant. The contributions made by activists such as Moody have been the subject of a wealth of historical research, examining both the man as well as the pioneering group he led. It is most interesting that the research work on this influential man reveals what seems to be a recurring pattern amongst the black political elite of this era, namely, the disjuncture that existed between their personal life experiences and those of the mass of their ranks and the extent to which this tension provoked an early identifiable black consciousness. Moody was certainly privileged in many senses, arriving in London from Kingston in 1904 and qualifying in medicine in 1912. In *Negro Victory*, a biography of Moody by Vaughan (1950), the story is told of how Moody was prevented from using a public beach in the United States in the summer of 1919 whilst *en route* with his (white) wife and four children. The entry in his diary regarding this episode reveals the deep impression it had left on him, an impression mirrored in a variety of ways in the personal experiences of numerous other black leaders of the early twentieth century. Moreover, his words also placed emphasis on the – arguably more hoped for than real – rights of educated black people:

> I pray that God will help me to do something to alter this awful state of things . . . I pray God to give me grace, strength, ability and tact to do something to show the world that character and not colour is the thing of ultimate importance. I will not and shall not apologise for my birth.
>
> (Quoted in Vaughan, 1950: 46)

The incident undoubtedly reinforced certain feelings Moody already had on the race issue and caused him to make the work of the League his life's work until his death in 1947. But Moody was not alone and nor was the League lost without his contribution when in 1934 he stepped down from its presidency after a three-year term.

The significance of the League rests not merely on its pioneering role but also in the deep, though not widely reported, conflict that emerged within its ranks. The divisions were based on two factors. First, the organisation had always prided itself on its wide-ranging eclectic leadership, ranging from vocal right-wingers through to committed Communists. Second, confrontation with the issues of the day forced the League to examine its own position, often revealing a tenuous bond among its leaders based on an ill-defined single issue, namely race. For example, a rising sense of colour consciousness put pressure on the League's leaders to define the organisation's formal title. Whilst Moody was able to successfully carry the executive committee with him in the view that it meant a body for and on behalf of the 'Negro race', his opponents remained unconvinced. To be sure, the source and nature of these conflicts of nomenclature were to rise to the surface of intra-organisational politics a generation later within one of the League's successors, the Campaign Against Racial Discrimination.

Overview and conclusion

This chapter has been concerned with charting a historical overview of the presence of black people in Britain. It has also examined the changing attitudes towards black people and various other 'aliens' or foreigners in British society. These attitudes, as we have seen, were often shaped by the requirements of Britain's foreign policies and external relations with other countries.

A key feature within this historical process was Britain's emergence as a world trading nation. With the dramatic increase in trade from the sixteenth century onwards, English society came into regular and wide-ranging contact with the non-white-skinned peoples of Asia, Africa and the Americas. English traders became incorporated into the slave trade which forcibly removed countless millions of black people from their indigenous homelands and transported them in sub-human conditions to work the sugar and cotton plantations of the Caribbean and the southern United States. In doing so, one of the earliest systematic debates concerning racial stereotypes took place in English society. This debate was chiefly about how to populate the New World most effectively and fears were aroused that a population drift might occur leaving the Old World without sufficient labour. However, as the chapter emphasises, it was the economics of slavery which lay behind its great rise, by which the efforts of several slaves could be bought for the price of a single white labourer. Moreover, much of the cultural and racialised explanations used to justify slavery at the time came largely *after* its inception and wide-scale practice. Thus, an important conclusion of this chapter must be that the development of systematic racial attitudes and assumptions has often occurred regardless of verifiable truths and has been used to rationalise forms of economic exploitation.

Another important feature of the chapter was the changing relationship between British society and India. Whilst this relationship has been dominated by the imperial link, it is interesting to note that beneath this link lay a curious fascination on the part of the outward-looking and adventurous English with what was seen as the cultural mysticism of the East. This close fascination was at least partly reciprocated by Indians over the years. However, the relationship was also punctuated by spells of racial stereotyping in which Indians were portrayed as untrustworthy and conspiring. Whether these periodic bouts of anti-Indian hostility were tantamount to an expression of systematic racism is perhaps a moot point, but what is clear is that it took the Indian Mutiny to precipitate a sea change in this relationship. In other words, it seems that external, largely unrelated events were principally responsible for the rise of a form of hostility expressed in racial terms.

The conclusion that can be drawn is that it is meaningless to examine the development of forms of British racism without reference to Britain's extensive and long-running relationship with different parts of the world. This relationship forms the hallmark of British history since the Tudor age and therefore the features of race and racism in contemporary Britain must be viewed within their historical context.

3

The Social Demography of Multiracial Britain

Introduction

Britain is a multiracial society, in the narrowly descriptive sense of that much overused expression. Large numbers of black people have now been settled in Britain for over thirty years. According to the 1981 General Census of the Population, around 2.2 million people with origins in the New Commonwealth (NCW)[1] lived in Britain, and whilst the figures for the most recent Census (1991) have yet to be published (see Addendum to Chapter 3 below), all the indications point to a significant growth in Britain's black minority population. For instance, recently published official data estimate that the black population already exceeds 2.5 million – a rise of more than a fifth during a decade in which most primary and secondary black immigration had come to a halt (Haskey, 1990).

The purpose of this chapter is to examine some key aspects of the social demography of Britain's black population. In several leading studies of the politics of race and racism in Britain it is not uncommon to find the barest passing reference to the size and nature of this population and its component groups (see, for example, Layton-Henry, 1984; Layton-Henry and Rich, 1986; Solomos, 1989). Indeed, it is rather as if specialist writers on the politics of race in Britain have been reluctant to study the black population, whose presence and position in British society is purportedly being examined. Such a discomfort with demographics is hard to fathom for two reasons: first, there is now a trove of useful and interesting research information available on the British black population as a whole; secondly, the collection and dissemination of demographic data on black Britons has itself become a politically sensitive part of the wider debate on race relations in Britain. The consequence of the collective by-passing of socio-demographic research in academic studies of race and politics has been that students are forced to rely upon several rather specialised academic journals devoted to human geography – as indeed are several parts of this chapter's reference to empirical knowledge concerning black Britons. However, the consequences are not merely technical ones centred on narrow pedagogic distinctions between academic journals. The more significant result has been that the *political* analysis of race and racism sits rather uncomfortably within the academic study of politics.

Putting these preliminary observations about the use of demographic research in the political analysis of race to one side for a moment, the work of social demographers remains an important feature of the evolving race issue in British politics. The need for a chapter such as this can therefore be supported on three principal grounds. To begin with, the question of the numbers of black people either settled, or arriving to settle, in Britain has been an inescapable feature of the political debate on race during the post-war years. As Chapter 4 below goes on to note, the so-called 'numbers game' intensified and reached a highpoint during the 1960s and 1970s. For that reason, it is well worth acquainting ourselves with the actual scale of black settlement during this epoch and its subsequent growth or contraction in the period since.

LEEDS METROPOLITAN UNIVERSITY LIBRARY

Second, although the original substantial issue of black immigration involved in the 'numbers game' has declined in salience in the past ten years, issues relating to the social patterns of black minority employment, housing and education continue to attract periodic interest from both black political activists and the major political parties (Booth, 1988). A closer inspection of the race and education policy debate for example reveals that virtually all of the contributors to the debate rely in one way or another upon statistical data on the performance of black children in the classroom.

These data originate from two main sources: small-scale surveys of black attainment, and the analysis of larger aggregated data on black population groups and educational performance statistics. Therefore, in order to move beyond the necessarily limited pictures provided by small area surveys, policy-makers are forced to rely upon more general data concerning the black population. Given that this population is not static either in its geographical location or its internal composition, it is vital that policy-makers have available to them reliable up-to-date statistical information about the black population.

Nowhere is this need more acutely felt than in relation to policies that seek to help black people overcome racial barriers in jobs, education, housing and so on. The clear identification of the size and location of the principal policy subject – black people themselves – remains central to the broader perceptions of the success of the several important government programmes aimed at redressing racial disadvantage. For that simple reason, policy-makers in Britain have grappled with the issue of whether or not to include a direct ethnic origin question in the decennial General Census (Bulmer, 1986). The argument, when stripped to its barest essentials, has been that the viability of certain areas of public policy would be compromised without the availability of such data allowing policy-makers to pinpoint the present position of black people in British social and economic structures.

Third, as a number of writers have suggested, there is a need for closer study of social and economic variations within the black population (Miles and Phizacklea, 1977; Robinson, 1990a and 1990b). For over thirty years social scientists and policy-makers have attempted to characterise the general position of black people in British society, using collective analytical categories such as 'black', 'ethnic minority' or, as was commonplace until about ten years ago, 'coloured'.

Notwithstanding significant academic debates that have arisen about the use and suitability of these different terms, emphasis has shifted in recent years towards examination of the lives, experiences and opportunities of different component sections of the black population. The most common of these distinctions has been that drawn between black people whose origins lie in South Asia as opposed to Africa and the Caribbean. Several further distinctions have drawn interest including those of religion, language, caste and regional ancestry within the South Asian population. Empirical research carried out by Robinson (1986), for example, has highlighted the considerable degree of residential concentration found among different sub-groups of the South Asian population in a northern mill town (Blackburn), whilst Peach (1984) has pointed to similar structuring of residential patterns among the various island components of London's Caribbean population.

More recently, it has been suggested that as a result of the variations in experience and current location in British social structures, it is no longer meaningful to continue to view Britain's black population as a single socio-political category. Some have gone further and argued that the historical failure to analyse discrimination and disadvantage through the various categories of South Asian ethnic sub-groups has served to drive a wedge between British Asians and political movements aimed at attacking the racism to which they have been subjected (Modood, 1988). Whatever the merits of this argument (and criticisms of it are examined later in the book), it is important to note that moves are afoot within academic research to study sub-groups of the Asian and Afro-Caribbean communities in greater detail. The grounds on which such studies are justified are that variations within these communities may either be accounted for by, or be the cause behind the persistence of, different forms of ethnicity and ethnic cohesion (Robinson, 1990a).

Size and composition of Britain's black population

As previously stated, the last General Census carried out in 1981 suggested that Britain's black population stood at some 2.2 million people. It should be stressed that the census only provided an indication of the size of the black population based on a methodology which counts as 'black' all those living on census night in households the heads of which were born in the New Commonwealth or Pakistan (NCWP). This methodology in fact tries to establish a link between NCWP birthplace and ethnic group and, to that extent, follows the basis of the previous 1971 General Census which also sought to equate birthplace directly with ethnic minority status. The main difference between the 1971 and 1981 procedures was that the latter sought to generalise outwards by assuming correspondence of ethnic origin between household members and their heads whilst the former merely counted birthplace as a measure of ethnic origin. Both censuses nonetheless relied heavily upon an indirect, *proxy* test of ethnic origin which viewed birthplace as being of central relevance in assigning respondents to ethnic categories. Partly for reasons to do with the growing numbers of British-born black children and young adults, and partly because of the difficulties associated with not counting those black people born neither in Britain nor the NCW, by the mid-1980s the efficacy of this methodology was being questioned. In recent years, even the government agency responsible for conducting the census has all but conceded that traditional, birthplace-based methodologies could no longer be assumed to be reliable (White, 1990: 11).

The 2.2 million total can be broken down into several key groups, of which black people from the Caribbean, India, Pakistan, Bangladesh and East Africa are the best known. Table 3.1 illustrates this breakdown and shows that in 1981 ethnic Indians comprised the largest single NCW-origin group in Britain.

Table 3.1 Britain's ethnic minority population originating from New Commonwealth countries and Pakistan, 1981 General Census

Place of origin	*Percentage of total ethnic minority population*
Caribbean/West Indies	24.7
India	30.5
Pakistan	13.4
Bangladesh	2.9
East Africa	8.2
Other	20.2

Source: OPCS and Registrar General for Scotland (1983)

Added together, these five NCW sub-groups account for 3.4 per cent of the whole population of Britain. If the remaining NCW-origin countries are added (that is, from other New Commonwealth countries such as Guyana, Nigeria, Malaysia, etc.), the total rises to 4.2 per cent of the population – or around one in every 24 people. Of these, Indians alone make up 1.3 per cent and their numbers far outstrip those of the smallest group – Bangladeshis – at just 0.1 per cent of the population. When the ethnic Indians, Pakistanis and Bangladeshis are added together, the South Asian-origin population accounts for over half the total black population of Britain. South Asians' numerical dominance has been the product of two processes: first, their broad pattern of migration to Britain between the 1950s and 1970s, and second, their relatively high birth rates once settled in Britain (further evidence on this latter point will be outlined later in the chapter).

Of course, terms such as 'Indian' are only of limited relevance since such groups are structured by several notable cleavages, including those of religion, language and regional origin. Since the Census does not contain data on these variables, it is necessary to turn to the evidence provided by large-scale sample surveys of the black population. Amongst the largest and best known of these have been the surveys carried out by the Policy Studies Institute (and its predecessor, Political and Economic Planning). The most recent PSI survey (Brown, 1984) was published in 1984 and we shall return periodically to make use of its findings.

Brown (1984) indicates that around two-fifths of the Indian ethnic population are Sikhs (mainly from East Punjab in what is now the state of India), whilst a little less than a third are Hindus, with Muslims accounting for around a sixth of this population group. A sizeable proportion of Indian Hindus have their origins in the north-western Indian state of Gujarat. Pakistanis, in common with Indians, are also dominated by Punjabis (although this time from West Punjab in the modern state of Pakistan – the region was divided following Independence in 1947); the vast majority are Muslims. The Bangladeshis too are a largely Muslim population sub-group and originate in the main from the Sylhet region of the post-1971 state of Bangladesh.

This breakdown of the Asian population is, however, further complicated once allowance is made for Asians who came to Britain from East African countries such as Kenya, Uganda, Tanzania and Malawi (particularly between the mid-1960s and mid-1970s). Several studies of the British Asian population have treated this migrant group as being rather separate to the Asian population from the India subcontinent, stressing the cultural, linguistic and psychological distinctions that are said to exist between Asians originating from these two continents (Smith, 1989; Saggar, 1986; Robinson, 1986). Against this is the view that, notwithstanding more than half a century of largely separate development, the two groups still retain more in common than they do not. According to this view it is pointless to attach great sociological or political significance to variations in dialect, dress and diet and several other factors.

Clearly the impact of the parallel development of Asian communities within and beyond the Indian subcontinent cannot be entirely overlooked. In recent years detailed studies have been carried out illuminating the discreteness of internal cultural mechanisms among East African Asians in particular. Bhachu (1985) in particular has produced an intricately detailed insight into the history and society of East African Sikhs from the artisan Ramgarhia caste in their dual migration from Punjab to Britain via East Africa. If East African Asians are included within the population of Asians in general – a reasonable view given the not insignificant scale of cultural variation even among Asians of the *same* religion and region of the Indian subcontinent – we can see that, whilst Sikhs remain the largest group, their proportion of the East African cohort drops whilst that of Hindus rises from a third to two-fifths.

Black Britons with origins in the Caribbean account for around a quarter of the NCW-origin population. Perhaps even more than their South Asian counterparts, Caribbeans have been largely viewed as originating from an homogeneous society. However, given the island-centred geographic identity of the Caribbean region, a number of traditions have evolved in parallel with one another, serving to differentiate Jamaicans from Trinidadians and Barbadians from Dominicans and so on. The majority of Caribbeans born in the Caribbean itself are from Jamaica (56 per cent), followed by those born in Barbados (8.5 per cent), Guyana (7.3 per cent) and Trinidad and Tobago (5.5 per cent), with the remainder made up of those born in numerous other islands (Peach, 1986; Smith, 1989). Linguistically, very little data exist on the dialectic variations in Caribbean English. However, occasional case studies have revealed that such variations both exist and indirectly serve to structure the ethnic bonds between Caribbeans from the same islands as well as shaping patterns of integration following settlement in Britain (Sutcliffe, 1982; Peach, 1984: 226-28).

Patterns of immigration

The black population of Britain could be said to comprise three chief groups based on their mode of settlement. To begin with, there are those who migrated from different parts of the world – principally South Asia and the Caribbean – during the 1950s and 1960s to seek better jobs and economic futures for themselves and their families. This first category are commonly referred to as primary labour migrants. Studies of their settlement have tended to highlight the economic factors underlying both their perceptions and experience of immigration (Robinson, 1986). Moreover, it has been this category of immigrant that has tended to shape most prominently perceptions within the mass media and beyond concerning the reasons underlying mass non-white immigration to Britain.

During the 1950s there was a steady flow of primary labour immigrants to Britain from the Caribbean and the Indian subcontinent. To counteract this flow the government introduced statutory immigration controls in 1962, but this new legislation could not prevent a massive bulge in primary immigrants suddenly arriving in Britain in 1961–62 in an attempt to try to beat the effects of new controls based on labour requirements and skills. The revealing aspect of this first category is the extent to which it was composed of young males (Brown, 1984: 28). The primary immigration of this early period of mass non-white immigration to Britain was a largely male affair in which significant numbers of young married and soon-to-be married men came to Britain to search for work. A wealth of detailed local case studies exists to illustrate this pattern in such diverse places such as Southall (Saggar, 1991a), Leamington Spa (Jenkins, 1971) and Manchester and Wolverhampton (Beetham, 1970).

This leads on to the second category of immigration, namely, the dependants of primary economic migrants. As primary labour migration was progressively checked by increasingly restrictionist immigration laws after 1962, so the actual flow of primary immigrants began to fall off. It was the 1971 legislation which, through the concept of patriarchy reflected in its much criticised 'grandfather' clause, served to reduce radically the ability of new labour migrants to enter Britain, a country with which many could not claim to have a close ancestral link. From 1971 large-scale primary immigration had effectively come to a halt. Thus, reports Smith (1989: 25), between 1971–83 the average flow of South Asian immigration was just over 18,000 individuals each year; almost all of these were dependants of primary immigrants who had entered Britain often ten or fifteen years earlier.

For this reason, this category has often been termed *secondary* immigration, consisting of the wives and children of male primary immigrants. As later chapters go on to describe, the politics of the immigration issue as debated by the major political parties has often encompassed both these categories of immigration. At times the key issue of concern has been to close the door to the primary immigrant, and events surrounding the 1962 and 1971 Immigration Acts tended to reflect this angle of the issue. However, at other times party political attention has shifted to the 'problem' of whether and when to admit the dependants of immigrants already entered, in other words the secondary immigrant. Indeed, much of the political controversy surrounding the issue in the late 1970s and early 1980s had to do with a populist arousal of fears about the scale of secondary would-be immigrants who retained, but had yet to be given leave to exercise, the right to rejoin their breadwinners.

But it would be a mistake to conclude that post-war non-white immigration as a whole was a narrow, economic phenomenon. It was not and was accompanied by significant numbers of black immigrants who came to Britain to escape political difficulties of one form or another. This third category of immigration comprised what is often known as *political refugees* and, in that sense, represents a continuation of a much longer tradition of refugee settlement going back to the Huguenots and the Jews of the seventeenth and nineteenth centuries respectively.

In the post-war period such refugees to Britain have come from all over the world, but three clearly delineated waves of Asian explusions from East Africa stand out. Between 1965–68 the rising temperature of domestic politics in Kenya meant that a growing stream of Asian emigrants turned into a full-scale torrent in late 1967 and early 1968. It may have been that this influx did not constitute refugee status in the sense that few could point to overt forms of oppression in the country of origin. At most, many held rather less tangible fears concerning the future for themselves and their children in an ever more Africanised Kenya of the future. But this group of immigrants is more akin to refugees because of the British government's response to them. The Asians' collective will to exercise the right of abode – that their British nationality had conferred upon them – was largely rejected by the government. As subsequent chapters note, a new immigration bill was passed through Parliament in a matter of days in February 1968 which stripped such rights from the considerable numbers of Asians who had not already entered, or joined the queue to enter, Britain.

Another similar nationality crisis arose in 1972–73 over British Asians in Uganda, although on this occasion their blatant expulsion over a strict 90-day period meant that the British government was forced to recognise their refugee status and admit them to Britain. Finally, a third refugee episode took place during 1976 when several thousand British Asians were forced to leave Malawi under not dissimilar circumstances. In all three episodes it is possible to see the common thread of British nationals opting or being forced to settle in Britain for reasons that were fairly far removed from the economic reasons which had fuelled Asian and Caribbean migration in earlier years.

The main distinctions that can be drawn between the previous two categories and this category of immigration are threefold. First, the former categories took place, or were the consequence of, large-scale international movements of labour and can be viewed as aspects of changing economic realities; the latter category was largely driven by post-independence political conflicts. Second, the former categories occurred over a long timescale because of the dynamics of successful primary settlement and subsequent family unification; in the latter category, comparatively few families were separated over long periods and full-scale migration occurred in a number of short episodes. Finally, the politics of immigration have changed enormously from primary immigration concerns to do with the needs of the economy (1950s and 1960s), to domestic responses to external political crises (1960s and 1970s), through to the social aspects of family reunification (1970s and 1980s).

It is interesting to note the different effects these various categories of immigration have had on some groups of black Britons in comparison with others. Data collected for the 1984 PSI survey revealed considerable variations in the peak years of male and female immigration. Among the sharpest contrasts were found among ethnic Bangladeshis: barely one in five male immigrants compared with two-thirds of female immigrants entered Britain after 1972. Table 3.2 provides information about other minority ethnic groups.

Table 3.2 Period of settlement for ethnic minorities in Britain (column percentages[1])

	West Indian		Indian		Pakistani		Bangladeshi		African Asian	
Period	*men*	*women*	*men*	*women*	*men*	*women*	*men*	*women*[3]	*men*	*women*
Pre-1962[2]	70	54	24	13	32	5	19	0	4	1
1962–72	22	36	51	54	53	44	63	48	55	53
Post-1972	2	4	21	27	14	49	18	65	35	41

Notes: [1] Column percentages do not equal 100 due to omission of 'don't knows' etc
[2] Column figures as given in original source.
[3] Up to July 1962
Source: Brown (1984), 27

Focussing on slightly different time cohorts, data from the Labour Force Survey (LFS) analysed by Saggar (1986: 403) showed that the bulge years of NCW immigration were between 1965–74 when 38 per cent of the total NCW population not born in Britain entered the country. Just 11 per cent had entered the country before 1955, a further 29 per cent during 1955–64, and the remaining 22 per cent between 1975–84. However this research revealed great variations in the settlement flow amongst different South Asian ethnic groups. A colossal 62 per cent of East African Asians first entered Britain during 1965–74 (in which two out of the three East African Asian nationality crises occurred). Among ethnic Bangladeshis, entry to Britain was a comparatively late phenomenon with some 57 per cent arriving between 1975–84; the survey figures recorded none who had first settled before 1955. But it was ethnic Indians and Pakistanis who exhibited the most evenly spread historic immigration patterns: between a fifth and two-fifths of each group settled in Britain in every ten-year spell from 1955 to 1984.

Geographic distribution

The geographic distribution of the black population has tended to reflect the patterns established following the early phases of immigrant settlement during the 1950s and 1960s. Consequently, it is the case that Britain's black population in the early 1990s is significantly more concentrated in the big cities than their white counterparts. Moreover, as we shall see, certain cities have proven to be more attractive areas of settlement for certain black communities than others. In general though, it would appear that the black population has located itself disproportionately in the inner and inner-suburban parts of Britain's cities rather than in the suburban and more outer-lying areas surrounding those cities.

Any analysis of the geography of black settlement must distinguish between two questions, particularly when drawing comparisons with patterns of white settlement. First, there is the question of the *national distribution* of either the whole black population or discrete groups within that population such as Indians or West Indians. By examining the national breakdown of the population, we can make comparisons between different groups and generalise about each group's strength of representation in various parts of the country. Second, there is the question of the *ethnic composition* of different regions and cities. Sub-national breakdowns show levels of individual group representation in a specific area of the country and can tell us a lot more about the sorts of minority–majority relations found in that area.

Thus, it is quite possible to find that a group is more heavily concentrated in one particular city rather than another but is by no means the biggest ethnic minority presence in that city. The case of ethnic Bangladeshis is illustrative of this point since most of them are located in London, a city whose ethnic composition is far more heavily made up of ethnic Indians as well as other minority ethnic groups. This sort of pattern is a reflection of the fact that there are minorities (and majorities) within minorities and, with this point in mind, it is important to remember that the local politics of race is often shaped by the particular sort of ethnic mix found in a given locality. However, in the case of other groups – ethnic Pakistanis in West Yorkshire for example – there is a general concurrence between their skewed geographical distribution in one area and overt strength of numbers among the black population in that area.

Using self-ascriptive ethnic origin data from the mid-1980s, Table 3.3 describes the regional distribution of the whole population across ten regions and compares this with the distribution of the black population.

Table 3.3 Comparison of the ethnic minority population distribution with the total population distribution by region in Britain, 1983–85

Region	*Percentage of total population*	*Percentage of ethnic minority population*
Scotland	9.3	1.8
Wales	5.1	1.6
North	5.7	1.6
Yorkshire/Humberside	9.0	7.4
North-west	11.7	9.0
East Midlands	7.1	6.5
West Midlands	9.5	16.8
East Anglia	3.5	1.2
South-east	31.1	52.2
South-west	8.1	2.0

Note: [1] based on averaged results of the Labour Force Survey for 1983, 1984 and 1985.
Source: adapted from CSO (1987).

These data show that the geographic distribution of the black population generally does not follow that of the population at large. In particular, two regions (the South-east and the West Midlands) comprise almost seven in ten of the entire black population; by comparison, around four in ten of the total population live in these two regions. Elsewhere, extremely small proportions of the black population (8.2 per cent) live in five of the ten regions (Scotland, Wales, the North, East Anglia and the South-west) – regions which contain almst a third of the nation's total population.

The chief reason underlying the skewed geographical distribution of the black population is that it reflects the pulling effects of business and industry at the time of black immigrants' original settlement. Thus, early waves of immigrants from the Indian subcontinent and the Caribbean settled in Britain during the 1950s at a time when the regional economic decline of northern England and parts of the Midlands was less apparent. At that time plentiful employment opportunities existed for the new immigrants in northern mill towns and the Midlands' manufacturing industries. However, as many of these once-booming regions went into slow decline, subsequent cohorts of primary immigrants settled in these areas in smaller proportions. Consequently, large northern cities which contain significant black minority populations such as Liverpool and Manchester experienced only limited post-war black immigrant settlement. Responding to the bleak job prospects in these cities, black immigrants opted to settle elsewhere.

Of greater interest perhaps is the regional distribution of each of the main minority ethnic groups (CSO, 1987). This breakdown of the data reveals that virtually no ethnic Caribbeans are to be found in Scotland or Northern England; instead, more than four-fifths of this ethnic group live in the South-east and West Midlands (with two-thirds in the former region alone). Bangladeshis also exhibit a similarly strong tendency to live in these two regions (67 per cent and 16 per cent respectively). Their ethnic Indian counterparts appear to be a little less heavily concentrated in the South-east (49 per cent), though more heavily concentrated in the West Midlands (22 per cent). Moreover, across all ten regions, ethnic Indians generally seem to be the most dispersed community among the minority ethnic groups. Finally, whilst other minority ethnic groups tend to be found in one or two regions (the South-east and West Midlands), the ethnic Pakistani population is concentrated in three regions (the former two regions plus Yorkshire/Humberside where 20 per cent of their number are found).

As the LFS data breakdowns are published on a regional rather than a city-by-city basis, we have to turn to the traditional General Census data in order to find out more about the conurbations in which black people live. According to the 1981 Census, almost 79 per cent of all NCW-origin groups live in metropolitan areas (OPCS, 1983). This level of urbanisation is extremely high compared with the non-NCW population (49 per cent), and is further underlined by two factors. First, a large proportion of the black population have their origins not only in New Commonwealth countries but in the rural parts of those countries (see for instance Ballard and Ballard (1977) on the case of the Sikhs from the Jullander district of East Punjab). The socio-cultural consequences of this abrupt move from rural to urban environments is a frequently overlooked aspect of the political and sociological analysis of migration. However, these factors have been pursued by a number of writers engaged in researching micro-level small group behaviour. Second, it should be stressed that black Britons display very high levels of urbanisation living in a country which, by international standards, contains an exceptionally urbanised populace. For this reason, it is virtually meaningless to explore the politics of race in Britain without relating the investigation to issues in urban politics, an area in which the academic literature has grown rapidly in the past twenty years.

It is also striking that among the non-NCW population in the South-east region there exists a rough one-third–two-thirds split between those living in Greater London and those living elsewhere in the region (OPCS, 1983). Among the NCW population, in contrast, the division is reversed and approximates a three-quarters–one-quarter split. Moreover, when it comes to the region's Caribbean-origin population, getting on for nine in ten are Londoners; the nearest comparable figures are found among the region's Bangladeshi-origin and East African-origin communities (around eight in ten). Other notable concentrations include the huge concentrations of all NCW groups living within the city of Birmingham in the West Midlands (approaching nine in ten in most cases), and the heavy concentration of ethnic Indians and Pakistanis living in the West Yorkshire cities of Bradford and Leeds (more than eight in ten of each group within the region).

Age and gender

Whilst black people in Britain are minorities and endure certain tangible consequences from their minority status (most notably as a result of overt forms of direct discrimination), they also differ from the majority white population along several demographic criteria. The accumulated effect of these contrasts places further pressures on their life-chances in British society. To begin with, the age structure of Britain's black population differs significantly from that of their white counterparts. In short, black people in Britain are more likely to be younger than white Britons. This younger age profile is illustrated in Table 3.4 which compares the proportion below 35 years of age among the majority white and minority black populations. Moreover, as Table 3.5 shows, in a few cases the contrasts are so sharp that Bangladeshis can fairly be described as a generationally distinctive community in their own right. To be sure, a colossal seven in every ten ethnic Bangladeshis are less than 35 years old and, according to these averaged LFS data, hardly any are beyond the age of retirement.

Table 3.4 Age structures of the ethnic minority and white populations in Britain, 1986–88[1]

Age structure	*Ethnic minority population[1] (%)*	*White population (%)*
Under 35 years	70	47
35 years and over	30	53

Note: [1] self-ascribed non-white ethnic group based on the Labour Force Survey averaged over three years, 1986–88.
Source: adapted from Haskey (1990), Table 2.

This skewed age profile has great implications for the future population sizes of minority ethnic groups since it is precisely these age cohorts that make up the bulk of the child-bearing and rearing generations. Moreover, if this largely young, child-bearing population is coupled with a high birth rate together with a low mortality rate, then significant growth in its total size is likely to occur in the short run. Therefore, insofar as certain ethnic groups have experienced significant growth in the period since initial settlement, it may be that a large part of this increase is accounted for by internal growth factors (recent evidence on this point is examined later in the chapter). Additionally, growth through fresh external immigration – particularly through family reunification – will have a decreasing impact on the overall size of the group population. Ethnic Indians and Pakistanis are also made up of large proportions of younger cohorts, though in the case of the former the contrast with Bangladeshis appears to be quite sharp and may be indicative of an underlying pattern. That said, the much larger size of the existing ethnic Indian population means that, even if it has a smaller differential birth–mortality rate compared with the ethnic Bangladeshi population, the greater part of Asian population growth is likely to continue to be made up of young Indians rather than young Bangladeshis.

In order to confirm or dispel any suggestions about the ethnic composition of Asian population growth, it would be necessary to examine data pertaining to births and deaths. In the case of the former, the ethnic group of new births are not recorded; however, data pertaining to birthplace of parents does exist in a form that we can at least draw some conclusions from. In the case of the latter, the ethnic group of deaths are not recorded; however, since the mid-1970s, the OPCS has published information on the country of birth of mothers whose babies died at or shortly after birth (Grimsley & Bhat, 1988: 179). The country of birth of the parents of live births is recorded by health authorities and are published by the OPCS. However, as these only pertain to parents' country of birth, they suffer from the same drawbacks as data generated through the General Census, namely the failure to account for British-born black parents, the obvious inability to attribute births to parents of different ethnic groups, and the general confusion between country of birth and ethnic origin. In the case of the last of these problems, it is fair to say that as we gradually move further away from the era of mass New Commonwealth migration, the proportion of parents of new-born black children who were born outside the United Kingdom will progressively diminish. As this chapter goes on to note, British-born black people already account for more than half of the total black population and, in the case of some specific ethnic groups, the proportion is increasing at an accelerating rate.

Finally, amidst this general picture of ethnic minority population growth, it is important to note that the case of the ethnic West Indian population appears to be moving in the opposite direction. According to averaged LFS data from 1986–88 prepared by the OPCS, a small but significant decline in the overall size of this group is intimated (Haskey, 1990: 36). Over a seven-year period up to 1988, this ethnic group appeared to contract in size by around 33,000 individuals; its total population at the end of this period stood at around 495,000 individuals. This estimated decline, whilst only modest in scale (6 per cent), is interesting for two reasons. First, it places West Indian population growth patterns into a position comparable to that of the white population (which stood more or less still over this period) and may mean that it will begin to experience similar labour market difficulties as well (Ermisch, 1990). Second, this trend runs counter to the picture of dramatic growth experienced by certain ethnic Asian groups, among whom Bangladeshis for example are estimated to have roughly doubled in numbers since 1981.

The real significance of the younger age profile of certain sections of the black population lies in the differential birth rate with which such profiles are associated. With optimum child-bearing ages grouped in the second cohort shown in Table 3.5, we can see the disproportionate size of West Indians and Indians of these ages. If coupled with a mortality rate that does not fully compensate, these groups' population growth rates through differential replacement will be high and, in turn, will yield net rises in the absolute and proportionate size of their numbers. In the case of Indians such a rise is discernible; in the case of West Indians it is not. This is because a great concentration among optimum child-bearing age cohorts does *not* necessarily mean that many more children will be born. To achieve this requires a high birth rate as well. Across all ethnic minority groups, averaged LFS data from 1986–88 indicates some 825,000 persons below the age of 15 whose future impact in terms of differential birth rates has yet to be seen (most notably among Pakistanis and Bangladeshis). However, statistical evidence also exists to suggest that over time the reproductive patterns of the black and white populations are gradually converging and will continue to do so at an ever-faster rate. Some early indications of such convergence are already visible in the case of Indians (whose large numbers – almost 800,000 – mean that the net difference in the total black population's size will be notable) and West Indians (whose comparatively low birth rate, in line with that of young whites, is likely to lead to a further small dip in their overall numbers over the next 10–20 years).

Table 3.5 Population age structures of selected ethnic groups in Britain, 1986–88[1]

	Age cohort			
Ethnic group	*under 15*	*15–34*	*35–59*	*60 plus*
Whites	18	29	31	21
West Indians[2]	24	40	29	7
Indians[2]	29	39	28	5
Pakistanis[2]	41	35	21	2
Bangladeshis[2]	47	31	21	2

Notes: [1] row percentages do not equal 100 due to rounding.
[2] self-ascribed non-white ethnic group based on the Labour Force Survey averaged over three years, 1986–88.
Source: adapted from Haskey (1990), Table 2.

The point to be made is that the child-bearing associated with younger age profiles of population sub-groups is just that: association, not prediction. Thus, West Indians and various Asian groups may share a similar concentration of their numbers in the key 15–34 age cohort, but this does *not* mean that significant population growth is bound to result. Instead, in order to explain such growths and contractions other factors need to be examined, such as actual birth rates, mortality rates and the effects of continuing secondary immigration.

The ratio of males to females among the black population varies in differing degrees to that of the white population. Partly as a continuing consequence of early migration patterns which mainly involved young males, most ethnic groups within the black population today contain a slightly larger number of men than women. Over the years the effects of marriage and family reunification have slowly reduced this over-representation of men but have far from reversed it entirely. As Table 3.6 makes clear, the gender ratio is greatly exaggerated for some groups (Bangladeshis and Arabs) and reveals a greater preponderance of females to males among the white and West Indian populations.

Table 3.6 Number of males per 1,000 females in selcted ethnic groups in Britain, 1986–88

Ethnic group	*Number of males*
West Indians[1]	940
Africans[1]	1,200
Indians[1]	1,000
Pakistanis[1]	1,070
Bangladeshis[1]	1,240
Chinese[1]	1,010
Arabs[1]	1,630
All ethnic minority groups	1,020
Whites	950

Note: [1] self-ascribed non-white ethnic group based on the Labour Force Survey averaged over three years, 1986–88.
Source: adapted from Haskey (1990), Table 2.

Finally, it is also interesting to note the evidence concerning the correspondence of ethnic origin between married couples.

Evidence from a single LFS (1984) showed that cross-ethnic marriages remained relatively unlikely phenomena (Saggar, 1987a). Around 93 per cent of Asian husbands were married to Asian wives, whilst almost 98 per cent of Asian wives were married to Asian husbands. Virtually all white husbands (99 per cent) were married to partners of the same ethnic group.

Jobs and housing

The relative concentration of black people in urban areas of Britain has meant that the problems affecting them are often those affecting urban areas in general. The decline of the urban infrastructure has led to further problems in the quality of public and private services. Added to this general problem are those experienced by black people as a result of racial discrimination and the cycle of disadvantage that this frequently leads to. Black people consequently face problems in employment, housing and education which merely compound the worse effects of urban decline.

In the employment market, recent LFS data reveal that ethnic minority unemployment rates stood at 14 per cent of the working age population compared with 9 per cent among white people (*Employment Gazette*, 1991). But behind these unemployment rates lies evidence concerning the structure of the labour market and the roles played by the various ethnic minority groups in different areas of employment.

To begin with there appears to be a clear distinction between ethnic minorities and white people who are self-employed (16 versus 12 per cent). The highest self-employed proportions were found among the Pakistani and Bangladeshi workforce (22 per cent), followed by Indians (20 per cent) and lastly West Indians and Guyanese (14 per cent). Interestingly, these LFS data suggest that the proportion of ethnic minority men in manual occupations was no different to that of their white counterparts. According to the 1982 PSI survey around 30 per cent of all ethnic groups were employed in skilled manual work, but Bangladeshis, Pakistanis and West Indians were all significantly over-concentrated in semi- and unskilled work (Brown, 1984: 197). Further discrepancies are found when the earnings of black and white workers are considered. The PSI survey reported that black men earned on average much less than their white counterparts: around 15 per cent less than the median earnings of white men (Brown, 1984: 167–69). Such differences were compounded by regional variations in earnings and did not change greatly once differential membership of occupational categories was allowed for.

The picture of disadvantage does not get any brighter when it comes to patterns of housing among black and white Britons. Disadvantage is reflected in the type of tenure, size, age and conditions of housing and, despite certain trends towards owner-occupation among Asian households, the sources and conditions of housing finance are often less attractive than among white households. The PSI survey revealed that white, Asian and West Indian households have very different housing tenure patterns. Some 59 per cent of the first group were owner-occupiers, with a further 30 per cent renting from local authorities. The last group were the least likely to be owner-occupiers (41 per cent) and the most likely to be council tenants (46 per cent). In between, Asians were the most likely to own their homes (72 per cent) and the least likely to be council tenants. However, an exception within Asian households are Bangladeshis: just 30 per cent owned their homes, whilst over a half rented from local authorities. Significantly, the level of home ownership among Asian households does not decline lower down the occupational scale: the percentage of home owners dips to just 66 per cent among non-professional, non-manual workers but stands at a colossal 72 per cent among unskilled workers. The comparison with white and West Indian households across the range of occupational categories could not be sharper as Table 3.7 demonstrates.

Table 3.7 Owner-occupation in Britain in 1982 according to occupational category of household head

Ethnic group	*Occupational category*				
	Professional/ managerial non-manual (%)	*Other non-manual (%)*	*Skilled manual/ foreman (%)*	*Semi-skilled manual (%)*	*Unskilled manual (%)*
White	86	64	52	40	21
West Indian	78	26	44	34	33
Asian	73	66	78	70	72

Source: adapted from Brown (1984), Table 33.

Another important difference lies in the reasons why black and white council tenants were initially allocated public housing stock. Whereas homelessness was the cause of this type of tenure for just 6 per cent of white households, for Asian and West Indian households the comparable figure was 23 per cent (Brown, 1984: 118). This difference undoubtedly masks the greater level of desperation and urgency surrounding black take-up of public housing.

But tenure pattern alone does not necessarily reflect housing quality. Here again the PSI reported that black people in both the public and private sectors lived in dwellings that were smaller, of inferior quality and with fewer amenities than their white counterparts. For instance, while just 3 per cent of white-headed households in the private sector comprised in excess of one person per room, among Asian-headed households this figure rose to a massive 35 per cent; Bangladeshi-headed households in the public sector were the most overcrowded of all (Brown, 1984: 109). Across a whole range of amenities often thought of as essential in the modern age – separate bathrooms, running hot water, indoor WCs, and so on – black households on average fared worse that white ones. When it came to the average age of properties, some 82 per cent of black households occupied properties built before 1945 against 56 per cent of white households.

A major factor affecting Asian households is the general undersupply of sufficiently large-sized public housing. In 1982 Asian households on average contained 2.6 children as compared with 1.7 and 1.6 children in West Indian and white households respectively. In addition Asians' overall household size is likely to be larger than that of other ethnic groups once account is taken of extended and joint family structures. This demographic profile has meant that housing stock suitable to the needs of Asians is very limited, particularly in the public sector, thereby putting short- to medium-term pressure on many Asian households to live in overcrowded conditions.

Furthermore, according to Brown (1984: 79), the startlingly high levels of owner-occupation among Asians is 'in part a response to the limited opportunity to find rented accommodation . . . and was often characterised by the outright purchase of relatively cheap, poor quality housing'. Finally, the cumulative effect of several factors such as difficulty in securing loans, low wages, high unemployment, and discrimination by banks and building societies, has helped to push many West Indians into poor quality public housing and Asians into poor quality private housing. Consequently, black people have tended to fare worse than their white counterparts from house price inflation and, in the meantime, their poor housing conditions are likely to have contributed indirectly to hygiene and health problems. An intolerable position has been the long-term outcome in which poor social conditions have fed upon poor housing and vice versa. 'Relatively poor share of size and equality of equity held by blacks in the housing market is likely to be a major contributing factor in the cycle of deprivation', writes Luthera (1988: 131).

Overview and conclusion

In this chapter we have seen that on a number of fronts the socio-demographic profile of Britain's black population differs from that of the white population. The aim has been to provide a sketch of the main features of this profile and to lay the basis for meaningful comparison across both black and white communities and between the component ethnic groups within the black population.

The need to inform the study of the social demography of multi-racial Britain has at least in part been necessary because of the paucity of such perspectives within many existing political analyses of race. But why does such a need rank so highly to begin with? At the outset of the chapter it was noted that the growing volume of work of social demographers could no longer be viewed as a distinct and therefore inconsequential area of social research. Rather, it was suggested that empirical knowledge about the size and dimensions of the black population had been at the heart of political controversy over immigration for more than thirty years. To put it another way, the 'numbers game' was the very stuff of the politics of race, and political scientists therefore neglected this valuable field of research at their own cost.

However, it was also fair comment to claim that the traditional 'numbers game' of the past had gradually declined in political salience. The old-style preoccupation with progressively limiting the flow of NCW immigration had tended to ebb during the 1980s, albeit periodically punctuated with moments of potential resurrection over the Hong Kong question. In its place there developed a new game of numbers, this time one geared more towards the political debate over the needs and demands of black people in the sphere of social policy. In areas such as employment, housing and education, increasingly sophisticated debates existed in which rival viewpoints were fuelled by the engine of empirical social-demographic knowledge. Lastly, it was also suggested that such knowledge was instrumental to academic enquiries into social variations within the black population. Moreover, sustained arguments have been put forward calling for the abandonment of broad analytical categories such as 'black' in favour of a more sympathetic treatment of the forces of ethnicity in contemporary Britain. Whether participants in this fairly esoteric academic debate are aware of it or not, the implications of future shifts in this direction for the world of public policy-making are likely to be great.

The usefulness of providing an introduction to the social demography of multiracial Britain in the present volume can be supported by examining the links between empirical observation, social structures and political processes. (Or to put it more formally, we need to be constantly aware of how theory, data and analysis form the basis of a social-science understanding of race and racism in a modern industrial democracy.) For instance, by looking at the geographic areas of concentration of the black community it has been possible to develop a reasoned argument that the black population – or at least parts of it – are disproportionately caught up in the problems of urban deprivation and decline. Black disadvantage cannot always be attributed to clear-cut acts of individual discrimination. Rather such disadvantage stems from the processes of discrimination which have been institutionalised into the affairs of public and private agencies.

Racial disadvantage can therefore be more fully understood by examining empirical data on black people's housing, education and employment in the context of social theory. That said, a brief word of warning should also be sounded about the use and misuse of statistical data on black people. There is always the danger that such data, if presented in a partial manner, can serve to mislead perceptions about black people in Britain. The high average level of Asian owner-occupation must be a good case in point since it masks the fact that much of this housing is old, of poor quality, and often utilised because of the difficulties many Asians encountered in renting or buying good quality housing. We should be careful not to let enthusiasm for socio-demographic information in general cloud or over-simplify the reality of the position of black people in contemporary Britain (Saggar and Rhodes, 1988).

Later chapters in this book will go on to explore more fully the role of racial and ethnic issues in policy-making. The main thrust of the present chapter has been to argue that, all too often, academic studies of the politics of race in Britain have shied away from providing even a rudimentary introduction to empirical knowledge about what is after all one of our key dependent variables, black Britons themselves.

Notes

1. See Notes on Terminology at the beginning of this volume.

4

The Problems of a Multiracial Society

Introduction

In a previous chapter the history of black migration to Britain was detailed. However, it did not specifically examine the dramatic wave of non-white immigration that took place during the post-war period. Whilst several noticeable pockets of non-white settlement existed in Britain at the end of hostilities in 1945, the scale of their presence did not compare with the new immigration that started a few years later. During the late 1940s growing numbers of black immigrants began to settle in Britain. The 1951 Census recorded a nominal 'non-white' population of around 75,000; by the time of the next count in 1961, this figure had mushroomed to around 337,000.

Post-war immigration differed from earlier waves of immigration principally because of the colour of the immigrants coming to settle in Britain. The heaviest flows of primary labour migrants came from the Caribbean and Indian subcontinent and began in the late-1940s and early-1950s. The bulge years of this migration occurred during the period between the 1956 Suez crisis and the passage of the first major non-white-oriented immigration legislation in 1962. Indeed, as if to further stoke the domestic voices opposed to the new immigration, a huge increase in immigrant arrivals took place between 1961–62, many trying to beat the impending deadline of the 1962 legislation. Over an eighteen month period during 1961–62 immigration into the country outstripped the total for the previous five years (Walvin, 1984: 111).

Scholars of the history of immigration to Britain during the nineteenth and twentieth centuries have noted on several occasions the various policies and programmes aimed not merely at restricting the entry of new settlers but also at making provision for the social and cultural adjustment of the newcomers to their new environment (Katznelson, 1973; Freeman, 1979; Miles and Phizacklea, 1984). The British state has periodically made notable overtures towards such an integrationist strategy but the most significant and concerted spell of activity in that direction took place during the 1960s. That decade undoubtedly saw intense political developments in the debate about racial issues in Britain, and not merely at the level of formal immigration control (where no less than three restrictive Acts were passed). This era also witnessed important developments in the building of the new infrastructure to aid the settlement of the immigrants. Two notable Race Relations Acts were placed on the statute-book (1965 and 1968) and two further selective instruments of policy (the Section 11 scheme and Urban Programme) were also established at this time. The primary tasks of this chapter will be firstly to examine the scale and nature of these events, and secondly to evaluate their significance in terms of fostering greater racial equality in British society.

In the years since the adoption of these reforms in the 1960s the approach and strategy of successive governments in managing the issue of race has endured recurring criticisms from both the Left and Right of British politics. Whilst the Left has argued that governments of both parties have lacked an unambiguous commitment to ensure full racial equality, those on the Right have countered that public policy programmes have merely served to entrench the notion of racial inequality and thus undermine racial harmony. As this chapter goes on to explore, the merits of both positions have been sufficient to attract strong and vocal supporters to their respective causes.

Moreover, the long road to racial equality in Britain has sadly included numerous diversions which have served to shift the focus of public debate away from substantive issues and towards a fierce controversy over the question of the need for race relations as an ongoing concern of government agencies. Following popular press reports in the 1980s in particular, there was little shortage of easily vilified targets in this battle between conservative and radical perspectives. The latter's often vocal onslaught against specific examples of racism were quickly and roundly condemned as at best the work of a nonsensical 'loony' fringe and at worst the precipitant of a new wave of racial conflict. A remarkable series of mythologised empires had come to dominate popular perceptions of the need for and work of the so-called race relations industry. The industry, claimed its most ardent opponents, was at work among a new wave of radical Labour local authorities. As one commentator put it in a recent critical essay on the future prospects for British race relations, the whole debate has become entrapped under the weight of fashionable humour:

> There is a brand of cheap humour which thrives on sarcastic references to 'the race relations industry'. The staff of the Commission for Racial Equality and the local Councils for Racial Equality make an easy target for such jibes. It seems as if the input into organisations for promoting racial harmony has been substantial; the output of actual achievement looks much smaller. Most commentators seem to be extremely disappointed with the degree of progress and many of the enthusiasts for the cause have been frustrated by their experiences.
>
> (Banton, 1985: vii)

In this chapter we shall begin by examining the political responses to mass non-white immigration during the 1950s, an era described by Katznelson (1973: 125) as the 'pre-political consensus' stage, culminating in the development of a 'coherent politics of race' by 1961–62. The core of the chapter is concerned with the substance and aftermath of the liberal reform of race relations over the period 1965–68. The chapter then turns to link the liberal legacy with the sharp polarisation that has occurred in recent years over public policy programmes geared to combating racial equality.

As we shall see, the most important factor or series of factors that led to the present picture was the framework created by the 1960s' reforms and the effect this had upon shaping and ultimately constraining discussion of the race issue by policy-makers. To that end, whilst the chapter includes a review of the events surrounding the various race relations reforms during the 1960s, its primary concern lies in sketching the parameters for future action that the reforms themselves set down. The longer-term consequences of such constraint are apparent throughout different areas of British society and politics. Aspects of the enduring influence of the *liberal settlement* – such as policy debates over education and the inner cities, and developments within the major political parties in coming to terms with racial politics – will be examined in more detail in later chapters.

The rising political saliency of immigration, 1945–62

Although many of the most significant developments of the 1960s took place following the election of the Labour Government in 1964, the race issue had been steadily rising up the political agenda since the late 1950s. As we shall see, after 1958 public debate shifted to questions concerning the possible restriction of immigration from the New Commonwealth. At this time Britain was very much in the middle of its policy of retreat from empire and, following the second wave of decolonisation, new independent states were established throughout Africa, the Caribbean and the Far East. The Conservative Government under Harold Macmillan was pursuing a new phase in British foreign policy, attempting to move from a familiar imperial role to a new role based on the leadership of a Commonwealth of independent and equal nations. Moreover, disturbances in Notting Hill and Nottingham during 1958 suddenly and rather dramatically brought the issue of the social dimension of immigration into the limelight.

It was against this backdrop that the earliest parliamentary voices were heard calling for a restriction in the numbers of immigrants entering the country. Those politicians, mainly on the Conservative benches, who now called for restrictions did not have to search far for an *ad hoc* leadership on the issue. Since the mid-1950s a small handful of Conservative backbench MPs had regularly asked parliamentary questions on the issue of 'coloured immigration' to their frontbench colleagues and had argued the case for immigration controls based on the spurious 'need' to combat disease and criminality. Their best-known figures included Cyril Osborne, the abrasive MP for Louth, and Norman Pannell, who represented Liverpool Kirkdale. The lone Osborne–Pannell campaign may have failed to attract large support from other Conservative MPs, but it nonetheless ensured that the issue remained close to the surface of most debates concerning social policy and inter-personal relations. In November 1958 Osborne stated to his parliamentary colleagues the principal motive behind his concern:

'It is time someone spoke out for the white man in this country', he said (quoted in Foot, 1965: 129). Earlier in 1954 he had displayed the nature of his basic message concerning discrimination against black people: 'In many cases a part colour bar has had to be imposed against people of a certain colour . . . . It is a pity that such things have to be done [but] these things have to be properly understood' (quoted in Miles and Phizacklea, 1984: 27).

The post-1958 debate concentrated on two key themes. First, politicians of all shades of party opinion expressed the view that caution ought to be exercised when it came to a domestic policy matter that touched upon Commonwealth policy. Many MPs felt they were addressing the much broader question of nationality and citizenship rather than questions concerning the social consequences of black immigration. For that reason the parliamentary debate at least focused upon the narrowly defined issue of whether or not to alter the existing legal basis of immigration, the 1948 Nationality Act. Of course, the basic proposition advanced by those who favoured reform was the implicit promise that such a move would help to restrict black immigration into the country. But the big question remained that of Britain's position within world and Commonwealth affairs (Deakin, 1968). According to a junior Home Office minister speaking in 1958:

> this country is proud to be the centre of an inter-racial Commonwealth . . . which is the greatest assortment of peoples of all races, creeds, and colours the world has ever seen. As a result . . . we have always allowed any of the people in what was the Empire and is now the Commonwealth to come to this country and go as they please.
> (Hansard, vol. 596, col. 1552)

Second, the debate also revolved around whether the introduction of controls was likely to affect domestic relations between established white communities and black immigrants already settled in the country. Contributors to the debate did not limit themselves to the domestic consequences of introducing controls. Rather, many began with the premise that the presence of 'too many' black immigrants was the cause of housing, employment and other problems. Moreover, allegations about immigrants' involvement in crime featured heavily in the calls for restriction. This second dimension of the debate was ultimately to cause the greatest political conflict in that it seemed to establish a putative linkage between the immigration issue on one hand and the issue of race relations on the other. The seductive logic of the 'numbers game', equating immigrant concentrations with social problems, had been sketched onto the map of British political discourse. For example, by August 1958 the traumatic events of the so-called race riots had prompted the following demand from a backbench Labour MP representing the constituency in which the London disorders had occurred:

> The government must introduce legislation quickly to end the tremendous influx of coloured people from the Commonwealth. Overcrowding has fostered vice, drugs, prostitution and the use of knives. For years the white people have been tolerant. Now their tempers are up.
>
> (Quoted in Miles and Phizacklea, 1984: 36)

Closing the immigration door

By the beginning of the new decade enormous pressure had mushroomed among Conservative ranks for some decisive action on the issue. The idea of regulating the flow of what were after all labour migrants from the Commonwealth countries was explored among government ministers. The possibility of setting up bilateral talks with individual countries seemed to be one way forward provided that it was accepted among Commonwealth governments that there was indeed a need for controls of one form or another. If this principle could be conceded, it was hoped that negotiations about the year-by-year capacity of the British economy to absorb fresh immigrant labour could then commence. Within this sort of arrangement the actual flow of immigrants into Britain would be put onto a precise footing, governed by certain objective criteria such as labour demand in growing industries rather than by the individual or collective whim of would-be immigrants.

Moreover, by moving to such an approach, it was also hoped that further immigration of unskilled or poorly skilled labour would be curtailed, allowing fresh immigration to be directed to areas where immigrants holding specific skills could be matched up with specific job opportunities. Against this desire for a voluntary solution to the issue lay the fact that large numbers of new immigrants were continuing to arrive daily and grass-roots calls for their restriction were beginning to sound less like isolated voices and more like a chorus of outrage. In short, the issue had steadily taken on mass proportions.

The emergence in October 1960 of the Birmingham Immigration Control Association reflected just one example of organised opposition to further immigration at grass-roots level. The Association and its supporters received considerable national publicity during 1960–61, reaching a crescendo in February 1961 as the pressure group stepped up their campaign to coincide with Cyril Osborne's presentation of a Private Member's Bill in the House of Commons to introduce immigration controls. Earlier in summer 1960 and again in spring 1961 a group of Conservative MPs who supported the Osborne–Pannell campaign confronted the Home Secretary on the issue and claimed to have achieved considerable success in shaping official policy (Foot, 1965: 129–38). The lobby's message was straightforward: the government was running up against public opinion in general and was provoking great resentment among its own supporters in particular.

Opinion remains deeply divided over the reasons behind the government's change of mind. By the latter half of 1961 the national mood on the issue could be clearly discerned: according to one survey, over four-fifths of all manual workers supported a fresh governmnent initiative to curb black immigration (McKenzie and Silver, 1968). Not only was a strong majority in favour of introducing controls, the majority also attached a greater degree of importance to the issue than ever before. The activities of the Conservative anti-immigration parliamentary lobby were undoubtedly important but, in the view of the then Home Secretary, not nearly as important as was commonly supposed (Katznelson, 1973: 132).

The Conservative Party at large played an important part in transmitting grass-roots feeling upwards to the leadership and the October 1961 party conference endorsed wholeheartedly a motion in favour of immediate controls. But the key factor seems to have been the impact that this heated debate had on the flows of immigrants actually entering the country. Through the Indian subcontinent and Caribbean the suggestion that draconian controls were impending was taken as granted. Thus, from mid-1960 onwards the pressure to emigrate grew, particularly amongst those who were planning to rejoin their family members. The domestic debate therefore had greatly magnified the scale of immigration and, according to some commentators (Katznelson, 1973; Deakin, 1968), of itself precipitated the sudden need if not to halt then at least to regulate the flow of immigrants.

The 1962 Commonwealth Immigrants Act

The cumulative result of this unprecedented level of mass campaigning on a single issue was finally seen in October 1961. Having concluded that there remained no further political reasons for the *laissez-faire* immigration policy, the Conservative Home Secretary, R.A.B. Butler, introduced into the Queen's Speech a commitment to bring in statutory controls on Commonwealth immigration. The notional bipartisan line of avoiding explicit policies that had existed on the issue since 1958 had been finally broken. The Labour Opposition reacted by rejecting the impending Bill, both in principle because of its impact upon Commonwealth relations and over fears that it would in fact damage local race relations. The party leader Hugh Gaitskell in particular spearheaded a sharp attack on the Bill, arguing that its impact would undermine his party's enduring commitment to socialist internationalism (Finer *et al.*, 1961; Deakin, 1968). For the time being at least Labour remained firmly opposed to both the principle and practice of control.

The new Commonwealth Immigrants Bill had, should the Conservative administration have chosen to exploit the situation, played directly to the growing public mood for controls (McKenzie and Silver, 1968: 152). The new legislation sought to control immigration by only allowing entry to those in possession of a Ministry of Labour employment voucher; alternatively, entrants had to be direct dependants of voucher holders or be students with intentions of leaving Britain at the end of their courses. The vouchers themselves were subdivided into three categories, thereby differentiating the backgrounds of immigrants in relation to the needs of the economy. Category A vouchers were allocated to those who could show that they had a specific job to take up in Britain; Category B vouchers were given to those holding specific skills thought to be in shortage and therefore likely to find jobs quickly; whilst Category C vouchers were distributed to all other applicants, though ex-servicemen were to be given some priority.

Building the new liberal consensus

The race and immigration public policy measures of the 1960s are listed in Table 4.1. This shows that, besides two notable Race Relations Acts, important initiatives were contained within two other new pieces of legislation. Whatever view commentators have taken of these various policy initiatives, virtually all are agreed that they reflected the general priority attached to both race and social policy issues by Labour administrations under which all but one of these Acts were passed.

Table 4.1 New race and immigration legislation and policy initiatives, 1960–70

1962	Commonwealth Immigrants Act
1965	Race Relations Act
1965	White Paper: *Immigration from the Commonwealth*
1966	Local Government Act (also known as Section 11 programme)
1968	Commonwealth Immigrants Act
1968	Race Relations Act
1969	Immigration Appeals Act
1969[1]	Local Government Grants (Social Needs) Act (also known as Urban Programme)

Note: [1] The Urban Programme was first announced by Prime Minister Harold Wilson in May 1968 but the enabling legislation did not follow until the following year.

In one of the earliest historical reviews of the race policy initiatives of the 1960s, Deakin (1970) described the advances made during this period as nothing short of a 'liberal hour' in British race relations. Quite what he meant by such a pleasing phrase is not altogether clear since the description must have at least partly been directed towards the immediate political debate at the time of writing. If the description is viewed with historical detachment more than two decades later, it would seem that the period between 1965–68 in particular signalled a dramatic shift in elite and mass opinion in favour of trying to tackle aspects of racial inequality. Alternatively, the description may have been a more accurate reference to the pace of developments in these years rather than their scope since, as political debates in the 1970s and 1980s have suggested, a lot of the demands for action and change remained unresolved. The 'liberal hour' should therefore perhaps be viewed as an era which saw a tremendous pace in policy debates and initiatives but, more even than that, reflected a unique period in which the civil and economic rights of black people were given some degree of priority by central government.

Katznelson (1973) has argued that in the period after the enactment of the 1962 Bill until Labour's narrow election to office in 1964, the politics of race became coherent in the sense that the political parties were able to construct their positions on the issue for the first time and chose to forge a new race consensus. The primary building block behind this new consensus on the race issue was the agreement 'which, it was hoped, would be capable of relegating race from the political plateau to the valley below' (Katznelson, 1973: 139). But before any government could begin to build on the 1962 Act in terms of legislating to outlaw selected forms of discrimination, a more sustainable consensus had to be built on the immigration issue. The 1962 Act had after all been vociferously fought by the Labour Party. The opportunity for the party to change its position on the basic question of whether controls should exist came before the ink had dried on the 1962 statute.

Three factors were responsible for the party's change of heart. First, by early 1963 the party had tragically lost one leader, Hugh Gaitskell, and found itself another in Harold Wilson. Although his first speech as party leader was largely devoted to renewing Labour's commitment to outlaw certain forms of racial discrimination, by 1964 the climate on the immigration question had turned once again. On a personal level Wilson, unlike his predecessor, held no principled opposition to the idea of statutory controls and signalled to all those around him that a pragmatic approach to the matter was now called for. Second, worrying questions were raised about the implementation and effectiveness of the 1962 legislation within months of its enactment. With the political debate quickly moving on to questions regarding the need for further supplementary restrictions, Labour's principled stand appeared to be far removed from the reality of grass-roots sentiment. Finally, if the party was not convinced of the opposition to immigration among its own supporters, it was soon to learn of this truth in the 1964 General Election at the hands of the electorate in the West Midlands constituency of Smethwick.

Smethwick: 'a cloud no bigger than a man's hand'

The 1964 General Election illustrated the tremendous potency of the immigration issue in British politics. Its impact has been described by Deakin (1970: 104) as 'a cloud no bigger than a man's hand'. However, the cloud certainly cast a very large and ominous shadow over the options open to the newly elected Labour administration.

The debate had been stimulated by the campaign fought in the Smethwick constituency held by Patrick Gordon-Walker, Labour's Shadow Foreign Secretary, who had established a reputation for a soft line on immigration. His Conservative challenger, Peter Griffiths, was able to mobilise successfully grass-roots public antipathy towards the presence of black immigrants in the constituency and surrounding areas and was able to ensure that the Labour Party's front bench was blamed for the perceived 'open door' policy. Griffiths' supporters included many traditional Labour voters who were alarmed by the projection of Gordon-Walker and his party as opposed to a hard-line immigration policy. 'If you want a nigger neighbour, vote Labour' became one of the more abrasive slogans in the bitterly fought contest which Gordon-Walker eventually lost following a sizeable swing away from Labour (whilst the national and regional swing was strongly pro-Labour).

The impact upon the Labour Government was to alter fundamentally perceptions of how far governments could resist populist hostility to black immigration. According to Deakin, the episode was

> generally seen at the time as a clear expression of popular resentment, frustrated too long by neglect, and acted as an immediate stimulus to action . . . it intensified pressure on the Government to devise some form of policy that could be put into early effect.
>
> (Deakin, 1970: 104)

Griffiths' victory was met with a mixed reaction from the Labour frontbench. On the one hand the new Prime Minister, Harold Wilson, greeted the Smethwick MP's initial arrival at Westminster by describing him as a 'parliamentary leper'. The clear implication of Wilson's remarks was that the Conservative Party had something to be ashamed of in their ranks. Yet, on the other hand, the potential haemorrhaging of the party's regular white working-class support alerted Wilson and many of his frontbench colleagues to the need to address the source of Gordon-Walker's defeat – the perception of the party as soft on immigration. As far as dropping the party's 'no controls' policy stance was concerned, events had already overtaken the disastrous Smethwick result.

Even before Gordon-Walker had lost his safe seat in spectacular fashion in October 1964, Harold Wilson had already begun to take action to reverse what he considered to be his party's vulnerable position on immigration. Barely a year into his leadership, Wilson announced in November 1963 to the House of Commons: 'On the general issue about the control of immigration . . . we do not contest the need for control of immigration into this country' (Hansard, vol. 702, col. 1254). With the principle conceded at the very top of the party at least, all that remained to be decided was the form of control required to meet this end.

Limitation and integration

A new consensus was emerging on the necessity for stricter immigration controls. The new mood first reached across the different strands of thought within the Labour Party and then embraced both major parties. The consensus aimed to keep political debate concerning race and immigration to questions of *means* rather than *ends*, with both major parties agreeing that prior restriction of Commonwealth immigration was a necessary precondition for harmonious race relations.

A great deal has been written about this conditional link and the impact it subsequently had on shaping the construction of race issues and debates in British politics. The argument ran that, as the numbers of black immigrants became more tightly controlled, so it would become easier to integrate them successfully into (a predominantly white) British society. Writers such as Miles and Phizacklea (1984: 57) have criticised the basis of this consensus. They have argued that the commitment to outlaw discrimination which lay at the heart of the integration side of the equation carried little weight since it was conditional upon a tight immigration policy that practised discrimination at the point of entry into British society. Within this very obvious constraint, these two writers have been joined by many other critics of the consensus who have suggested that the commitment to limitation was much stronger than it was to integration (Foot, 1965; Katznelson, 1973; Ben-Tovim and Gabriel, 1982).

Another related, though distinct, criticism of the post-1965 consensus has chosen to lay less emphasis on the immediate contradictions it involved. According to this view, the consensus went further than merely establishing a trade-off between limiting the entry of new immigrants and integrating those already in the country. Rather, it involved a deeper and more enduring settlement in thinking about approaches to and substance of public policy in a multiracial society. It was upon this settlement that the race relations reforms of this period were constructed. This criticism has highlighted some of the problems inherent in these reforms, and argued that the new consensus should be viewed at best as a mechanism for removing race from party competition (Messina, 1985 and 1989), or at worst as a device for exploiting a window of opportunity on the immigration issue (Saggar, 1991a and 1991b). Finally, it should be remembered that the favourable immigration climate in which many of these reforms were adopted was fairly short-lived. By all accounts it stretched from 1965 when Labour agreed to go along with and renew the provisions of the 1962 Act to 1968 when Labour's emergency Immigration Act limiting East African Asians' rights of entry was rushed through Parliament.

Labour's new strategy

After entering office in autumn 1964 Labour's first initiative was to renew the annual provisions of the 1962 Act whilst it turned to consider what could be done by way of a more permanent solution to the problem. However, following the Labour leadership's decision in the previous year to concede that in principle Britain needed to have formal controls on immigration, the new government's strategy offered only a new packaging of old familiar policies. Where it did differ however was first, in the commitment to attack discrimination by introducing new laws and setting up a watchdog body, and second, in the commitment to foster better integration by building a machinery for community relations work.

Other themes of the strategy involved a new initiative to examine grass-roots integration difficulties and the possibilities of organising government help in combating local problems. To this end in March 1965 the Prime Minister despatched his new minister for race relations, Maurice Foley MP, on a nationwide fact-finding tour. Foley was then called on to investigate what could be done 'to see that speedier action is taken on integration . . . in terms of housing, health, education and everything that needs to be done' (Hansard, vol. 708, cols. 248–50). Thus the job of a ministerial co-ordinator was established who, despite the *ad hoc* nature of his appointment by Harold Wilson, nonetheless demonstrated that institutional initiatives were possible to signal the priority attached by the new administration to the issue. Shortly after the Foley mission began, the Home Secretary, Sir Frank Soskice, announced plans to implement the 1964 manifesto pledge to 'legislate against racial discrimination and incitement in public places' (quoted in Hindell, 1965: 390). Within several months of taking office, expectations had risen enormously of what lay ahead. The 'liberal hour' had begun.

The 1965 Race Relations Act

The decision to move forward and introduce legal redress against racial discrimination was entered into after great thought. It should be remembered that implementation of the Labour Party's 1964 manifesto promise involved two things: first, the use of the law in this area had been widely thought of as being unfeasible; and second, the issue had not been considered sufficiently popular to warrant pioneering legislation. On both grounds Soskice, Wilson and others embarked on a route which aroused deep suspicion across many areas of British politics. However, one area of the British political terrain that did not share – or at least voice – this suspicion was the front bench of the Conservative Opposition. For the purposes of holding together the two-party race consensus, the Conservative leadership had agreed to work alongside Soskice and not oppose the Bill. According to Katznelson (1973: 126) the successful enactment of the new legislation marked the high-water mark of the two-party consensus to de-politicise the race issue. Therefore, a unique era in British racial politics underscored the passage of the Race Relations Bill through the House of Commons although, as we shall see, it was also here that its essential character was altered.

The new administration did not approach the task of passing the Race Relations Bill in a complete vacuum, for three reasons. First, it is often overlooked that the Labour Party had been committed to introducing a law to outlaw racial discrimination for some time prior to its decision to formulate such a policy following its 1964 election to office. In fact, for many years during the 1950s a Bill had been introduced annually by one its leading backbenchers, Fenner Brockway, to prohibit racial discrimination (Hindell, 1965). Moreover, every year since 1962 the party conference had voted by a two-thirds majority for such a commitment to be included in the manifesto.

Second, the first draft of the new legislation took its cue from the recommendations of the Martin Committee, a small committee of specialists set up by the Society of Labour Lawyers to examine the feasibility of operating anti-discrimination laws. Third, a certain amount of experience had already been accumulated from the adoption of anti-discrimination laws in the US during the early and mid-1960s, aspects of which informed the evidence put forward by the Martin Report and several leading liberal journals and newspapers. This putative climate of optimism over the capabilities of legislation has been remarked upon by commentators who have suggested that it characterised a unique era in the history of British race relations. Writing in the immediate aftermath of the period which saw the adoption of the second Race Relations Act, the team led by E.J.B. Rose wrote in *Colour and Citizenship:*

> For race relations in Britain the liberal hour has already passed. It lasted at most two years. 1968, the year in which it ended, was . . . *année zéro* for those who believe that there are solutions to be found to problems arising from inter-racial contact and that the way to achieve them is through the traditional devices of discussion, bargaining, and legislation.
>
> (E.J.B. Rose *et al.*, 1969: 10)

The first Race Relations Act has often been criticised as being scarcely more than an item of window dressing in the campaign to attain racial equality. At one level this criticism carries substantial weight since the Act was based not on providing the courts with criminal sanctions against proven discriminators, but rather on a voluntary mechanism to investigate allegations and offer conciliation wherever it was accepted. However, pitted against this charge is the perspective which stresses the contribution of the Act in laying a foundation for future extension of race legislation. Banton

(1985), for instance, has described the intellectual shift in opinion surrounding the Act as being of greater significance than the precise authority – or lack of authority – that the new law introduced to eradicate discrimination. His argument has gone as far as to describe the underlying debate concerning discrimination and its impact on a civilised industrial society as one about attaining a *public good*. The bases for this view and others ranged against it are taken up in an evaluation of the 'liberal hour' reforms in the final section of this chapter.

The Act has been chiefly criticised for its 'softly, softly' approach to the problem of discrimination. To begin with, during its committee stage through the House of Commons the Act was altered fundamentally from one which proposed criminal penalties for racially discriminatory actions to one which settled for a voluntary, conciliation-based approach. Thus, the new body set up to operate the legislation was deprived of even basic authority to allow it to investigate complaints and intervene to stop discrimination where it found it. According to Calvocoressi:

> The [1965] Act goes a long way indeed in separating conciliation from compulsion. Too far. In my view Parliament failed to distinguish between two kinds of compulsion. There is a difference between complling a man to desist from discrimination and compelling a man to attend to answer questions in relation to a complaint that has been made about him.
>
> (Calvocoressi, 1968: 51)

An allied weakness of the Act was its non-applicability to large areas of economic and social life such as housing and employment. These changes were postponed until future legislation could be introduced, although no timescale was spelt out. Furthermore, radical interpretations of this period have claimed that the Act merely served to racialise British politics by placing emphasis on legislating *for* race relations instead of *against* racism (Miles and Phizacklea, 1984: 58). In other words, the 1965 Act thus merely built on and confirmed processes of racialisation in the construction of the ideological parameters of post-war British politics (Miles, 1990).

Shortly after the new law reached the statute-book the government published its long-awaited White Paper *Immigration from the Commonwealth* spelling out the themes and goals of future public policy (Cmnd. 2739). Significantly, before it spelt out the government's planned strategy, it proposed a further tightening of the immigration rules governing the 1962 Act. Unlike many other policy statements at this time, the White Paper went into significant detail about the future strategy the government envisaged. Its best-known measure was to establish the National Committee for Commonwealth Immigrants (NCCI) to 'coordinate on a national basis efforts directed towards the integration of Commonwealth immigrants into the community' (quoted in Messina, 1989: 37). In other words, it involved a major policy initiative to build good race relations at grass-roots level and centred on a new infrastructure of local voluntary bodies co-ordinated by the Committee.

The other, less widely reported, aspect of the White Paper was its definitive statement on immigration and controls to ensure that 'immigrants . . . do not outrun Britain's capacity to absorb them' (Cmnd. 2739: 2). To achieve this end, the number of annual work vouchers issued to would-be entrants were cut back from 20,000 to 8,000 and the vouchers available to those without specific jobs or skills were to be ended altogether. At a stroke the government had both addressed worries about the effectiveness of the original 1962 Immigration Act and, in doing so, had made more scrupulous use of a law it had doggedly opposed only a few years previously.

The 1968 Race Relations Act

The period between the 1965 and 1968 Race Relations Acts is a most interesting one because of the extraordinary coalition that was built both within and beyond liberal circles to support the extension of anti-discrimination law into new areas. When in December 1965 Roy Jenkins became Home Secretary he immediately signalled his wish to try to build on the modest base of the 1965 Act and pass a second piece of legislation to ban racial discrimination more widely. However, as he also made clear, the new Bill would not be embarked upon until a firm alliance had been created to persuade both political elite and mass public opinion of its need. In that sense, Jenkins viewed his task as being as much about changing hearts and minds as about stewarding a new law through Parliament.

Within months of taking up his new post Jenkins set out the terms of his vision of the multiracial society he wanted to aim towards. In a speech to NCCI officers and community relations activists he defined the goal of policy as 'an integrated multiracial society' characterised by 'equal opportunity'. 'Integration', he continued, was *not* to be seen 'as a flattening process of assimilation but rather as equal opportunity, accompanied by cultural diversity, in an atmosphere of mutual tolerance' (Jenkins, 1966). The emphasis was placed on a more pluralist interpretation of what could be achieved through race relations policies. The traditional view of such policies and initiatives as steps to a fully assimilated society, in which cultural differences would eventually disappear, was effectively rejected. If the purpose of policy was not to encourage a British version of the US 'melting pot', then the challenge was placed before policy-makers to devise new instruments of policy which – directly or indirectly – helped to preserve and even promote the cultural heritage of the new communities. Many writers have argued that this challenge, more than any particular reform, was the most significant legacy of the 'liberal hour'.

Jenkins' short-term aim, however, was to enact a second Race Relations Act, but he sensed the weak political footing of his own government holding a slender Commons majority. Thus the plan to put a new Bill before Parliament was deferred until a stronger working majority could be relied upon following the impending general election. In the meantime, Jenkins concentrated on lobbying support for the general idea of extended legislation so that, when it came to publishing his new Bill, the principle of the argument had already been resolved.

In 1966–67 he took three initiatives to this end. First, he commissioned a small team led by Professor Harry Street of Manchester University to examine the relevance and applicability of anti-discrimination laws in the United States; the published findings known as The Street Report provided powerful evidence on the efficacy of a proper framework of law (Street, 1967). Second, in spring 1967 Political and Economic Planning, an independent research body, published their much-awaited report on the scale of racial discrimination in Britain (PEP, 1967); the report added weight to the argument that the problem 'was not a defensive fantasy in the minds of interested parties . . . but a harsh reality scarring British life' (Heinemann, 1972: 136). Finally, a wide-ranging campaign was launched to influence elite opinion through the semi-orchestrated publication of sympathetic newspaper articles and television and radio broadcasts highlighting the problems faced by black immigrants. The new Bill was eventually unveiled in July 1967 after several months of saturation coverage in the media of its broad theme. Most commentators viewed its impending passage through Parliament as largely a matter of tactics and fine detail, with the principle essentially beyond reproach. However, ominous clouds were beginning to gather on the horizon in the latter half of 1967 threatening not only the new law but also the political coalition upon which it was based.

The real risk that underlay Jenkins' strategy for delaying new legislation as long as he did was that it made his policy a hostage to the immigration issue. Whilst the 1965 White Paper had moved a long way towards arresting popular fears regarding current immigration, it did not perceive structural changes in the flow of immigrants to Britain. The principal structural change that occurred from late 1967 onwards was the escalation of the policy of Africanisation that was being pursued by the Kenyan government. The result of this policy was to place pressure on thousands of Asian British passport holders who had remained *en masse* in the newly independent state after the severing of its colonial ties in 1963. With the trickle of Asian immigrants growing steadily from 1965 onwards, the flow had assumed torrent proportions within two years. Moreover, the growing public alarm over this new chapter in immigration ensured that renewed pressure was placed on the Labour Government to intervene to stem the Asians' entry. The increasingly populist debate that ensued served only to swell the numbers entering Britain in late 1967 and early 1968 hoping to beat the barriers of any new tougher legislation that might be introduced.

Within a few short months the general optimism that had underscored the 'liberal hour' of reform had all but evaporated. The Kenyan Asian crisis ensured that the immigration issue – rather than the question of integration flagged so clearly by Jenkins in 1966 – returned to centre stage. The rise of Enoch Powell's own brand of popular opposition to black immigration was undoubtedly the most immediate cause of this turbulence (see also Chapter 5). Elsewhere, destabilising fractures in the coalition put together by Jenkins began to occur, further testimony to the basic weakness of his strategy to combat racial discrimination. For example, in late 1967 one of the most important pressure groups that had supported Jenkins' strategy, the Campaign Against Racial Discrimination (CARD), began to split openly on a variety of interrelated issues to do with the role of radical independent black politics (Heinemann, 1972; Saggar, 1991a: 35).

The Bill was finally brought before the Commons in the spring of 1968, just a few weeks after a hastily drafted Immigration Act to curtail the Kenyan Asian influx had been rushed through the division lobbies. Its basic features included an extension of the scope of the earlier 1965 Act to take anti-discrimination laws into the spheres of housing and employmemt. The declared intention of liberal enthusiasts to extend the law had been achieved, albeit in pessimistic circumstances and with Jenkins no longer at the Home Office to oversee the implementation of the Act (Jenkins had become Chancellor in autumn 1967 and had been replaced by James Callaghan).

Perhaps even more significant than these changes in the law were the changes in the bureaucratic organisation of race relations policy brought about by the Act. To begin with, the Act took the view that the work of the Race Relations Board was hampered by a failure in its enabling legislation (the 1965 Act) to distinguish between its role as a body to promote good race relations and its duties to enforce the law against discrimination. The Board was effectively operating as a watchdog and as a co-ordinator at one and the same time, and for this reason the Act relieved it of the latter of these tasks. To give a new impetus to grass-roots racial harmony initiatives, a new Community Relations Commission was established with a more tightly specified task of co-ordinating the local work of voluntary community relations organisations. So whilst the ideals of the 'liberal hour' may have been in retreat after 1968, the effect of the second Race Relations Act had been to revise dramatically the organisational structures and capacities of race relations policies. The opportunity to exploit these revisions would, however, have to be deferred pending the return of a more favourable climate on the immigration issue. In the event, any further developments in public policy were held in abeyance for several years under the 1970–74 Conservative Government and the question was not properly reopened until the mid-1970s.

Additional policy instruments

Although the first and second Race Relations Acts have been the subject of substantial writing, it is commonly forgotten that this period also yielded two further policy initiatives pertinent to the future of British race relations. The first of these was known as the Section 11 funding programme which was introduced as part of a much larger Local Government Act in 1966. The programme fulfilled a long-standing pledge of the Labour administration to do something to help those local authorities facing the brunt of additional financial costs involved in the mass settlement of Commonwealth immigrants. By providing for a 75 per cent subsidy for approved funding schemes, the programme went a long way towards targeting national resources to local difficulties.

As several writers have reminded us, it was at the local level in particular that many of the most bitter conflicts over race were fought in the immediate aftermath of immigrant settlement (Rex and Moore, 1967; Lawrence, 1974; Rex and Tomlinson, 1979). Unlike most other reforms from this period, the Section 11 programme has progressed largely intact to the present day, although it has undergone several reappraisals of its ability to target funds to those groups the programme was originally intended to assist (Smith, 1989: 78). The real significance of the programme rested on the precedent it created in making *specific* provision for black people within local government spending. The mechanism by which it did so was to limit funding to those projects aimed at assisting the smooth integration of New Commonwealth immigrants who had entered the country over a ten-year period. This restriction became known as the 'ten year rule' but was eventually abandoned once it was more widely accepted that the social and other problems faced by black immigrants frequently extended far beyond the first decade of settlement. (The significance of this approach to race policy is discussed more fully in Young and Connelly, 1981.)

The last remaining major policy initiative of the 1960s was the formal establishment in 1968–69 of British urban policy. As the following chapter notes, one of the immediate consequences of the Powell anti-immigrant speeches of 1968 was the announcement in May of that year of a new drive to combat the social and economic decline of Britain's inner-city areas. Although the initiative seemed to be one of the most unplanned policies of the post-war years, the decision taken by Harold Wilson to combat directly the damaging impact of Powellite rhetoric ensured that that it was given high priority by both officials and Wilson's Cabinet colleagues.

The legislative outcome of the political initiative taken by the Prime Minister was the 1969 Local Government Act which launched the administration's Urban Programme. Having identified the need to arrest inner-city decline, the Programme sought to measure areas of acute deprivation and channel resources accordingly. Its inclusion within an inventory on British race policy is warranted on the grounds that one of the criteria for measuring deprivation adopted by the Programme was the significant local presence of Commonwealth immigrants (Edwards and Batley, 1978). The Urban Programme was launched on this rather unsatisfactory basis in 1969. Later in 1976–77 it underwent a wide-ranging review to enable the Programme to concentrate on tackling structural causes of urban decline, although the racial dimension remained a part of its general approach (McKay and Cox, 1979). As with the Section 11 programme, the urban policy of the Labour Government introduced a limited degree of group-targeting of central government resources, although in the latter case the perception remained that the problems of the inner cities – rather than their inhabitants – were the principal objects of public policy.

Evaluating the liberal legacy

This chapter has been mainly devoted to reviewing the chronological developments surrounding the race and immigration policies of governments during the 1960s. The core of these measures was concentrated over three short years between 1965–68, widely known as the 'liberal hour' in British race relations. In the remainder of this chapter we shall turn to examine critically the longer-term consequences of these measures and to consider how far they have shaped an underlying policy framework around which the politics of race have been constructed.

To begin with, no assessment of the reforms of these years would be complete without reference to the role played by Roy Jenkins. Jenkins' tenure at the Home Office has often been thought of as the high-water mark of the 'liberal hour' in British race relations. There appear to be two reasons for this characterisation. First, Jenkins undoubtedly managed to push through several key reforms at great pace, building on the 1965 Race Relations Act which had been the work of his predecessor, Soskice. It was Jenkins, perhaps reading the signals from the Smethwick disaster, who took the tactical decision to delay extension of the 1965 Act until a solid parliamentary majority was in place after the 1966 General Election.

Second, it would be difficult to assess his contribution without taking account of the force his personality played in helping to raise the saliency of the race issue, and in successfully lobbying to move quickly to thoughts of a second Act within a few years of the first. For example, in keeping with his decision to give race relations a higher priority, Jenkins chose Mark Bonham-Carter as the first chairman of the new Race Relations Board. Bonham-Carter, a noted liberal on the race issue, stressed that his decision to take the job was on a conditional basis depending on the performace of the new anti-discrimination law; his involvement undoubtedly gave an important boost to the credibility of the exercise.

The downside of this view of Labour's reform-minded Home Secretary was that his rather privileged social and intellectual background made it difficult to foster much empathy with the daily discrimination faced by black immigrants that his supporters may have wished for. He was and remained the product of a narrow social class, albeit one that had taken on board the egalitarian values of intellectual socialism. But despite this, perhaps his greatest weakness lay in his naïve belief that government initiative and social education could together overcome a form of discrimination that was still widely perceived as a personal, self-regarding act. 'Jenkins', writes Deakin (1970: 108), 'set out his criteria for a civilised bourgeois socialism' – criteria which perhaps mistakenly viewed ordinary individuals' outlook to the changing racial character of Britain as optimistically as his own. Whatever the truth of Jenkin's contribution, his name has often become synonymous with the Labour Party's initial record on race and immigration. The most obvious reason for this characterisation is that he occupied the post of primary responsibility for both race and immigration for longer than any other Labour politician (he returned to the Home Office for a second spell between 1974–76). It is only in the Thatcher era that other politicians on both sides of the party divide – notably William Whitelaw and Roy Hattersley – have also become as closely associated with the race issue.

Whilst it is the case that writers are divided in their assessment of the 1964–70 Labour Government's strategy, it is often not apparent *why* such disagreements exist. Following Banton (1987), it could be argued that opinion is divided between optimists and pessimists, with the former taking a sympathetic view over what was achieved in these years and the latter stressing the limitations and contradictions of Labour's strategy. Banton's own assessment is set out in his extended essay *Promoting Racial Harmony* (1985) and falls squarely into the former camp. He describes the period as worthy of the label of a 'liberal hour', principally because of the institutions created during this era for the subsequent promotion of racial equality. In doing so, however, there may have been some confusion over the policy goal of racial harmony as opposed to racial equality since the former is not necessarily synonymous with the latter and may even be in conflict with it (see also Chapter 9 below). But even more important than the institutional achievements of these years is Banton's claim that this era served to promote an underlying liberal philosophy that 'pins its faith upon the ability of institutions to mould the behaviour of individuals' (1987: 40).

Other, less sympathetic, writers have gone further in suggesting that the period spelt the ascendancy of a *liberal settlement* in the underlying ideological debate over what could legitimately be included within policy debates on race and what could not (Saggar, 1991a). Banton's argument appears to dwell on the politics of the feasible insofar as it is careful not to evaluate the Labour administration's record by reference to abstracted principles. Indeed, such an approach has been used to characterise another important evaluative study, *White Man's Country*, by Miles and Phizacklea (1984). These authors advance the argument that Labour's strategy was doomed to failure because however hard progressive politicians pushed for the legal protection of the rights of black people, their efforts were ultimately undermined by the exposed flank of the appeasers in the party who wished to fall into line with public opinion deeply opposed to black immigration.

This perspective is certainly convincing when we recall the strains under which the strategy was placed following the 1967–68 immigration scare. Moreover, it could be said that Jenkins and his supporters were only able to introduce the reforms that they did on the basis of a stable immigration climate that resulted from Labour's decision not to repeal the Conservatives' 1962 Act. That is to say, all that may be concluded about the strategy was that a window of opportunity was successfully exploited by the reformers but nothing more. The difficulty here is that this position denies the link in terms of ideology and values between the reforms on one hand and on the other the framework for race policy debates in the period beyond. A number of critics of Labour's record seem content to focus exclusively upon the appeasement of anti-immigrant sentiment at the expense of trying to explain the longer-term impact of the values and assumptions that made up the strategy, however flawed they may have been.

The criticisms of the strategy do not merely stop at highlighting the electoral hostility that Labour was said to be running one step ahead of, in the years between Smethwick and the Kenyan Asian crisis. Miles and Phizacklea (1984) have argued that the strategy was flawed in the crucial sense that it failed to disassociate itself from popular calls to halt further black immigration. The public could hardly be expected to take the need for laws against discrimination seriously when no less discriminatory laws governed who was allowed to enter Britain and who was not. In the words of Roy Hattersley, then a junior Home Office minister, the goals of racial integration and immigration control were mutually interdependent: 'Integration without control is impossible but control without integration is indefensible', he stated in the House of Commons in spring 1965. A form of dualism had effectively been established whereby measures to improve the former could not be pursued without action on the latter:

> Hattersley's clever syllogism was really arguing that in order to eliminate racism within Britain, it is necessary to practise it at the point of entry into Britain. But the Labour government's commitment to 'limitation' was rather stronger than its commitment to 'integration'.
>
> (Miles and Phizacklea, 1984: 57)

The debate over Labour's reforms has also been joined by sceptical voices who approach the question from a conservative outlook. It is impossible to identify such a viewpoint set out in a single volume devoted to a political analysis of race and immigration from 1962. Instead, we must look to a series of disparate sources in order to gauge the Conservative perspective. To begin with, the emphasis of the conservative critique is not the unintended social consequences of political actions such as immigration policies which distinguish between New Commonwealth and other immigrants (Rich, 1986a). Rather, the emphasis is placed upon the ability of measures aimed at combating racial discrimination to deliver the goods in terms of individual or group behaviour. In other words there is a deep scepticism about the efficacy of public policy programmes and legal mechanisms in the field of race relations. For example, the public bodies established during the liberal reform era have been criticised as being elitist and aloof (Rich, 1986b: 55). Perhaps more significantly, the strongest criticisms have been reserved for the apparent failure of the two major parties to discuss openly the social consequences of large-scale black immigration (Deedes, 1968).

Beneath these misgivings lies a more general observation concerning the integration-centred goal of public policy. There are some considerable grounds, suggest conservatives, for doubting that integration can be achieved by focusing exclusively upon the majority group and its willingness to accept the ethnic pluralisation of society and culture that accompanied black immigration. Moreover, the success of any such strategy must ultimately depend upon the behaviour of those groups that are to be integrated. Of course, once attention is shifted to the conduct of the new black immigrants, it is likely that the debate will also shift towards goals that have traditionally been described as assimilation-centred. These sort of goals place little weight on the idea of a meeting of minority and majority cultures and life-styles in which a climate of mutual tolerance and respect is fostered.

It should be stressed that commentators are far from agreed about the motives underlying the scepticism of conservatives. We must therefore be careful not to rush to the conclusion that this position is only sustainable on the basis of a more general lack of value and regard for the cultural heritage of black Britons. To do so would be to impute a single motive to a variety of views held by commentators who have freely professed their pessimism about the ability of government to intervene in race relations. So for example, it may be that the sceptics' disagreement with the liberal reforms of Jenkins and others is not so much about the desire to build a racially harmonious society but more about the instruments deployed to that end. Jenkins, as we have already seen, was keen to highlight his opposition to a 'flattening process' which he suggested was all that could come from traditional thinking on integrating black immigrants into British society. Instead, he wanted to gain the confidence of black immigrants by offering a vision of a multiracial society which valued their presence and background. A two-way process was envisaged as the route forwards. However, this process, conservatives persistently argued, has been incapable of gaining sufficient white confidence and has tragically underestimated black willingness to conform to the common values and traditions of British society.

Having briefly outlined the bare bones of these important analytical perspectives, we shall return to examine their influence in British politics in later chapters.

Overview and conclusion

The primary concern of this chapter has been to review and evaluate the developments in politics and policy-making during the most concentrated period of reform seen in modern times. This era has been dubbed as the 'liberal hour' in British thinking and approaches to the problems of a multiracial society. As one commentator has written, the significance of this era 'reflected the ascendancy of liberal over conservative assumptions about race relations' (Banton, 1985: abstract). Whilst there is considerable controversy among liberal, radical and conservative writers over the merits of the race strategy pursued by the 1964–70 Labour administration, there is widespread agreement that key elements of political discourse about race were forged during this era. Moreover, it has been suggested that these developments can be characterised as nothing short of a *settlement* in the framework for the future pursuit of race-related public policy. If that is the case, then the racial conflicts and tensions that have arisen in British politics in the years since the 'liberal hour' must be interpreted in that light. Subsequent chapters will survey the nature of several of these conflicts and put forward the view that they are as much about the legitimacy of the *liberal settlement* as about narrowly defined policy issues.

A bipartisan consensus existed on the race issue in Britain for a little over a decade, beginning in the mid-1960s. Several commentators have argued that this consensus was an illustration of the relative inability of British political parties to confront the dilemmas of the issue (Katznelson, 1973; Layton-Henry, 1984). Some writers have stressed the intentional nature of this consensus, claiming that it formed part of a pattern of the management of issues not thought of as belonging to the 'high politics' of the central state (Bulpitt, 1986). Other writers have contended that the consensus was in effect a mask for the sustained drift to the Right among both major parties on the issue of black immigration (Nandy, 1967; Miles and Phizacklea, 1984), whilst still other writers have concluded that the consensus was designed to allow elite politicians to keep the lid on an issue which could not be managed successfully by successive governments (Messina, 1989). All of these perspectives are essentially reflections of contrasting approaches to the analysis of the politics of race since 1962. Moreover, it should be remembered that certain aspects of this experience are undoubtedly stressed in some analyses more than others.

These perspectives are all based on general characterisations of the impact of the race issue in post-war British politics. We still need to explore the political role of race in two additional senses: first, as a factor within the major political parties, and second, as a factor shaping the political participation of black people. It is to these topics that we shall now turn in Chapters 5 and 6.

5

Race and Party Politics

Introduction

In January 1978 Margaret Thatcher, then Conservative leader of the Opposition, gave a television interview in which she displayed considerable empathy with the feelings of white voters hostile to black immigration. Among other more remembered remarks, she stated that politicians should 'Never be afraid to tackle something which people are worried about. We are not in politics to ignore people's worries; we are in politics to deal with them' (Granada Television, 1978). At a stroke the Conservative leader had addressed the issue of non-white immigration head-on. Since the early 1960s, however, both parties had sought to keep the lid on the issue and generally avoided discussing it in the context of electoral competition. The golden age of the 'non-politics' of race came to an abrupt end in the controversy that followed the interview. The editorial of *The Sunday Times* for instance criticised her for 'giving aid and comfort to the National Front' (26 February 1978).

The episode tended to exaggerate the tranquillity of the bipartisan consensus that had preceded it. For one thing, the ensuing 1979 General Election campaign was by no means the first in which the race factor had played an important part. Both the 1964 and 1970 campaigns had been shaped by the issue, such that several researchers have claimed that the Conservatives' unexpected victory in June 1970 was at least partly due to the so-called 'race card' (Deakin and Bourne, 1970; Studlar, 1974 and 1978; Miller, 1980).

Several writers have made great play of the *de facto* agreement that was forged by the party leaderships in the mid-1960s. As outlined in the previous chapter, this era saw a number of important developments in public policy aimed at fostering the integration of black immigrants. However, signs of the shallow roots and inherent fragility of the consensus were apparent from the outset. The major parties did not so much end disputes over the issue once and for all, but rather they succeeded in temporarily calming its known volatiity.

In this chapter we shall trace the record of each of the major parties on the race issue in the post-war period. The chapter highlights both the changing nature of the issue as well as the changing responses of the parties. It is apparent that the parties faced considerable difficulties in engineering and maintaining a consensus between themselves. One of the principal reasons for this was the disunity over the issue within each of the parties. Among the Conservatives, the smooth shift from the party of empire to the pragmatism of the Heath years was constantly under threat from right-wing opponents of black immigration.

The intervention of Enoch Powell in 1968 was therefore merely a more dramatic illustration of ongoing internal disquiet over the policy stance of the party leadership. In the case of the Labour Party, the liberal progressive lead of Jenkins, Hattersley and others was the object of resentment from the party's old guard, right wing who shared many of the misgivings of their working-class supporters. From the late 1970s onwards the main source of internal disunity shifted to the radical left. A new orthodoxy emerged in the party's urban local government strongholds based on the commitment to fight overtly the inequalities of race, gender, disability, sexuality and so on. This important development placed further strains on the party's unity on the race issue.

The central aim of the chapter is to demonstrate that the original race consensus was based on very weak foundations. It survived at its strongest for a ten-year period from around 1965 to 1975 and was centred on the commitments of the party leaders. Most significantly, it did not always extend further down into the rank and file of the parties and it singularly failed to de-politicise the issue in any lasting way. In order to understand the reasons for this record, it is necessary to examine several key phases in each party's approach to, and thinking about, race-related issues in general.

it is necessary to examine several key phases in each party's approach to, and thinking about, race-related issues in general.

The main parties' internal debates and electoral strategies since 1945 appear to fall under four phases. First, there is the period of the 1940s and 1950s culminating in the abandonment of the policy of unrestricted entry of New Commonwealth labour migrants between 1958–62. Second, the parties pursued a largely successful policy of containment in which the immigration issue, having already been racialised by virtue of the 1962 Immigration Act, was kept off the agenda of party competition until the mid-1970s. The third phase stretched from about 1976 until the 1983 General Election and encompassed the Conservatives' fairly deliberate move to the right to capture the support of those strongly opposed to continued black immigration. Finally, there has been the period since 1983 in which a more consolidationist strategy has been deployed on the Right coupled with a sharp polarisation of opinion on the Left.

Among the Conservatives this new climate has at least partly been a consequence of a closer climate of trust and co-operation with conservatively inclined sections of the black communities; for the Labour Party, the 1980s have witnessed a new era of radicalism particularly at grass-roots levels in the party's urban strongholds.

Industrial recovery and labour shortages, 1948–58

Table 5.1 Chronology of key political developments relating to race and immigration, 1948–58

Labour in office	1947	Independence for India and Pakistan
	1948	Nationality Act
	1948	Arrival of SS *Windrush*
Conservatives in office	1953	Fenner-Brockway's first anti-discrimination Bill
	1954	Commonwealth immigration first discussed at Cabinet
	1956	Suez adventure
	1958	Notting Hill and Nottingham 'race riots'

reconstruction was placed at the head of the Attlee administration's priorities, it was slower to reflect the upturn in living standards. In 1949, the young Harold Wilson, then President of the Board of Trade, made a speech pronouncing a 'bonfire of controls' which marked the beginning of the end for wartime rationing (Greenleaf, 1983: 65). By the time the second Churchill Government took office in 1951 the turnaround was fully under way and, in some cases, had resulted in temporary shortages of labour. The incoming Conservative administration sensed that the problem might get worse before it got better and stated in its first King's Speech: 'My Government views with concern the serious shortage of labour, particularly of skilled labour, which has handicapped production in a number of industries' (quoted in Foot, 1965: 124). Earlier, the first post-war legislation on immigration, the 1948 Nationality Act, had created a common British citizenship for all Commonwealth citizens and thus pointed to the Commonwealth as the most likely source for additional labour. By the mid-1950s the tacit support for Commonwealth workers to fill gaps in domestic production had begun to shift to a more deliberate policy of labour recruitment.

Oddly, there is evidence to suggest that the formal extension of common citizenship, with all its implications for the right of abode in Britain, was barely discussed by politicians of all parties at the time. Foot quotes the 1958 words of a junior Conservative minister who was forced to re-examine the basis of the 1948 Nationality Act:

> [The granting of citizenship] was not due to a deliberate act of policy formally announced and embodied in our law. It is not even a policy which gradually grew up and became established by custom . . . . It is simply a fact which we have taken for granted from the earliest days in which our forbears ventured forth across the seas.
>
> (quoted in Foot, 1965: 125)

It was on this basis that the notion of an *insoluble* Commonwealth ideal was founded. Conservative politicians as much as their Labour counterparts were at the forefront of the transformation of the ideal into firm policy. This important transformation was to apply both to British foreign policy and to the future debate on the rights of black Commonwealth citizens who wished to settle in Britain.

A large part of the failure to examine the immigration implications of the 1948 law stemmed from the wide acceptance that the entry of black labour was purely a temporary phenomenon. For that reason, it is hard to discern a clear domestic political debate over immigration until at least the late 1950s, by which time attention had not so much shifted to the permanence of existing black settlement but rather to the scale of numbers involved and the putative link with domestic social cohesion.

The rate of entry of black Commonwealth citizens averaged 36,000 per annum during the second half of the decade (Foot, 1965: 126). The prospect of seemingly unlimited resources of labour from overseas was viewed with approval by British industrialists suffering from chronic labour shortages particularly in areas of low-skilled and/or low-paid work. However, pitted against this approval was a growing sense of unease about the social implications of black immigration. The unease originated at grass-roots level in local communities and slowly filtered through into elite policy discussions in Westminster and Whitehall.

Carter *et al.* (1987: 4) have reported that as early as April 1954 the case for legal controls over immigration was considered by the Colonial Office. The outcome was an agreement to defer a decision until more evidence could be collected to show that the local impact of immigration necessitated controls. Despite the unwillingness to take action, the Chancellor, 'Rab' Butler, nonetheless managed to get the matter debated in Cabinet in February 1954. At this meeting the Prime Minister, Winston Churchill, stated that the increase in Commonwealth immigration 'sooner or later would come to be resented by large sections of the British people' (quoted in Seldon, 1989: 86). This time broad agreement was found to legislate but the plan was apparently shelved in the face of backbench opposition. Banton (1985: 35) has argued that the bond between white British people and the Empire remained strong throughout this period and only really began to be questioned after the 1958 riots in Notting Hill and Nottingham. To be sure, until as late as 1956 several surveys reported that anywhere between 46 and 72 per cent of people supported the principle of free entry for Commonwealth workers.

Suez and the shattering of idealism

The 1950s early experience of black immigration is particularly interesting because of competing attitudes that were found within the Conservative Party, not merely on the narrowly defined question of black immigration but also on the question of the future of the Empire. It should be remembered that during this decade Britain had already embarked on a policy of decolonisation, a policy which had begun in 1947 with the decision to quit India. The 1950s had quickly developed into a period in which Britain's continued colonial presence in a number of African, Caribbean and Asian colonies was under threat from nationalist independence campaigns. So whilst Conservative politicians had taken a largely pragmatic line on immigration matters for most of the 1950s, they had also been preoccupied with the future of Britain's scattered colonies.

The pivotal factor in attitudes about the future of the colonies came in 1956 when Britain, together with France and Israel, was forced to accept the loss of the Suez Canal. Following the Egyptian nationalisation of the Canal, Britain had agreed to spearhead a trilateral attempt to recapture the Canal Zone by force, a policy which resulted in military failure and political humiliation. At home the Conservative Prime Minister, Anthony Eden, had to contend with the wrath of the Labour Opposition who had denounced the policy as military adventurism. Suez had also split the Conservatives and Eden was subjected to the scathing criticism of numerous fellow Conservative MPs. The episode illustrated the scale of Britain's swift decline from a world power to its new status as a middle-ranking European regional power.

The foreign policy that accompanied its new status was caught between several competing priorities. But the greatest impact was felt in the sudden deterioration in relations with Commonwealth governments. In India, Prime Minister Jawaharlal Nehru was amongst the strongest critics of Britain's Suez policy: 'I cannot think of a grosser case of naked aggression' he stated (Childs, 1986: 89). Further afield, the US administration headed by President Eisenhower complained that at the moment when the Americans had to respond to Soviet aggression in Eastern Europe (Hungary): 'we should be forced to choose between following the footsteps of Anglo-French colonialism in Asia and Africa or splitting our course away from their course' (Childs, 1986: 89). The realisation was fully brought home by Commonwealth leaders and US Presidents alike, that Britain would find few friends in pursuing a foreign policy that so closely resembled its nineteenth-century policy of gunboat diplomacy. Nehru's point had been that British action was fundamentally at odds with its declared intentions of retreat from its colonies.

But for British policy-makers, another more pertinent lesson could be drawn from the Suez experience, namely that the Commonwealth would never be more than an ideal that had been used to rationalise its imperial retreat from power. If the Commonwealth was not working for Britain and British interests, argued those disenchanted by the Suez fiasco, what use was it? Moreover, they asked: why should British immigration policy be so firmly based on the notion of a common Commonwealth citizenship? The answer, they concluded, was that the principle was a flawed ideal which had permitted the entry into Britain of large numbers of 'alien' workers. Furthermore, the immigrants' supposed link with Britain was more imaginary than real, based as it was on the same principle that had led Britain to give up its Empire. Others dismissed altogether the idea that Britain could successfully resist domination by 'coloured' races within the Commonwealth. In *The Unarmed Invasion*, published in 1965, Lord Elton argued that 'the Commonwealth is almost as far as it could possibly be from multiracialism' since it consisted 'overwhelmingly of coloured citizens' (quoted in Rich, 1986b: 206-7).

'Race riots' at home

If the events of 1956 had fundamentally shaken Britain's perceptions of its place in a post-imperial world order, they had also managed to put onto the agenda the question of the unrestricted right of Commonwealth citizens to enter Britain. With this principle widely conceded, attention returned to the factors said to be behind the need to qualify this right. Conservatives sceptical of the worth of black immigrant workers had little to base their argument upon given the growing output of British industry and its need for reserve labour. However, the events of summer 1958 in west London and the East Midlands introduced a new factor in the debate and shifted its focus away from economic prerogatives and towards questions concerning social order.

The events of 1958 served to heighten dramatically concerns that had been voiced among Conservatives for several years about the social consequences of black immigration. Simmering tensions between black and white people in Notting Hill in west London and Nottingham in the East Midlands erupted into open street conflict during the summer months. The street conflicts soon involved the police as an added object of mistrust on the part of the black community (Pilkington, 1988).

The primary response to these incidents was to label them as illustrations of a 'race/immigration problem'. Between 9–13 September *The Times* ran all four of its headline stories on the issue. 'Frank Talks on Racial Issue: Move to Control Immigration: Voluntary Curb Suggested' stated one of the headlines. Norman Pannell and Cyril Osborne, two Conservative MPs who had persistently called for controls since the mid-1950s, once again attacked their front bench for their apparent failure to act (Miles and Phizacklea, 1984: 35). Several commentators have been at pains to point out that the racial attacks upon black people which lay at the heart of these events were obscured by their presentation as 'race riots'. To dub them as a 'white riot' might have been more fitting therefore (Pilkington, 1988). Popular coverage of the riots had jolted Conservative thinking into examining what should be done. The option to leave the matter on the back burner, where it had effectively remained for the best part of a decade, was no longer open. One writer has described the impact of the riots in terms of the uncovering of the disjuncture between official government policy and everyday reality:

> Although race-related issues were not prominent in the 1959 general election, the disturbances highlighted the goverment's lack of explicit policy on immigration. Moreover, public anxiety over non-white immigration in the affected constituencies helped to elect a number of illiberal Conservative parliamentary candidates, thereby strengthening that party's anti-immigrant lobby.
>
> (Messina, 1989: 23-4)

By the late 1950s the party had moved within the space of a few short years from a position which saw Commonwealth labour migration as a valuable opportunity for British post-war recovery, to a view that was increasingly sceptical about the notion of a universal Commonwealth citizenship. The party was also determined to address the new-found 'problem' of black–white relations within Britain's cities. It has been commonly assumed that the years up to 1958–59 signalled a *laissez-faire* policy on immigration (Freeman, address the new-found 'problem' of black–white relations within Britain's cities. It has been commonly assumed that the years up to 1958–59 signalled a *laissez-faire* policy on immigration (Freeman, 1979; Messina, 1989). However, it would seem from the evidence that Conservative governments were increasingly preoccupied with the immigration question in one form or another. The debate within government from department to department certainly suggests that the issue was of significant concern in the sense that it was rarely examined as an aspect of employment or industrial policy alone. The relationships with housing, law and order, welfare and education were intertwined into the immigraton debate at an early point and by the close of the decade had become widely accepted dimensions of the issue. The Right of the party had won the argument as to whether there was an issue based on *black* immigration to begin with, but, as we shall see, this did not mean that the right had succeeded in terms of shaping the party's policies on the issue.

The triumph of pragmatism, 1958–76

Table 5.2 Chronology of key political developments relating to race and immigration, 1958–70

Conservatives in office	1960	Harold Macmillan's 'wind of change' speech
	1962	First Commonwealth Immigrants Bill enacted
Labour in office	1964	Smethwick defeat for Labour
	1965	*Immigration from the Commonwealth* White Paper
	1965	First Race Relations Act
	1965	Outbreak of rioting in Watts, Los Angeles
	1967	Collapse of the Campaign Against Racial Discrimination
	1967	Start of Kenyan Asian influx
	1968	Second Commonwealth Immigrants Bill enacted
	1968	Powell's 'rivers of blood' speech
	1968	Second Race Relations Act
Conservatives in office	1971	Immigration Act
	1972	Ugandan Asian influx

'The wind of change'

Following the debacle of the Suez affair in 1956, British governments faced a number of choices in the development of foreign policy. Winston Churchill had previously described these choices as competing and overlapping circles of influence, suggesting perhaps that weaknesses in British foreign policy arose from being too thinly committed to all three concomitantly. However, Suez did serve as a more immediate impetus for British foriegn policy-makers to accelerate the process of decolonisation that had been started in the 1940s.

The Conservatives had been perpetually divided on their responses to the calls for 'Home Rule' in India since the 1920s and had fought bitterly amongst themselves over the final retreat from the Raj in August 1947 (Childs, 1986: 43-46). By the time Macmillan became Premier in 1957, the agenda had changed dramatically with the emphasis now less on *whether* the Empire should be kept and more on *when* it should be abandoned. The most important factor leading to this change had been the the rise of anti-colonialist movements throughout Africa, Asia and the Caribbean, several of which had led to open revolts in places such as Kenya (the Mau-Mau rebellion) and Guyana (the left-wing Jagan government).

With pressure mounting in the colonies for independence and a growing vacuum developing in the *ad hoc* responses of successive Colonial Secretaries to individual revolts, Macmillan decided finally to seize the initiative to outline the long-term goals of Britain's policy. Thus, in January 1960 Macmillan travelled to the South African Parliament and said:

> the most striking of all impressions I have formed . . . is of the strength of African national consciousness. The wind of change is blowing through this continent, and, whether we like it or not, this growth of national consciousness is a political fact.
>
> (Quoted in Childs, 1986: 111)

The wind of change may not have been welcomed nor accepted by his hosts but it signalled the second wave of decolonisation that the Conservatives had decided to embark upon during the early 1960s. Among the products of his policy were the ending of the West Indies Federation in 1962 (with Jamaica and Trinidad both opting to go their own ways followed by a succession of smaller island states) and the Central African Federation in 1964 (yielding the newly independent states of Zambia and Malawi). Elsewhere, the retreat from Empire was formally sounded in *inter alia* Kenya

(1963), Uganda (1962), Tanzania (1964), Malaysia (1957), Cyprus (1961) and Nigeria (1960). Several took up Commonwealth membership at the encouragement of the Conservative Government.

The upshot of this period of intense change was that by the time Labour inherited the now structured immigration issue in 1964, it was possible to distinguish between an old and a new Commonwealth. Within the Conservative Party it was therefore possible to begin to get around the traditional principle of an indivisible Empire, the subjects of which shared everything in common in terms of their legal identities. It was clear that the second round of decolonisation had created a whole host of new independent states around the globe whose common feature was their non-white people and governments. Some Conservatives had initially tried to oppose Macmillan's policies on the simplistic grounds that he had sold out the white settler communities throughout Africa. For example, The Monday Club, a right-wing caucus opposed to the 'surrender' of Britain's colonies, was founded in 1961. Macmillan's Colonial Secretary, the liberally inclined Iain Macleod, turned out to be an early casualty of internal dissent when he was moved to the job of Leader of the House in October 1961 following a strong attack led by the Marquis of Salisbury.

But many other Conservatives, no less hardline on black–white relations, saw in Macmillan's doctrine a new opportunity to try to repudiate the Commonwealth ideal once and for all. If the non-white former members of the Empire wanted to go their own way, then, it was argued, they should be allowed to do so. Britain's place in world affairs should no longer be shaped by an outdated attachment to a past which, following the 'wind of change', was largely composed of self-determined black and brown peoples with little or nothing in common with the metropolitan British. The argument was a forceful one, not least because it uncovered the deep fissures that ran through the emergent British Commonwealth. Added to this was Macmillan's decision in 1961 to begin negotiations for Britain's entry into the European Economic Community. The early reactions to this move saw it as potentially detrimental to Britain's trading relations with Commonwealth countries, thereby further heightening the implicit choice that faced the British.

An internal party consensus that emerged at this time sought to introduce legal controls over black entry into the country. The consensus was based on an assumption that black immigrants were not only culturally and ethnically distinct from the indigenous population but were also politically set apart. Commonwealth immigrants were thus those very people who had fought to liberate themselves from British rule. According to opponents of black immigration within the Conservative Party these immigrants had little right to enter Britain on the basis of the 1948 Nationality Act which had orginally offered them a completely different deal to that of full independence. The 1962 Act, which formed the foundation of the party's strategy for more than fifteen years, was *de facto* a measure aimed at immigrants from the newer, non-white Commonwealth. According to an ex-minister involved in the Act's original passage, 'the restrictions were applied to coloured and white citizens . . . though everybody recognised that immigration from Canada, Australia and New Zealand formed no part of the problem' (Deedes, 1968: 10).

The campaign to introduce formal controls

At the level of popular perceptions and the formulation of explicit party policy, the debate on race and immigration can be dated from about 1958 (Katznelson, 1973). However, within government a reluctance to act swiftly in response to public opinion lingered on. Consequently, from the time of 1958 disturbances until 1961 the issue received growing attention from politicians and the press and revealed the lines along which the Conservative Government had revised its approach to the issue. On the one hand, some writers have argued that this public debate was indicative of a process of racialisation of the immigration issue in general and the origins of the new, post-Empire racism within the Conservative Party. Miles and Phizacklea (1984: 38) for example talk of a 'significant advance in the racialisation of British politics' at this time because the 1958 disorders had allowed racists responsible for attacking West Indians a national platform for their anti-immigrant views. These writers are especially interested in the new cohort of Conservative MPs returned at the 1959 general election who 'soon proved themselves to be supporters of the cause long advocated by Osborne and Pannell'. The arrival of this new group of MPs meant that the Conservative Government now had to contend with a sizeable anti-immigrant lobby from within its own ranks, a lobby which was heavily influenced by the views of grass-roots white supporters. Two of the most vocal MPs among the anti-immigrant group of Conservative backbenchers were Harold Gurden (Selly Oak) and Martin Lindsay (Solihull), the latter having been at the forefront of post-1958 parliamentary debate:

> 'We must ask ourselves to what extent we want Great Britain to become a multiracial community . . . . A question which affects the future of our own race and breed is not one we should merely leave to chance.'
> (Quoted in Foot, 1965: 130).

The consequence of developments leading up to the 1962 Act, contend Miles and Phizacklea, was that the Conservatives had made themselves hostages to future changes in public opinion. The role of party thus became to aggregate and reflect popular pressure from its own supporters and, in doing so, it effectively surrendered the high ground of policy-making it had once enjoyed. This view of the party as merely responding to public opinion on the issue is also shared in the writings of Home Secretary Butler (1971) and Prime Minister Macmillan (1973), the two principal politicians involved in the 1962 Act, though neither, unsurprisingly, describe the surrounding debates as symptomatic of the racialisation of British politics.

On the other hand, some commentators have stressed the extent to which the Conservatives under the leadership of Macmillan and Butler were able to absorb the pressure for controls and manage them in a masterly and bold way without yielding sovereignty to extra-parliamentary groups. Thus what was important was the relative success, by appeasing anti-immigration pressures, in guiding the debate towards arguments about the need for controls on a temporary basis and subject to the needs of the economy (Rose, 1969). Although statutory controls formed the corner piece of the party's declared policy after 1961, the element of continuity cannot be overlooked since one of the major justfications for the 1962 legislation was that it would introduce greater coherence into the equation linking labour migration and industrial growth. In addition, it is significant that the policy was not an attempt to completely end Commonwealth immigration and therefore landed a long way short of the blunt 'closed doors' calls of many members of the party.

Labour's surrender

As the previous chapter noted, the record of the 1964–70 Labour

Governments has been the subject of intense scrutiny and disagreement by a wide community of scholars. One writer though, Zig Layton-Henry (1984: 74), has managed to capture a broad span of opinion though his description of

> the policy of appeasement [which] led to concession after concession by the Labour government which encouraged right-wing Conservatives to believe that they had a winning issue which commanded widespread popular support and which could be used against the Labour government.

The experience of losing the Shadow Foreign Secretary at the hands of the Smethwick electorate in 1964 meant that, from its earliest days, the Labour administration felt vulnerable and defensive on the immigration issue. Significantly, in 1964 the Conservatives only enjoyed the slenderest of leads over Labour (seven percentage points) as the party seen by the electorate as most hardline on the issue (Butler and Stokes, 1974: 306). Therefore, the sense of self-conscious defensiveness shown by Labour politicians must be viewed as largely self-inflicted. Critics have charged that, at this early point in the development of the debate over public policy towards black immigration, Labour still retained the ability to turn its back on right-wingers' calls for ever-tighter controls. John Rex (1968) for instance has characterised Labour's strategy as little short of a catastrophe. His argument has emphasised the extent of the rude shock Labour front-bench politicians endured during this formative period. The message that the electorate had little sympathy for the case of would-be immigrants was first delivered at Smethwick. However, if it had not been received clearly at Smethwick, it was repeated a few months later at Leyton when an engineered by-election failed once again to secure Patrick Gordon-Walker's election to the Commons.

The strategy that Labour then banked its entire credibility upon was to reach a bipartisan agreement with the Conservatives to effectively de-politicise race. In order to do this, great effort went into the presentation of Labour's immigration regime being no less hardline than that of the Conservatives. The aim was to defuse the possibility of one party or another making electoral capital out the issue. Certainly, following the experience of a gradual concession of the principle of control between 1958–62, the Conservative leadership knew at first hand of the difficulties associated with management of the issue. The support of the new Conservative Leader, Edward Heath, and that of his Home Affairs spokesman, Quintin Hogg, was therefore achieved relatively quickly and with few complications. The price demanded by liberal reformers within Labour's ranks was to introduce modest race relations legislation. The cross-party deal was struck and both leaderships felt that they had found a semi-permanent formula to excise race from party politics. The leaderships were mistaken and the consensus was broken a few years later by Conservative hawks led by Powell. But the consequences of its abrupt demise were considerably more damaging for Labour than for the Conservatives, and have contributed to subsequent perceptions of Labour's strategy as cynical, flawed and unprincipled.

It had been the Labour Party after all that had stood out so firmly against the need for formal controls until as late as 1963. One of the reasons for this stance proffered by the Labour leadership had been the movement's commitment to socialist internationalism. Additionally, the party saw itself as the party of Commonwealth and had been in the vanguard of the decolonisation process. These principles were seemingly jettisoned by the leadership whilst in office in an ultimately failed bid to avoid electoral unpopularity. Interestingly, there is little evidence to suggest that there was a rational basis for this strategy. Indeed, it seemed flawed: the more the party moved to the right on immigration, the less convinced the electorate became. Survey evidence shows that the Conservatives' electoral edge over Labour as the tougher party on immigration grew streadily from 13 points in 1966 to 53 points by 1970. The profit in following the crowd appeared to be one of the myths of Labour's record in office.

Finally, it is hard to avoid concluding that Labour's strategy was not merely founded on populism but was also cynical in that it continued to boast of its progressive record on integration. Whilst it was undoubtedly Labour politicians who were the driving force behind the two Race Relations Acts, it should not be forgotten that the Conservatives' support was vital to both. But Labour's appeasement of the anti-immigrant right meant that its integration-oriented measures needed to be as weak as possible. The simple logic of the strategy was that fewer immigrants were a precursor to good race relations. Of course, several commentators have observed that Labour's case for outlawing discrimination was at odds with its own immigration policy of discriminating against black people. The eventual outcome of this linkage was that setbacks in domestic race relations could always be blamed on the scale of immigration, which would have to be restricted ever further.

The point would come when it would no longer be possible to further tighten immigration policy without countenancing the removal of citizenship rights from countless numbers of British passports holders all over the world. In the short term this option was off the agenda but in 1968 Labour was forced to introduce such fundamental changes in response to the Kenyan Asian crisis. Once again the strategy revealed itself as an exercise designed to take available actions to limit fresh immigration. If the design involved the betrayal of both legal and ethical obligations to British citizens in Kenya or elsewhere, the Labour Government considered it worthwhile. Yet again the policy failed, not least because of the damning critique of appeasement presented through the intervention of Enoch Powell.

The impact of Enoch Powell

The most remarkable feature of the years between 1962–76 was the degree of continuity and stability in the parties' *front-bench* stance towards race. Such continuity was doubly significant given the acrimonious nature of the public debate that raged for much of this period. However, whilst the Heath leadership managed to steer clear of direct exchanges with Labour, the same cannot be said of prominent voices within the Conservative Party. It was during this period that some of the deepest intra-party disputes over race and immigration surfaced and, as we shall see, led to the greatest public row over the issue in modern British political history – the Powell affair.

Relations between different strands of thought within the parties during the consensus period are most revealing in terms of the Conservatives' long-running difficulties over perceiving Britain as a multiracial society. For many years, there had been a small number of voices within the party which warned that non-white immigration could not be controlled; rather, it had to be ended altogether as part of a wider policy involving the repatriation of many black immigrants. As we saw earlier, it had been left to MPs such as Osborne and Pannell to articulate this position in the 1950s. Their supporters continued to have reservations about immigration during the period of the bipartisan consensus, but for the most part the focus of attention was elsewhere, on the reforms of Roy Jenkins. The question of the longer-term social and cultural impact of non-white immigration was largely in the reformers' court. The intervention of Powell therefore represented a return to this fundamental question and involved a conservative critique, not merely of the fact of large-scale black immigration, but also of the multiracial society liberals believed they were in the process of shaping.

During the closing months of 1967 rumours circulated about the future citizenship policies of the Kenyan government. Their impact on British passport-holders in Kenya – ostensibly of South Asian origin – was enormous and precipitated a growing exodus from the country. In fact the exodus had first begun in 1965 and had been growing steadily until the near-panic flight of 1967–68. The response of the Labour Government was to force through Parliament an emergency immigration Bill aimed at stemming the flow of Kenyan Asians. The Bill constituted a further dilution of principle by subdividing the categories of British citizenship. According to one member of the Cabinet, the key difference on this occasion as compared with the passage of the 1962 Act was unmistakable (Crossman 1977: 679). Whereas six years earlier it had been a shameful betrayal of the ideals of the Commonwealth, virtually all leading politicians now subscribed to the view that the denial of entry rights to British nationals was a necessary and desirable thing to do. *Civis Britannicus sum* was dead, presumed murdered.

The hasty, somewhat panicky actions of the government were seized upon by Powell as an illustration of the seeming lack of any guiding rationale for public policy on race and immigration. The Kenyan Asian crisis, however, was not the only backdrop to Powell's speeches. It should be remembered that his attacks were principally directed against the second Race Relations Bill which was due to come before Parliament during spring 1968. Together with Duncan Sandys, a former Conservative frontbencher, Powell launched a campaign to stop the influx of Kenyan Asians and thereby undermine the Race Relations Bill.

The chief instrument of their aims was to shift public and press debate away from the question of discrimination in British society and back onto the question of black immigration. Earlier, in July 1967 Sandys was reported to have said that 'the breeding of millions of half-caste children would merely produce a generation of misfits and create increased tension' (*The Daily Telegraph*, 25 July 1967). It was striking that he failed to receive a public rebuke from his own party leadership, but even more significantly, calls for his prosecution under the 1965 Race Relations Act were turned down by the Attorney-General (Saggar, 1991a: 45). The Sandys controversy came in the wake of the arrest of Michael Abdul Malik (also known as Michael X) of the Black Power Racial Action Adjustment Society for allegedly inciting racial hatred in a speech given in Reading. These two controversies suggested that the mood was ripe for the Right to launch a more concerted attack on the liberal consensus.

Powellism rested largely on a collection of hearsay incidents aimed at bolstering public fears about the immigrant influx. Although his views were given credibility by the manner in which he expressed them, at their simplest they relied on stoking the flames of anti-immigrant racism. His conception of a mono-racial nation that would be lost forever undoubtedly struck a populist chord in the country at large. But his warnings went further than simply highlighting the impending end of white British society. Rather, they evoked the spectre of black people in Britain gaining the upper hand over the indigeneous white community. Such a prospect could not be reconciled with his belief that the white population were entitled to defend their own interests against 'alien invaders', but had not been allowed to do so by the major parties:

> We must be mad, literally mad, as a nation, to be permitting the annual inflow of some 50,000 dependants who are for the most part the material of the future growth of the immigrant-descended population. It is like a nation busily engaged in heaping up its own funeral pyre.

These words were part of Powell's now legendary Birmingham speech given in April 1968. The nub of this speech had been to attack the Race Relations Bill which was due to come before Parliament. He had waited for some considerable time before choosing to launch his attack in April and his immediate dismissal from Heath's Shadow Cabinet can have come as no surprise. This was because the speech deliberately tore a gaping hole through the race consensus. That said, when it came to the passage of the Bill through the Commons, it was significant that the Conservatives remained deeply divided. The liberal wing of the party succeeded in getting the front bench to support the principles of the legislation whilst rejecting its detailed content.

Powell had therefore triumphed in splitting his party on the issue which no end of procedural deals could disguise. Numerous Conservative backbenchers, who for so long had felt frustrated by the spirit and pace of race relations legislation, had suddenly found a leader for their cause. Moreover, sensing the magnitude of popular support for Powell's message in the country, many Conservatives felt they had the ingredients of an election-winning platform. It was precisely for this reason that Heath hesitated before dropping Powell, for he knew that to dismiss the dissenter would only have added weight to Powell's claim to lead the party in the future. In the event the dismissal was immediate and reflected Heath's high-risk strategy of repudiating such naked displays of racism; moreover, there was little doubt that his Shadow Home Secretary, Quintin Hogg, would have resigned had Powell not been sacked.

The political impact of Powell's intervention had been to stretch the bipartisan consensus to near breaking point. He had split his party on the issue. The shadow front bench nonetheless managed to keep alive the party's commitment to the consensus, although the cost of doing so was considerable. It involved a significant lurch to the right on immigration policy which ensured a proportionate shift to the right in Labour's policy stance. The result was that the 1970 general election was fought against the backdrop of tough restrictionist policies being promised in the manifestoes of both major parties. The electorate however perceived a difference between the parties on the issue and had seemingly linked Powell's message with Conservative Party policy.

Powell had put the parties on the defensive over immigration and effectively bounced them into taking the arguably contrived fears of his supporters seriously. By 1969, so confident had he become of his grass-roots support that he unveiled his all-too-serious plan for the creation of a government Ministry of Repatriation. He had now turned his attention to what should be done about his prediction of a future in which black people in Britain held 'unfair' rights over their white counterparts. The fallacy of his case was the total absence of evidence to support his prediction. Moreover, he also suggested that future generations of black people would remain outsiders to mainstream British society which he defined in cultural and racial terms. He stated:

> The West Indian or Indian does not, by being born in England, become an Englishman. In law he becomes a United Kingdom citizen by birth; in fact he is a West Indian or Asian still.

Nationhood, according to Powell, was defined in terms of common heritage and ancestary, terms that his supporters – though not Powell himself – took to be racial. An important debate had been opened in British politics. We shall return to consider the development of this debate in Chapter 7.

The beginning of the end for the consensus

The Conservative Party's approach to issues of race and New Commonwealth immigration has traditionally been viewed as hardline and sober in the sense that the party has neither encouraged such immigration nor particularly championed the rights of black people settled in Britain. However, the party has in fact experienced a variety of approaches to the issue from among its own ranks. These approaches have competed for exposure within the party and have captured the policy-making stance of its leadership in different ways and at different times. If perceptions of the issue positions of political parties count for anything, then perhaps all that can be said reliably is that the party has undoubtedly been perceived by key sections of the electorate as less receptive to black immigration (Butler and Stokes, 1974: 306). Whether this broad perception – only clearly identifiable in survey data from the 1970 election onward – has made a significant difference to voting behaviour is, however, a moot point.

In the face of all the evidence, the Conservative Party did not consciously exploit the race issue to its advantage at the 1970 General Election (Layton-Henry, 1984: 77). Survey evidence analysed by Butler and Stokes (1974: 306) demonstrated beyond doubt that the Conservatives were perceived as the tougher of the two major parties on immigration. The Powell controversy had succeeded in shifting perceptions – if not the substance – of the party substantially further to the right. The response of Heath was to stand firm in his opposition to the populist rhetoric of the Powellites whilst simultaneously refusing to condemn a fellow Conservative candidate. Layton-Henry (1984: 78–79) notes that, realising that the chances of returning to Heath's front bench had been extinguished forever, Powell wisely planned ahead for the possibility of becoming party leader himself. He prudently stayed within the Conservative fold and urged his supporters to back the Conservative Party, in spite of his own very obvious disagreements with the party's immigration policies.

Meanwhile, a number of important developments took place which further undermined the already weakened race consensus. First, organised, quasi-factional opposition to the consensus began to surface within the Conservative Party. The Monday Club, first founded in the early 1960s to campaign against decolonisation policies, re-emerged as a powerful lobby within the party. Important new links were forged by the Club with anti-immigration pressure groups such as the Immigration Control Association. In 1969 a leading member of the Monday Club, George Young, wrote a pamphlet which attacked the prevailing liberal consensus, arguing that its goal of 'integration' was fundamentally at odds with the rising force of global racial tensions (Young, 1969). Building on the critique developed by Powell, Conservative MPs and activists on the right of the party, contended that the party had been duped by nothing short of a 'neurotic' regard for individual rights. As Rich (1986a: 56) notes, the model of racially divided South African society was both the logical end-point and intellectual inspiration for the 'aggressive ethnocentric line of politics' of the Club.

The second development that was to shake the Conservative leadership's stance towards immigration to its core came in 1972 when it emerged that up to 50,000 fresh Asian immigrants were planning to enter Britain. In 1971 the Conservative Government had passed its own Immigration Act in the belief that its tougher controls would bury the immigration issue from sight. For a while it seemed that the hope was based on a realistic assessment of immigration queues, not least because the new legislation scrapped altogether the issuing of employment vouchers carrying permanent residency rights. This state of cautious optimism was obliterated virtually overnight in early August 1972 when the regime of President Amin of Uganda announced the immediate expulsion from the country of all Asians holding British nationality. An entirely new immigration crisis had been created and one which placed Heath's administration in a position it had neither planned for nor knew how to manage. The fact that most of the Ugandan Asians were British citizens placed a clear obligation to allow them to exercise the right of entry that went with their citizenship. To interfere with, let alone unilaterally withdraw, that right was virtually unthinkable since such a policy would have been universally condemned by Britain's allies. However, to accept their right of entry and allow their settlement involved a major policy reversal since the party was explicitly committed to closing the immigration door. The wrath of not only the right-wing of the party but also moderates awaited the leadership if it opted to permit the refugees' entry.

After frantic negotiations to explore the feasibility of other Commonwealth countries accepting some of the refugees (notably Canada and India), the Government eventually agreed to accept just over half of them and set up the Ugandan Resettlement Board to oversee the exercise. The reaction within domestic politics was largely negative, involving considerable media publicity portraying the Ugandans' arrival as a further invasion of British society. The Monday Club established its own 'Halt Immigration Now' public campaign, whilst Powell, now on the verge of a lasting split with the party, stated quite plainly that Britain had little legal and certainly no moral responsibility to accept the refugees. The party was thrown into turmoil on the issue, culminating in the October party conference. After heated argument, both on the substantive issues as well as on procedural matters arising from the inclusion on the agenda of a motion challenging the government's policy, the conference supported a Young Conservative resolution which backed Heath's position. Notwithstanding this victory, the writing was on the wall that large numbers of the party's activists would no longer wear the policy of acceding to fresh large-scale immigration. The ground had been laid for a major shift to the right on the issue initiated by, and as a result of, a reappraisal by the party leadership of the electoral incentives for doing so.

Third, the experience of Labour in office during the 1960s had disillusioned many of those on the left wing of the party. A new wave of Labour activists emerged within the party after its 1970 defeat, many of whom had not been involved in formal party politics beforehand. The party underwent a dramatic shift to the left during the early 1970s on a wide variety of policy issues (Whiteley, 1983). The issue of non-white immigration posed a number of difficulties for the party in position since its leadership, at least, had been made acutely sensitive to its latent volatility and exposure to the forces of populism.

Labour's initial reaction to its unexpected electoral defeat had been to point the finger of blame at racism within the Conservative Party, recognising the electorate's difficulty in distinguishing Conservative policy from Powellite rhetoric. But by 1972 the Labour Party had published its own discussion paper, *Immigration and Integration*, which made a bold leap from internal party thinking on the issue just a couple of years previously (Labour Party, 1972). The document stated the case for a major revamp of the legislation governing citizenship, calling for an end to distinctions between the notions of, and rights attached to, colonial and non-colonial UK citizenship. On integration matters, recommendations were endorsed for a major shake-up of organisations and ministries overseeing race relations legislation.

Commentators have not surprisingly contrasted the comparatively liberal policy line taken by the Conservative Government over the Ugandan Asian crisis with the hardline, reactionary policy of the previous Labour Government towards the Kenyan Asians. However, even before the 1972 crisis, a number of awkward questions were being raised in relation to Labour's immigration policies in opposition. The key test of this dilemma for Labour came in 1971 in the debate over the Government's promised Immigration Act. This, by now infamous, piece of legislation sought to curtail dramatically the scope of further fresh immigration. It did this using two principal instruments. The first was to introduce a system of tightly regulated work permits in the place of the system of issuing employment vouchers; the second was to explicitly identify the doctrine of patriality as the basis of deciding which category of UK citizens would be exempt from otherwise draconian immigration controls. Labour's own track record of tight immigration policy in the 1960s meant that it naturally approached the debate on the new legislation with extreme caution. Its position of opposing the new Bill was founded entirely on the view that a wholesale review of citizenship was required – hardly a commitment to block the principle of the proposed law.

Therefore, whilst sections of the party became radicalised on key aspects of public policy during the opposition years of the early 1970s – notably on the economy and industrial planning – it was clear that on race and immigration the party still retained its earlier posture of nervous realism. The key factor that did emerge at this time, however, was the capacity of the Labour Left in particular to launch attacks on the strict immigration regime both promised and largely delivered by the Heath administration. Such attacks may not have seemed terribly credible given Labour's own drift to the right between 1965–70, but they placed the party in a new position. In the early 1960s the Labour leadership had fought the principle of the 1962 Act introduced by a Conservative Home Secretary. By 1971 Labour found itself once again opposing a Conservative Immigration Bill but on this occasion, unlike the 1962 Bill, there was little doubting the clear aim of public policy – to shut the immigration door completely.

The populist ticket, 1976–83

Table 5.3 Chronology of key political developments relating to race and immigration, 1976–83

Labour in office	1976	Malawi Asian crisis
	1976	Third Race Relations Act
	1977	Anglo-Asian and Anglo-West Indian Conservative Societies established
	1978	Mrs Thatcher's 'swamping' interview
	1979	Southall anti-National Front disorders
Conservatives in office	1980	Riots in St Pauls, Bristol
	1981	Nationality Act
	1981	Riots in Brixton, Toxteth and numerous other cities
	1981	Scarman Report published

The repoliticisation of race

The period between the mid-1970s and early 1980s witnessed an intense rise in domestic anti-immigrant political sentiment. In the short run, this development was precipitated by the concession to the Ugandan Asian refugees in 1972, followed by a further wave of Asians from Malawi in 1976. Protest campaigns against these further 'betrayals' of the indigeneous white population escalated and were spearheaded by far-right political parties such as the National Front (see also Chapter 7 below). But the emergence of a coherent, legitimised form of anti-black political discourse at this time has also been explained in terms of longer-term processes. In *Race and Party Competition in Britain*, Messina (1989) argues that the rapid repoliticisation of race after the 1974 general elections owed a great deal to the conspiracy of silence of the two major parties on the issue since 1965. Further, he links the rise of fierce inter-party disputes over race with a more general decline in the consensus politics of the post-war settlement. He writes:

> Why the Conservative and Labour parties diverged after 1975 is fairly clear. Impelled by distinct internal pressures and attempting to woo different constituencies, each side gravitated towards race policies which offered the best prospect for internal party coherence and electoral advantage.
>
> (Messina, 1989: 126-49)

Miles and Phizacklea (1984) have suggested that this era ought to be viewed as part of a longer-running drift in the major parties' policies towards the hardline Right. Indeed, they trace the turnaround from the controversial 1971 Immigration Act and claim that it cleared the way for the articulation of a discourse aimed at 'repatriating' black immigrants. These authors note the extent of the right-wing clamour pushing both parties towards embracing the underlying assumptions – if not the policies – of Powell. Their interpretation lays weight on the 1971 Act's internalisation of the ideology of resisting the 'black invasion' within Conservative Party ranks. Messina's interpretation, in contrast, stresses that the Conservative Party made no clear attempt to move to the right on immigration for electoral gain until after the change of leadership in 1975. Both perspectives, however, agree that the experience of Labour in power between 1974–79 contributed heavily to popular perceptions of policy failure on non-white immigration. The scale and nature of these perceptions have in turn been linked by different commentators to the rise of (a) the National Front (see Messina, 1989: Chapter 5), and (b) the electoral exploitation of such dramatically skewed public opinion by the Conservative Party between 1976–79 (see Rich, 1986a: 57–63). It is the second of these links that we are concerned with in this section of the chapter.

Mrs Thatcher's leadership

The election of Margaret Thatcher to the leadership of the Conservative Party in 1975 brought about a major transformation in the intellectual basis of the party's policies. This transformation was not merely restricted to certain litmus test issues of right-wing purity such as immigration but extended to a whole range of social and economic policy concerns. The new Conservative leadership reflected the ascendancy of neo-liberalism designed to revive British capitalism. To bring about such a goal it was necessary to restrict the scope of government activity in economic affairs. In doing so, neo-liberals insisted that the strategy would enhance the personal freedom of the individual (Gamble, 1986: 29–32).

But that is not to say that Mrs Thatcher's leadership could be described in such simple terms. Rather, as Rich (1986a) has argued, Thatcherism should be viewed as a fusion of several political traditions, including economic liberalism but also that of moral authoritarianism. In the non-economic, social sphere, Thatcherism has often embraced a greater degree of state control over society (Gamble, 1988). It was the influence of non-economic values that shaped Mrs Thatcher's approach to the questions of race and immigration. Indeed, several commentators have linked hardline, populist views towards immigration with views regretting the alleged moral decline in British society since the Victorian age (see for example Hall *et al.*, 1978; Jessop *et al.*, 1988).

Of course, the influence of a single individual in the Conservative Party's rapid move to the right on race can easily be exaggerated. It is important to note that Mrs Thatcher may merely have been responding to and voicing the policy perceptions of the electorate. To be sure, Heath *et al.* (1991: 177) report that levels of negative public sentiment towards black minorities themselves barely changed during the 1970s and 1980s: in October 1974, 26 per cent of voters thought that attempts to give equal opportunities to black people had gone too far; over the course of the 1979, 1983 and 1987 elections (all resounding Thatcher victories), the figures were 28, 18 and 28 per cent respectively. A similar line of argument is signalled in Messina's (1989) thesis which portrays both major parties as having come significantly adrift of public opinion on race in the period up to 1976.

This rider to the data apart, that clear overtures were made towards authoritarian populism on race and other issues is unmistakable. From 1976 onwards an apparently orchestrated strategy was deployed by the Conservative leadership to alter public perceptions of the party's position on immigration. Interpretations of this strategic move, however, vary from those of supporters who emphasised the need to bring public opinion and policy commitments back into line, to those of critics who asserted that it merely pandered to crude racism. According to the latter interpretation, the logical outcome of the strategy did not merely end with enhanced Conservative electoral support, but would result in a *bipartisan* policy of repatriation through incremental steps:

> The government argues that the 'fears of our people' about . . . being 'swamped' by 'alien cultures' are justified. It does so in circumstances where it is not immigration but natural reproduction which maintains that population, and therefore the 'problem' can only be resolved by a policy of 'repatriation'.
>
> (Miles and Phizacklea, 1984: 105)

Following the change of leadership, the Conservatives moved to attach greater prominence to the immigration issue. This in itself ran counter to the spirit of the race consensus which had operated since 1975 and which had tried – often unsuccessfully – to avoid bringing the issue into the heart of party politics. The real difference made by the new leadership was that calls for the party not to ignore public opinion were now the basis of Mrs Thatcher's own political style. Mrs Thatcher was keen to present a firmer, more high-profile line on immigration but also to project a more hospitable image towards potential supporters among the ethnic minorities themselves. On immigration, the Conservatives' policies looked beyond the 1971 Act which so many within the party had believed would bury the issue by virtually severing the source of fresh immigration. Instead, the party now emphasised the growing problems of secondary immigration and backed a policy to establish a register of dependants. In addition, it promised a new Nationality Act which would streamline citizenship rights with the right of entry to the country. The former of these two main commitments was particularly attuned to Mrs Thatcher's own political instincts which suggested that white public opinion was anxious about the unknown scale of future growth in the black population. Therefore, the argument ran, it was vital to assess the scale of immigrants planning to enter Britain for the purposes of family reunification.

The new approach was first sketched out by Mrs Thatcher's Shadow Home Secretary, William Whitelaw. He told the 1976 party conference that the long-term success of all race relations policies ultimately rested on policies which brought non-white immigration to an early end. He went on to say that the 1971 Act remained the starting point of the party's future policy insofar as it would honour the pledge to allow the family reunification of all primary immigrants who had entered Britain before 1 January 1973. However, that commitment did not prevent a future Conservative government from introducing a queuing mechanism for such dependants and setting up a register of their numbers (Conservative Central Office, 1976).

With this package of policy commitments in place, the attention turned to ways in which the Conservatives' immigration strategy could be best used to gain electoral advantage. The temperature of the debate was raised dramatically in January 1978 when Mrs Thatcher was interviewed on Granada Television's *World in Action* programme. In the course of this much quoted interview, the Conservative leader went considerably further than any major party leader before her towards adopting a nakedly populist posture on black immigration. At its most controversial point, Mrs Thatcher spoke of 'the British people's fear' of 'being swamped' by 'alien cultures'. Her comments were a personal statement of her own political creed, both conspicuously unfamiliar with and unwelcoming of the long-standing black presence in Britain. But her views were also intended to be a channel of articulation for the white majority who both feared and resented the creation of a multiracial society.

The only questions which remained were conflicting views about the motives behind her remarks. Supporters saw her remarks as proof of her loyalty to 'the ordinary folk' of the country who had been misled (at best) and deceived (at worst) by elite politicians on the immigration question. But for her critics, the parallels were too close with the last Conservative politician who had used a similar rationale for his own intervention on the question. On that occasion, Powell had found himself drummed out of the party's leadership and eventually out of the party. On this occasion, it seemed that Mrs Thatcher was rewarded with the support of the party and, in turn, the electorate.

Building bridges with the ethnic minorities

The surprising feature of the Conservatives' race strategy under the new party leader was the positive attempt to win the confidence of black voters. Since the days of Powell's 1968 speech, relations had been severely strained and the party had assumed that black voters were amongst the most loyal of Labour voters. To some extent this perception of the black electorate was a reasonable one confirmed by most independent research (Butler and Kavanagh, 1974 and 1975). However, following their two 1974 election defeats, the Conservatives were keen to discover the social characteristics of voters in marginal seats lost to Labour. As the following chapter shows, the publication of a report on the second 1974 election by the Community Relations Commission gave new credence to the view that the Conservatives had forfeited – because they had ignored – a number of so-called ethnic marginals (Anwar and Kohler, 1975). Thus was born the 'ethnic marginals' electoral strategy, based, it would seem, on a rather shallow understanding of the relationship between black voting patterns and floating voters.

Conservative Central Office responded to this analysis by organising a major rethink of its attitude towards ethnic minorities. In January 1976 Central Office established a Community Affairs Department to oversee new initiatives aimed at specific social groups within the electorate. Soon after, its new Director, Andrew Rowe, launched an Ethnic Minorities Unit. The Unit's tasks were two-fold: first, it was to be responsible for making existing party members more aware of the importance of black voters, and second, it was to promote the party to potential black voters. To that end, its first move was to set up an Anglo-Asian Conservative Society and an Anglo-West Indian Conservative Society. Both Societies were to have a national body accompanied by a number of local organisations.

In practice, the former Society turned out to be the more successful, running to over 30 local branches at one time. It even managed to attract such prominent names as William Whitelaw, Michael Heseltine and Lord Carrington to serve as vice-presidents. This success largely endorsed the view taken by Rowe and others who stressed the potential deep reservoir of support among middle-class Asians who, it was claimed, shared many of the values of thrift, self-help and family discipline promoted by the party at large. Among West Indians the initiative was rather less successful, though several highly active branches were launched in parts of London, most notably in Haringey. The launch and early history of both Societies suggested that the Conservative Party had fundamentally rethought the question of black participation in mainstream party politics. Even more significantly, given that both organisations were granted the status of special associations, they were entitled to representation in the party's internal structure, namely the National Union. This direct fusion into the mainstream party structure demonstrated that a place existed within Conservative ranks for distinct ethnic bodies. Therefore, whilst both Societies fell a long way short of the principle of black autonomy – which was to afflict internal developments in the Labour Party in the 1980s – they did nonetheless demonstrate a fresh approach to meeting the political aspirations of black Britons.

The split line of thinking towards race and immigration issues masked an underlying tension within the Conservative Party. On the one hand, the party leadership had made a firm decision to move further to the right on immigration in order to address the sense of powerless drift that shrouded the policy debate. Electoral gain was undoubtedly one of the motives behind this shift. The calculation depended not merely on the public perceiving a clear policy difference between the parties but also on the issue continuing to be highly salient. From 1976 onwards, with the influx of Asian refugees from Malawi and the dramatic rise in anti-immigrant agitation by the far right, both these criteria had been met. The Conservatives stood poised to reap significant numbers of disillusioned Labour-identifiers. These *de facto* floating voters had come adrift from their traditional class-derived Labour moorings because they perceived that Conservative policies stood a better chance of dealing with their resentments.

On the other hand, the party's traditional paternalistic values were given expression through the lobbying of black supporters and recruits. This strategy was also motivated by electoral concerns as a result of post-mortems over the unexpected 1974 defeats. The success of both strategies ultimately rested upon the party's ability to keep both groups of target voters fairly isolated from one another. Distinct and rather dissimilar messages had to be communicated to each group. White floating voters, resentful of black immigration, were told that immigration would end definitively under a future Conservative administration. Meanwhile, aspiring black voters, often eager to participate in the party they felt best mirrored their class and economic interests, were told that the days of prejudice and bigotry were over. In both cases, the question of the protection of the rights of black people through public policy remained conspicuously off the agenda.

Party strategy and issue management

The two-track approach of the Conservative Party was a high-risk strategy designed to extract maximum political advantage from an issue which had lain dormant for a decade. Signs of its inherent tensions were apparent from an early point, as illustrated by the case of the party's relations with the anti-racist movement. In 1977, the two major parties were invited to nominate joint chairmen of the newly formed Joint Campaign Against Racialism (JCAR). Mrs Thatcher's Shadow Home Secretary, William Whitelaw indicated his support for the new campaign body. The Conservative choice for the post was John Moore MP but his nomination was abruptly blocked by Mrs Thatcher who objected to such close links with an organisation she perceived to be dominated by far-left activists. The dispute heightened when the National Union of the Conservative Party tried to persevere with its plans to support JCAR; once again the plan was vetoed by the party leader. As Layton-Henry (1978) has observed, it was rare for the party to go against the wishes of the leader and the fact that it tried to was an indication of how strongly the left of the party felt about being seen to oppose racism. The eventual Conservative nominee was chosen from outside the parliamentary party and was selected to achieve a face-saving compromise for both sides.

The Conservative position was further complicated by Mrs Thatcher's 'swamping' remarks at the beginning of 1978. Press reports had appeared prior to the Granada interview indicating that the party was engaged in a fresh trawl for ideas to curb immigration. At the same time relations between the leader and backbenchers from the left of the party were increasingly strained by continuing reports of Mrs Thatcher's staunch opposition to the party's involvement in anti-racist campaigns. The leader seemed determined to try to keep the issues of race and immigration on separate and parallel tracks. Evidence of the electoral arguments for being seen to be tough on immigration was soon apparent. In February 1978 the *Daily Mail* commissioned an opinion poll which showed that in the weeks since the Granada interview, the party's ratings had shot up by 9 per cent; moreover, the poll reported that the proportion of the electorate who thought that immigration was an 'urgent issue facing the country' had climbed from 9 to 21 per cent (NOP, 1978).

The pressure to play to the populist ticket did not stem from Conservative readings of public opinion alone. In fact, there were growing signs of Conservative backbench MPs adopting a more right-wing stance on race. A survey conducted by Messina in 1982 revealed that no less than 42 per cent of Conservative MPs favoured the idea of the voluntary repatriation of non-whites in Britain. The survey also showed that 22 per cent thought that current immigration policies were 'too lenient' (quoted in Messina, 1989: 129). Furthermore, opinion among the rank and file of the party was even more right-wing. In a survey of delegates to the 1983 party conference, 14 per cent supported the compulsory repatriation of non-white citizens and a massive 56 per cent felt that their own government's immigration policies were not strict enough (quoted in Messina, 1989: 131).

On all sides, therefore, the Conservative leadership was subjected to pressure to exploit the so-called race card. In order to do so, it was necessary for the party to be fairly certain that it could in fact manage the dimensions of an issue which had proven to be so volatile under earlier Conservative and Labour governments. More importantly, authoritarian populism did not merely involve posturing whilst in opposition. It also involved the sustained delivery of policies to meet the expectations generated both among the party faithful as well as among the less partisan electorate at large. On this criteria, Heath's government had clearly surrendered some credibility between its 1970 victory and the 1972 decision to admit the Ugandan refugees. Consequently, during the first 1979–83 Thatcher administration, the leader's guiding aim on immigration

– like so many areas of public policy – was to avoid the pitfalls that had sunk her Conservative predecessor.

One Nation Toryism versus radical race politics, 1983–92

Table 5.4 Chronology of key political developments relating to race and immigration, 1983–91

Conservatives in office	1985	Riots in Brixton and Tottenham
	1986	Labour Left breakthrough in London local elections
	1986	Ray Honeyford affair receives national publicity
	1986	Establishment of Conservative One Nation Forum
	1987	Election of four black Labour MPs
	1990	Islamic Party of Great Britain launched
	1990	Paul Boateng appointed to Shadow Treasury post
	1991	John Taylor selected as prospective parliamentary candidate for safe Conservative seat of Cheltenham
	1991	Ashok Kumar elected as Labour MP for an overwhelmingly white constituency, Langbaurgh

The end of the immigration issue

After the Conservatives' election to office in 1979, enormous pressures existed for the government to take swift and decisive action. In the field of immigration policy at least, many of these fed into policy change. A White Paper outlining the new Nationality Act was published within months of entering office and the Act itself was on the statute book by 1981. The government implemented most of its 1979 manifesto promises on immigration and several additional policies to shut tight the door of immigration. The 1981 Nationality Act was the culmination of several years of policy planning and its chief aim was to introduce a far higher degree of coherence into Britain citizenship laws. Its main feature was the creation of three categories of citizenship: first, British citizens were those with close personal links with the UK; second, citizens of British Dependent Territories were those who held or acquired citizenship in an existing dependency; and third, a residual group of British overseas citizens were those who did not fall into the former two categories. The object of the last category was to avoid the possibility of a future nationality crisis similar to the successive waves of East African Asians who had entered the country in the 1960s and 1970s. By taking away the right of abode from other British passport-holders spread around the world, the government was making it clear that Britain would not be a potential receiving country; the incentives for such groups to treat their newly defined residual category of citizenship for what it was worth – and elect to become citizens of the countries in which they actually lived – was all too clear.

The domestic political impact of the Act was to drive a horse and coach through bipartisan attempts to manage immigration policy. The Labour Party opposed the Act doggedly through its passage through the Commons and in its 1983 manifesto formally promised to repeal it. However, it should be remembered that Labour had earlier promised to scrap the 1971 Immigration Act but had failed to do so throughout its 1974–79 term of office. Cynics retorted that the chances of repealing the 1981 Act were therefore slim, not least because of the long period of its operation during the Thatcher years. The more likely course would therefore be revision of aspects of the Act under a Labour government.

There had been considerable doubts expressed by sections of the left about the race strategy of Mrs Thatcher's first administration, with many issuing warnings about the resurrection of the repatriation option. In the main, these doubts largely failed to materialise. Writing in the mid-1980s, one set of writers (Miles and Phizacklea, 1984: 106–114) emphasised the inability of the Conservatives to restrict immigration policy reforms to the legislation and rules governing potential new entrants. The influence of the far right within the party, they argued, would ensure that the continuing problems of a multiracial society would be met with a search for a permanent solution to the 'problem'. These predictions in reality turned out to be rather hollow, not least because they mistook the discussion of the far right on the issue to be reflections of official party policy.

More importantly, the impact of the 1981 Nationality Act was to remove much of the heat out of attacks on official policy from the party's right wing. Questions to do with its fairness and principle aside, the legislation represented the largely intact implementation of a manifesto commitment. By tackling the matter head on, the Conservative Government effectively removed the basis of popular resentment of the 'conspiracy of silence' among elite policy-makers. The views of the radical right, therefore, could not be launched from a widespread belief that the matter had been neglected. Moreover, the actual scale of immigration declined sharply in the early 1980s and has remained low ever since. Studlar (1985: 4–5) has noted that the 1981 Act ended the long dominance of the immigration side of the race question in British politics. Governments had found it easy to reduce the flow of immigration incrementally as the only or main policy response to race-related issues, and this approach had preoccupied policy-making for twenty years between the early 1960s and early 1980s. 'However much some far right philosophers . . . and politicians . . . might want to revive the repatriation option, immigration has taken a back seat to race relations', writes Studlar (1985: 4).

Academic opinion remains fairly divided about whether developments centred around the 1981 Act actually ended the immigration issue altogether. Psephological evidence presented by Crewe (1983b) from the 1983 General Election has shown that 'immigration . . . dropped off the bottom of the political agenda'; just 1 per cent of all respondents reported that it was one of the two most important issues facing the country. Of course, whilst this evidence remains credible, we should not overlook the possibility that it only refers to the numbers question of mass non-white immigration that clouded political discourse during the 1960s and 1970s. For the issue to drop off the agenda in 1983 is not incompatible with greater or exclusive attention shifting in the 1980s to questions about domestic race relations and social stability (Studlar, 1985: 12–13).

In any case, there are a number of other factors which might lie behind the apparent demise of the immigration issue. One view, as outlined above, is that this merely reflected the efficacy of the 1981 Nationality Act in stopping fresh immigration. Alternatively, it is likely that the issues of concern to second and third generation descendants of non-white immigrants, such as social mobility and tackling indirect discrimination, have played an increasingly prominent role since the 1980s. The decline of the immigration issue has therefore been more relative than absolute (Banton, 1987). Another interpretation, frequently cited by sympathetic politicians and commentators, was that the agenda in fact gave way to more pressing matters such as the urban disorders of 1981 and 1985 (Benyon and Solomos, 1987).

Inner cities and racial disadvantage

During the early 1980s the Conservative Government was suddenly confronted by the outbreak of street rioting in several British cities. Fuller consideration of these events will be reserved for a later chapter, but it is important to note here that the riots had a dramatic impact on Conservative thinking towards the idea of multiracial Britain.

The outbreak of rioting linked to race issues was far from a new feature of the British political landscape. Since 1945 there had been several examples of 'race riots' beyond the 1958 disturbances; demonstrations organised against National Front marches in 1973 (Red Lion Square) and 1979 (Southall) had left a civilian fatally injured on each occasion. The distinctive feature of the riots of summer 1981, however, was the apparent surprise and shock of politicians of all shades of opinion. In April 1981 Brixton exploded into anti-police rioting and in July fierce battles broke out in Toxteth in Liverpool. The response of the Government was essentially two-fold. First, it warranted the maximum support to the police to bring about a short-term end to the rioting. The disorders were characterised in strict law-and-order terms, the breakdown of which would not be tolerated: 'what we are talking about is sheer criminality', protested one Conservative backbencher (quoted in Benyon, 1984: 4).

The other response was to launch what would turn out to be a far-reaching inquiry into the social and other dimensions of rioting and racial disadvantage. This latter approach was initiated by the Government's appointment of Lord Scarman, a widely respected senior Law Lord, to oversee an investigation into the riots and their causes. It was through this initial move that a wider debate was begun about the role and efficacy of public policy measures in tackling racial discrimination and disadvantage. Concerted, though organisationally limited, attempts were subsequently made to assess how central government could play a more active part in policy programmes affecting or involving the black population. Of course, the substance of this redirection of government strategy was regularly underestimated, usually because of its more limited scope compared with developments in a number of Labour local authorities. Changes that nonetheless transpired from the altered climate of policy-making included several revisions of the Section 11 programme, the launch of a major new phase in urban policy relating to economic regeneration, and the expansion of the pre-existing Urban Programme.

The changing face of black political activism

The 1980s saw a number of major developments in the parties' attempts to recruit and maintain the support of black voters. The Conservatives had first started the ball rolling in the mid-1970s with the establishment of a Community Affairs Department comprising a small bureaucracy geared to oversee various local and national initiatives. Whilst the branches of Anglo-Asian and Anglo-West Indian Conservative Societies had a mixed record of achievement, the real significance lay in the breakthrough they represented in attitudes towards mobilising black support. The notion that black votes were part of an immovable Labour urban heartland was questioned by the findings of a Community Relations Commission report (Anwar and Kohler, 1975). With the close result of the 1974 general elections close to mind, the Conservatives began an ambitious programme of trying to win over black voters. The weak link in this chain, as the next chapter notes, was that there was only limited evidence to sustain the putative belief that large numbers of black voters were floating voters. Both Societies were highly active in the 1979 and 1983 election campaigns. Together with Central Office, they were instrumental in clustering the party's handful of black parliamentary candidacies in several Labour-held Birmingham seats.

More importantly, a number of Asian and Afro-Caribbean activists took pride in the political socialisation vehicles provided by the Societies. Both putatively fostered a warmer climate of mutual respect between the party and its black members. This view of the Societies was endorsed by successive party chairmen, most notably by Norman Tebbitt between 1985–87. The strength of such bodies, the argument ran, was that they operated in conjunction with the internal ethos of the party precisely because they rejected all notions of autonomous black organisation within the party. But it was the black autonomy question which also contributed to these Societies in the mid-1980s.

In 1986, following protracted factionalism within the Anglo-Asian Conservative Society between supporters and opponents of Sikh separatist claims, the party chairman intervened to disband the body altogether. The crunch point for the party's central bureaucracy had come when it became apparent that recent recruits to the Society were motivated by issues pertaining to the politics of the Indian subcontinent. The guiding philosophy of the Society had been to promote cross-cultural contact in order to accelerate black participation in the party; it had deliberately couched such contact in terms of a learning process for minorities' activists subscribing to party values and policies. However, the experience of the Anglo-Asian body suggested that potential recruits remained unclear about the basic function it served. A short while later the party chairman launched a new body to succeed the disbanded Societies. Known as the One Nation Forum, the new body was to be presided over more closely by Central Office and it aimed to bring black members more directly into the activities of the mainstream party.

The 1980s also witnessed key developments in the relationship between the Labour Party and segments of its black activists. As the next chapter outlines, this relationship was characterised by a long-established record of strong and stable levels of voting for Labour. By the mid-1970s, however, the terms of black electoral loyalty began to be scrutinised by younger, more radical cohorts of black activists within the party. In 1975 the Labour Party Race Action Group (LPRAG) was set up to act as a lobby for black issues and interests in party affairs. It was not long before LPRAG began to reorient its agenda away from a broad discussion of racism and towards party policy aimed at tackling racial inequality.

Following the 1979 election defeat, attention turned to Labour's record in government and its election strategy, and in October of that year LPRAG issued a circular to all local parties entitled *Don't Take Black Votes for Granted* (LPRAG, 1979). Its line of argument was straightforward in accusing the party of sidelining black political interests and thus aiding a climate whereby black voters were exploited because they were assumed to have no electoral alternative to Labour. Meanwhile, the party's central body, the National Executive Committee, was also busy in formulating its own revised approach to the issue. In early 1980 it published an advice note entitled *Labour and the Black Electorate* which went some considerable way towards conceding that the previous Labour administration 'failed to deliver' on a variety of policy fronts relevant to ethnic minorities such as immigration and equal employment opportunities (Labour Party, 1980).

It was against this background of accepted self-criticism that activists within the party began to campaign to have the discussion of race placed further up the party's policy-making agenda. Their demands were essentially threefold (Roberts, 1984). First, to give greater exposure to the specific interests of black people in policy-making, thus developing the notion of race or ethnic issues in British politics (see Chapter 6 below for an extended discussion of this point). Second, to press for measures to improve black participation in the party in general and in the party's policy-making structures in particular. Third, to lobby for enhanced levels of representation by black politicians at both local and national levels. In practice, however, the second and third of these demands were frequently confused by activists and the press who attached disproportionate attention to the lurking 'problem' of the absence of black MPs at Westminister.

During the early 1980s many of these demands were channelled into the Black Sections Movement. Messina (1989: 166) reports that between 1984 and 1987, the annual party conference received more than a dozen resolutions calling for black sections to be formally incorporated into the party's constitution. All were heavily defeated by conference votes, largely because of the emphatic opposition of the NEC to the proposal. Three counter-arguments have been used by the party establishment against black sections: first, it was claimed that such sections would merely siphon off black participation within the party as a whole; second, they would merely divide the working class along lines of race; and third, they would inevitably generate a new culture of racial explicitness which the party was keen to avoid being associated with. The arguments were in the end often reduced to a single issue, namely the widespread belief that black sections would create a *de facto* apartheid-style system of segregation between black and white activists. The contradiction this presented to familar ideals of equality meant that prominent Labour politicians such as Hattersley saw no role for them in the party:

> 'We cannot insist that all men and women be treated the same . . . if then we choose to treat the races differently within the Labour Party itself. Treating them differently would involve . . . breaches of absolute principle.'
>
> (Labour Party, 1985: 37).

Throughout the mid-1980s Black Sections activists returned to conference year after year only to have their plans decisively rejected on each occasion. Meanwhile, a number of unofficial Black Section groups remained active at the local level, often closely associated with attempts to select rising black politicians as parliamentary candidates. In 1988 the national Black Section published a detailed paper, 'A Black Agenda', which set out the campaign's stance on a wide variety of policy issues; this document made clear the broad left-wing stance the organisation took on many issues whilst concomitantly maintaining a distinctly radical approach to tackling racism. With the conflict over formal Black Sections no nearer to a solution, after the 1987 election the National Executive Committee (NEC) began trawling for a compromise. Under the stewardship of Jo Richardson MP, a committee was appointed by the NEC to seek what support it could for the idea of a Black and Asian Socialist Society with the status of an affiliated socialist society. The model for this proposal was Poale Zion, the Jewish Social Democratic Labour Party that is also affiliated to the party (Levin, 1978). The plan met with some success but failed to undermine support for the Labour Party Black Section itself.

It is unclear what the future course of events will be on this most contentious of race-related issues within the party. Messina (1989: 169) suggests that the misgivings of Labour's leadership about the electoral impact of Black Sections should not be underestimated. No early acceptance of any proposal to establish autonomous black organisations within the party is therefore likely. However, the pressure to seek new and more effective ways of incorporating black participation into the party will be hard for the NEC to ignore and a future compromise solution must remain on the cards. In the meantime, it is interesting to note that, with one notable exception, the support given to the movement by the 1987 crop of black Labour MPs has all but disappeared. The politics of backbench loyalty and internal party discipline have had a major – and unanticipated – impact on the debate over black autonomy within the Labour Party.

Overview and conclusion

In this chapter we have seen that intra-party disputes over race and immigration have often been at least as important as the better-documented disputes between the major parties. It has therefore been impossible to characterise either of the major parties' approaches and policies to race in simple or stable terms. In fact, both Labour and the Conservatives have been bedevilled by periodic internal quarrels on the issue and front-bench policies have often been held together by the flimsiest of agreements between internal factions. The 1964–70 Labour governments, for instance, were only able to push ahead with plans to introduce race relations laws on the condition that immigration control was tightened. This agreement was reached as much with the party's own right-wing MPs, conscious of their vulnerability to white working-class resentment, as with the Conservative Opposition which had shown itself willing to remove the issue from party competition. Another illustration of compromises struck within the parties can be seen in the case of Mrs Thatcher's initial leadership of the Conservative Party. Between 1976–83 the party adopted a decisively restrictionist line on immigration whilst concomitantly spearheading moves to bring black activists into Conservative ranks.

The chapter has also argued that too much weight is commonly attached to the characterisations of race and party politics of writers such as Katznelson (1973) and Messina (1989). Both have described distinctive pre-consensus (1958–65) and consensus (1965–75) eras in the political history of race and party competition. Whilst these perspectives are useful starting points for an appreciation of the changing climate of political debate about race, they can be criticised on the grounds that they remain inflexible. Enormous change has occurred in the development of race issues in British politics since 1945, but it is vital to recall the extent to which there was considerable overlap from one era to the next. A bipartisan consensus clearly did exist on the issue from the mid-1960s to the mid-1970s, but beyond that, the analytical lines of distinction remain rather blurred.

Finally, the chapter has drawn attention to the context and impact of the Conservative Party's short-lived attempt to use the issue of non-white immigration to its own electoral advantage. The politics of race during the Thatcher years has been the subject of intense disagreement among academic writers, many of whom have argued that this period represented an unparalleled attack on the rights of black people in Britain. The argument advanced in this chapter has emphasised somewhat different evidence, noting in particular the ascendancy of the liberally inclined One Nation brand of Conservatism.

The period following Mrs Thatcher's accession to the leadership has been described as the 'repoliticisation of race' by one commentator (Messina, 1989), suggesting that the strategy not only succeeded but also persisted into the 1980s. This chapter, however, has contended that the rationale that underpinned this strategy was no longer in existence by the 1983 Conservative election victory. The 1981 Nationality Act effectively closed the immigration door and thus killed the salience of the issue; moreover, as Studlar (1985) has argued, following the urban unrest of 1981 and 1985, the race relations side of the race question took precedence over immigration. The Conservatives' abrupt and risky lurch to the right on immigration during the late-1970s was accompanied by a more pragmatic and less hostile approach to black people legitimately settled in Britain. The origins of this progressive streak lay in the mid-1970s when the party took action to court upwardly mobile Asian and Afro-Caribbean voters. The growing sense of pragmatism was an important influence within the party after its first term of office between 1979–83. Government thinking on race and immigration after 1983 was also subject to a second term devoted to consolidating, rather than extending, the policies of the reform-minded first term. Whilst the cries of doctrinaire supporters of a white British nation could still be heard throughout sections of the party during the Thatcher years, for the most part the triumph of the One Nations Tories in shaping Conservative attitudes towards race was complete.

6

Black Political Participation

Introduction

Most black voters support the Labour Party and have done so with such regularity and strength that their votes have sometimes been thought of as safe and subsequently possible to neglect. Based on this perception, Conservative strategists have argued that a valuable opportunity exists for their party to attract the support of at least those disillusioned with Labour's mixed record of helping black people to overcome the problems they face. To that end, recent years have witnessed a mushrooming of initiatives to try to lure black voters to the Right.

One of the most celebrated examples was seen during the 1983 General Election when the Conservative Party launched a major advertising campaign featuring the profiles of two smartly dressed and socially mobile Asian and Afro-Caribbean young men. The slogan attached to these powerful images was 'Labour Says He's Black. Tories Say He's British'. The posters soon became one of the most controversial aspects of an otherwise unremarkable and one-sided election campaign. Labour politicians suggested that they represented an attempt by the incumbent Conservative Government to bring the so-called race card into the electoral battle. However, given the overwhelming lead enjoyed by the Conservatives throughout the campaign and the obvious certainty of re-election, it seems doubtful that the motivation was purely to mop up wavering white, anti-black voters. Others have contended that the aim of the posters was to target party symp minority black electorate. The detailed messag certainly couched as if directed towards black v potential rewards in terms of extra votes can ha justified the effort.

How can the Conservatives' strategy be exp this question we must first place the episode into the wider context of the development of black political participation in Britain. Throughout the thirty or more years of mass black settlement in Britain, the question of the political participation of black people themselves has tended to be overlooked by academic researchers who have instead focused more readily upon the consequences of the non-white immigration issue on the British party system (Deakin, 1965; Foot, 1965; Studlar, 1978; Layton-Henry, 1978). It is only since the mid-1970s that interesting questions have been developed and researched about black people's role in British politics.

Indeed, following the two elections of 1974, there was a significant rise in academic and press interest in black voting behaviour. This apparent discovery of race within the world of psephology was largely initiated by the publication of an empirical study by the Community Relations Commission which implied that black voters had played a pivotal part in helping to elect a majority Labour Government in the October 1974 general election (Anwar and Kohler, 1975). So was born the notion – and a largely mythologised one at that – of an 'ethnic marginal' in British electoral competition. A number of subsequent studies of black voting behaviour have been obsessed with this rather narrowly-conceived question. The underlying dynamics of black voting have become overshadowed by the rush to make claims and counter-claims for 'ethnic marginals' in determining election outcomes.

This chapter is concerned with the reasons why British politicians have from time to time paid a disproportionate amount of attention to the so-called 'ethnic vote' in spite of the very small potential rewards for doing so. The other major theme of the chapter is to go behind much of the psephological data and explain the reasons why black participation is so strong in terms of registration and turnout and yet so weak in terms of influencing public policy. For the purposes of these questions, the chapter *intentionally* concentrates on formal electoral politics in which West-

…ter (as well as town and county halls) are the focus of participation. In doing so, it leaves out (though defers to a later chapter) consideration of pressure group politics based on influencing Whitehall civil servants, local government officers and others.

The chapter begins with a discussion of the term 'the ethnic vote'; this section considers problems associated with defining and measuring it as well as debates over interpreting empirical evidence (usually derived from sample survey methods). The chapter then briefly examines the data on black voting behaviour in recent elections and the attitudes that lie behind such behaviour. The third section is devoted to sketching a profile of the influence of various social factors such as age and class on black voting patterns. Finally, the chapter turns to assess the ability of black participants to influence politics and policies given the features of the established British political system. Drawing upon some of the work of Crewe (1983a), the merits of several different routes to political influence potentially open to black citizens are looked at.

Ethnic votes and voting: definition and interpretation

Before we can proceed to examine the voting patterns of black Britons, it is necessary to devote some attention to questions concerning definition and conceptualisation of the so-called ethnic vote. Most writing on this subject has tended to confuse substantial support for one party among black voters with the belief that such skewed support is uniformly caused by a single set of factors. The reasons why this confusion exists are not hard to see and largely reflect the tendency among researchers firstly to collapse Asian and Afro-Caribbean cohorts of voters together – the previous sentence being a prime example of this custom! – and secondly to assume that 'ethnic' or 'race' issues monopolise the political concerns of non-white voters.

Moreover, the importance of ethnicity in shaping voting behaviour is often muddled by writers in this field. Importance may be attached to a variable in the sense that it yields a strong influence upon change in another variable, typically associated with a high regression coefficient. However, it may also be a variable that applies to a small proportion of the electorate and therefore is unable to have an important impact on the election as a whole. In this sense, it clearly is not an important variable. As Heath *et al.* (1991: 99) correctly observe, the force of ethnicity has such a two-edged effect: 'black and Asian respondents are much more likely to vote Labour than are white respondents, but only a small proportion of the electorate is black'.

If we begin to scratch away at the causes and components that lie behind the voting behaviour of ethnic minorities, we can see that it can be one of four phenomena (or combinations thereof). First, ethnic minorities may vote according to a completely separate and discrete set of criteria made up of issues and concerns not shared in any way by the white electorate. So it may be possible to conceive of cases of black voters who feel not only that racial divisions are widespread and fundamental in British society but also that their political view of the world is based *exclusively* on these divisions.

It must be said, however, that empirical research suggests that few black voters have articulated such a position; the nearest illustrations of such political language are probably found among some sections of the Pan-Africanist and Islamic separatist movements active in contemporary British society. If it is hard to accept the view that ethnic minority voters are subject to an exclusive black agenda – and therefore not subject to any other agenda whatsoever – it may be easier to think of this agenda as comprising aspects of minority ethnic experience and traditions. That is, the exclusiveness of the agenda does not of itself mean that it is a racially based agenda, but rather that it is shared either by members of the same racial group or members of minority groups at large. Moreover, the relationship of the agenda to racial criteria may be tangential at most, in that it reflects areas of socialisations and cultural background which are peculiar to these minority communities. For example, it can be argued that the cultural heritage and distinctiveness of a given South Asian community may provide its members with a unique outlook and perspective on the world which entails an *ethnically related way of thinking and acting politically*. However, it may not, and several commentators have suggested that the ethnicity of black voters only serves as an additional influence on their political actions – over and above that of a wide variety of non-ethnic factors (Rath and Saggar, 1990).

Second, the political outlook of ethnic minorities may be based on the same range of issues and policy concerns as those of white voters but slightly reordered in terms of priorities. Thus, it may be that white voters feel more strongly about defence than housing for instance, whilst for black voters it is the other way around. But even here, it is not entirely clear *why* their priorities differ whilst the range of issues that makes up the agenda of both groups is the same. One explanation may be that as black voters are more likely to be Labour supporters, they are more likely to attach priority to certain issues over others. Thus, their different priorities may in fact be less a reflection of any fundamental difference of outlook and more to do with support for a party's ideology. For example, a higher priority attached to housing issues may be part of a wider picture in which housing is of greater importance to Labour supporters and sympathisers, among whom black voters are over-represented.

Third, the ethnic minority electorate may have precisely the same agenda of issues as the white electorate but concomitantly perceive all issues to be ethnically related in one form or another. So, black and white voters may attach equal weight to defence, housing, schools, pensions and so on, but the former group is distinguished from the latter by its belief that race factors do – as opposed to ought to – play a part in deciding what happens in each of these areas. The common thread, of course, might be a sense of overt discrimination against black people in all these areas of public policy. On a day-to-day basis this position is perhaps more likely to take the form of a more generalised sense of resentment towards society based upon white domination of public life. Many politicians and commentators have dubbed this line of thinking as the 'race dimension' which underpins *all* areas of politics and society.

Fourth, black and white political agendas may match fully and do so because the former is merely a microcosm of the latter. In other words, this position holds that there is nothing really distinct about black voters' outlook on politics and that the truth of the much-quoted 'black political agenda' is that it is the same as the white agenda, writ small. It must be said that one of the most significant pieces of evidence used to justify this particular argument has been actual voting behaviour. Whilst such behaviour is heavily skewed towards support for the Labour Party – around seven in ten black voters in 1987 – it is explained as the consequence of a skewed class structure among black communities.

The tendency among black people to be employed in manual occupations far outstrips that of white workers and results in a significant black working-class community and level of support for the principal working-class party. Therefore, the argument runs, as the black class structure evolves to mirror more closely that of Britain in general, so too will the political outlook and actions of black people also begin to match that of their white counterparts. Writers interested in putting forward this view have been less concerned with front-end evidence of voting itself and more interested in the attitudes and beliefs underlying voting, claiming that the voting behaviour of black people is at present merely undergoing a period of transition based on the distorting affects of the initial job opportunities of black immigrants.

However, it is claimed by some writers that these opportunities can be expected to improve and enable a degree of upward mobility over time; eventually black voting behaviour will all but match that of the existing, more evenly spread behaviour of white voters. In the meantime there is nothing much to be explained in the figures for black voting – except perhaps to measure the pace of black occupational mobility and accompanying drift towards voting for parties other than the party of the traditional black working class. Robinson's (1990a) recent analysis of black social mobility suggests that whilst the pace of change has been fairly dramatic for certain minority ethnic groups, it has been minimal across ethnic minorities at large searching for social and economic parity with the white population.

It is not at all surprising therefore to find this view of the ethnic vote promoted vigorously within the Conservative Party, most notably among younger activists associated with the liberal left and interested in the prospects of economic change leading to political change. Of course, for Conservatives at large the question is more likely to be thought of as 'the votes of ethnic minorities' rather than the 'ethnic vote', thereby negating the view that ethnic minority voters act as one and for reasons to do with their common ethnicity.

According to empirical investigations of black political attitudes the evidence appears to point to a remarkable degree of similarity between black and white outlooks, with a few notable – but also easily explicable – differences of emphasis. Table 6.1 describes the two chief issues specifically cited by different ethnic groups at the

1987 General Election. The most interesting aspect of these data is undoubtedly the low salience of issues to do with race for Asian and Afro-Caribbean voters (in what was, after all, an open-ended survey question). Further, it is noteworthy that unemployment, health, education and defence are among the four most salient issues for all three ethnic groups, save for the housing issue which is ranked third by Afro-Caribbeans (far higher than among the other two groups). In general, it would seem that the black and white voting agendas were remarkably similar in character and that variations were largely a matter of degree. It should be noted that these data do not preclude Asians and Afro-Caribbeans from also perceiving there to be a race dimension to all the issues cited since the survey's recording of responses about 'race' cannot necessarily be equated with sentiment about such a dimension. FitzGerald's (1987) survey of political attitudes revealed similar findings, confirming once again that, broadly speaking, race-specific issues do *not* play an important role in the political priorities of black voters.

Table 6.1 The most important issues for voting in the 1987 General Election, by ethnic group (per cent mentioning).[1]

Issues	*White*	*Afro-Caribbean*	*Asian*
Unemployment	45	70	65
Health	32	25	34
Education	19	13	17
Defence	37	18	32
Law and order	6	4	11
Pensions	9	7	6
Housing	5	21	0
Prices	7	15	10
Race	1	0	1

Note: [1] Respondents were asked to list their *two* most important issues.
Source: BBC/Gallup (1987).

There are several further problems that need to be addressed before moving on to consider the evidence of black voting behaviour. These problems have crept into a great deal of writing on this subject and have been the focus of a protracted debate over the existence and behaviour of so-called ethnic marginals, that is, seats in which it is claimed that the votes of black electors can or have made the difference between the election of one candidate against another. The 'ethnic marginals' debate will be returned to later in this chapter but in the meantime we shall concern ourselves with the conceptual and methodological aspects of researching black voting behaviour and its impact upon candidates in marginal seats.

First, we should be aware of the limitations of claims about the electoral behaviour of a discrete ethnic group. This wariness is the inevitable outcome of a lack of clear and precise information about the ethnic minority electorate. As we saw in Chapter 3, until the most recent 1991 Census a direct ethnic origin question was not to be found in the census data and therefore calculations are based on rather inadequate data relating to New Commonwealth birthplace. Researchers cannot always be certain that black voters in a particular constituency have been responsible for a particularly significant swing in the overall vote. One way in which researchers have tried to overcome this limitation has been to try to match up self-evidently Asian surnames on the electoral register with visual checks at polling stations for evidence of Asians who have, or were about to, cast their votes (see, for example, Le Lohé, 1975). Of course, there are problems with taking such an approach, not least its seeming inability to address the measurement of Afro-Caribbeans on the electoral register who generally do not have obviously distinctive surnames.

Second, researchers have to be careful to draw a distinction between the size of black *population* and the size of the black *electorate* in a given area. The latter will always be a sub-group of the former and will be shaped by the age structure, levels of electoral registration, propensity to turn out on voting day, and the political geography of the constituency in question. What remains to be researched is the proportion of the former made up by the latter across constituencies as a whole. Moreover, estimates about the size of the ethnic minority population are just that, *estimates*. Account has to be taken of all the misleading permutations that can arise from using NCW birthplace of household heads as a proxy measure for ethnicity.

Third, a great deal of the research has broadly opted to collapse Asian and Afro-Caribbean voters together, a practice which, claims Crewe, may be mistaken. 'In religion, language, origins and culture they have little in common and political collaboration between the two groups is limited' (1983a: 260). It is not entirely clear, however, whether by drawing a distinction we are likely to discover very much that is different in the voting patterns of these two groups and it may be that the largest variance is to be found between different sub-groups of Asian and Afro-Caribbean electors. In 1987, for example, the difference between Asian and Afro-Caribbean support for the Labour Party approached twenty percentage points (67 versus 86 per cent), but we simply do not have sufficiently detailed data to assess how far distinctions of religion or even caste affected the propensity to vote Labour (Harris Research Centre, 1987 and 1991). Further empirical research in this area will certainly be eagerly awaited by those commentators who have argued that the cultural dimensions of Asian ethnicity have become submerged within the umbrella of black anti-racist politics (see for example Modood, 1988).

Finally, extreme caution should be attached to interpreting the claims of ethnic minority candidates and activists who try to draw a link between their own ethnic origin and that of the electorate they face. There have undoubtedly been cases where such a link did exist and could be demonstrated but, for the most part, these claims are widely exaggerated. Indeed, there may be more to be said for candidates who take a particular position of direct concern to their ethnic minority voters as a factor that serves to influence votes (for example the response of several Labour MPs such as Max Madden and Keith Vaz over the Rushdie affair). However, even here the real difficulty lies in not being able to match up reliably ethnic-related claims about the voting patterns of ethnic minorities with the votes themselves, thereby leaving the issue open to acts of considerable self-rationalisation. Interestingly, the evidence concerning ethnic minorities' perceptions about having an ethnic minority MP representing their interests is far from conclusive: in 1987 47 per cent of Asians and 35 per cent of Afro-Caribbeans thought it would make no difference whatsoever! (Harris Research Centre, 1987).

Black voting behaviour

In order to understand the recent voting behaviour of black Britons it is necessary to know something of their behaviour at earlier general elections. In order to do so, we shall refer to a number of studies of black voting patterns during the (October) 1974, 1979 and 1983 polls.

The October 1974 General Election

In a report prepared for the Community Relations Commission, Anwar and Kohler (1975) argued that black voters played a pivotal part in the outcome of the autumn election in 1974. The thrust of their argument was that black voters swung more decisively to the Labour Party between the February and October polls than the electorate as a whole; this swing, they suggested, was due in part to the minority Labour Government's actions and policies designed to woo the black electorate.

But beneath this argument lay another motive, namely to draw attention, however ill-founded, to the growing importance of the black electorate. Far from being isolated in safe Labour seats, the authors of the CRC report claimed that many black voters were to be found in a number of Labour and Conservative marginals. Furthermore, these voters should not be thought of as a 'bloc vote' inseparable from the Labour Party, but rather as a key section of the so-called 'floating vote'. As such, black floaters, like white floaters, could be expected to respond positively to policies targeted at them. The study probably received the enormous attention that it did from party strategists, journalists and academics for a combination of two reasons. First, the then most recent Census figures (from 1971) revealed a marked growth in the size of the black population, implying a concomitant – though not necessarily proportionate – rise in the number of black voters. Second, the striking closeness of the two 1974 general election results had nudged many politicians to take more notice of, and show greater sensitivity towards, the votes of small groups of voters. Indeed, in spring 1976 Conservative Central Office established its own unit to monitor the party's performance and potential in attracting the votes of ethnic minorities.

The CRC report sought to give an indication of the scale of importance of the black vote by making comparisons between the size of the non-white population in a particular constituency and the electoral majority of the constituency's sitting MP. In those seats where the former exceeded the latter, they asserted, black voters were in a position to exert electoral influence. They identified no less than 76 such seats at the February 1974 General Election, a figure which had risen to 85 seats by the time of the October poll. The authors concluded that around 1 in every 8 seats could be dubbed as 'ethnic marginals'; this estimate, as we shall see, grossly exaggerated the case. The report then focused on the 59 seats in which their conditions for ethnic marginality were met in both of the 1974 elections. Labour had made a net gain of 17 seats from the Conservatives from the first 1974 general election to the second, no less than 13 of which had been on Anwar and Kohler's list of 'ethnic marginals'. It was on this point that the authors based their claim about the pivotal role played by black voters in determining the outcome of the October election, an election in which a minority Labour administration had managed to secure office with fewer total votes than the defeated Conservative administration.

Table 6.2 Voting patterns of the black electorate in the 1974 and 1979 general elections

Party	*1974[1] (%)*	*1979 (%)*
Labour	81	86
Conservative	9	8
Liberal	10	5
Other	0	1

Note: [1] October 1974 general election.
Source: Anwar and Kohler (1975); Anwar (1980).

Both Crewe (1979 and 1983a) and Layton-Henry (1983) have been at pains to point out that the CRC study overstated the significance of the black electorate on four grounds. First, the study was simply misleading in using the proportion of a constituency's population born in the NCW as the black electorate base. For instance, this figure took no account of the proportion of the NCW-born population under 18 years of age and therefore unable to vote, and nor did it take account of black voters who were not born in the NCW. Second, it ignored the possibility that the black population over 18 years of age might have been under-registered to vote (compared with the registration rate of the white population). Third, it also side-stepped the equally important question of differential turnout of registered black voters relative to that of registered white voters. Finally – and no doubt most damaging to the study – little evidence was put forward to substantiate the claim that black voters formed part of the floating vote. In fact, as Table 6.2 makes clear, quite the reverse was true: the black electorate was overwhelmingly predisposed to supporting the Labour Party, with less than 1 in 5 black voters deviating from this pattern.

The May 1979 General Election

In 1979 the Commission for Racial Equality sponsored another study into the part played by ethnic minorities in the general election of that year. The report, authored by Anwar (1980), persisted with the broad line of argument of the earlier CRC study, claiming that where parties other than the Labour Party made a bid for the (hitherto loyal Labour) black vote, they had met with some success. More specifically, in no less than 5 out of the 7 constituencies which featured in both studies, Anwar reported that there had been a modest swing among Asian voters towards the Conservative Party. The notion of a differential swing between Asian and Afro-Caribbean voters was thus introduced into the debate for the first time, with considerable interest shown in the prospect of a significant desertion from Labour to the Conservatives among middle-class Asians in particular.

The extent to which these findings were indicative of a wider trend among black voters remained open to some debate, however. On one hand, the inference of a slight pro-Conservative swing among Asian voters was based on the small handful of seats for which Anwar had collected comparative data from 1974 and 1979. To generalise about the wider picture on this base was always going to be hazardous. On the other hand, given that the survey was limited to various inner city constituencies (where the task of surveying black voters was simply more practical), those black voters who had migrated out into suburban areas were grossly under-represented. Anwar and other commentators might have speculated that middle-class, suburban black voters – and Asians in particular – were in theory more likely to support the Conservative Party than their working-class urban counterparts. However, even the proposition that they were less firmly attached to their Labour moorings remained undemonstrated and speculative.

Notwithstanding the criticisms levelled by Crewe, the 'ethnic marginals' thesis was restated in modified form by Anwar. As in the ill-considered CRC study, the CRE analysis overlooked questions of differential black–white age distributions, registration rates and turnout rates. In 1979 Anwar listed some 41 seats that conformed to the crude 'ethnic marginal' test, though in this case the consequences of black electoral patterns in these seats were not of the same order as its impact in 1974 (when a slender victory for one party was laid at the feet of floating black voters). By 1979 the decisive majority won by the Conservatives meant that the outcome of the general election itself was not subject to 'ethnic marginals' changing hands because of the black vote. What could be argued – though not demonstrated by Anwar's data – was that black voters in the 'ethnic marginals' may have played a part in assisting the Labour Party in holding onto many of its vulnerable seats and therefore limiting the size of the Conservatives' parliamentary majority.

The CRE study's survey data helped to shed new light on the electoral registration and turnout rates of black people. Compared with 1974, the registration rate of Afro-Caribbeans had shot up from 63 to 81 per cent, whilst among Asians there had been little change from 73 to 77 per cent (the white registration rate meanwhile remained much higher at 93–94 per cent). When it came to turnout rates among registered Asians voters, these persistently outstripped those of registered white and Afro-Caribbean voters. Given that inner-city turnout rates usually fell considerably short of those found elsewhere, the unusually high turnout rate of Asians – often exceeding 90 per cent of registered voters – seemed to be a clear indication of Asians' willingness to participate in British electoral politics. The implication once again, suggested Anwar, was that black voters had helped Labour to cling on to some of its marginal seats in the face of a considerable national swing to the Conservatives.

The June 1983 General Election

The voting behaviour of black people in the 1983 election was the subject of a larger number of studies including, *inter alia*, Studlar (1983), Saggar (1984), Anwar (1984) and Layton-Henry and Studlar (1985). Two main data sets were collected on black voting behaviour in this general election: the first was a pre-election survey carried out by the Harris Research Centre (1983) for London Weekend Television, and the other was an exit poll conducted on behalf of the CRE based on a large sample of 2,050 black voters in 25 constituencies (Anwar, 1984: 35). In addition, a pooled pre-election survey carried out by Gallup for the BBC contained data on non-white voting intentions, though the number of cases involved was rather small compared with the Harris or CRE surveys. The Harris data in particular provided researchers with greater insight into many of the points of debate between Anwar and his critics in studies of previous elections.

Unsurprisingly, both the Harris and CRE data sets confirmed heavy support for the Labour Party. Excluding non-responses and 'don't knows', Table 6.3 tells the story. 'Deviant' non-Labour voting accounted in every case for less than 1 in 5 black voters and, in some cases, for barely 1 in 10 voters. As in 1974 and 1979, there could be little doubt that in 1983 the votes of black Britons were conspicuously *not* part of the floating vote.

Table 6.3 Voting patterns of the black electorate in the 1983 General Election, by ethnic background

	Asian		*Afro-Caribbean*	
Party	*Harris*[1] (%)	*CRE*[2] (%)	*Harris*[1] (%)	*CRE*[2] (%)
Labour	82	80	88	86
Conservative	9	6	6	8
SDP/Liberal Alliance	9	12	5	5
Other party	1	1	1	2

Note: [1] pre-election survey of voting intentions.
[2] election-day exit poll of voting.
Source: Harris Research Centre (1983); Anwar (1984) 11.

Previous studies had suggested that the registration rate among eligible black people was lower than that among their white counterparts (Anwar and Kohler, 1975; Anwar, 1980). However, both 1983 data sets confirmed that registration rates had improved greatly: 94 and 82 per cent for Asian and Afro-Caribbeans respectively according to Harris, while the CRE survey indicated rates of 79 and 76 per cent respectively. Perhaps more striking than the registration rates of black people was the evidence concerning turnout. As Table 6.4 makes clear, the gulf between Asians' and Afro-Caribbeans' propensity to vote was noticeable and the subject of growing interest from commentators and party strategists alike.

Table 6.4 Likelihood of voting among the black electorate in 1983, by ethnic background

Voting intention	*Asian (%)*	*Afro-Caribbean (%)*
Absolutely certain/ certain to/probably will vote	94	72
Probably/certainly will not vote/ don't know/unsure	6	28

Source: Harris Research Centre (1983).

Closer inspection of the Harris data reveals that absolute certainty about voting among Afro-Caribbeans between 18–24 years of age was as low as 1 in 4; moreover, even among those who normally identified with the Labour Party, clear commitment to turn out stood at a paltry 44 per cent. The comparable rates for Asians were 1 in 2 and 62 per cent respectively. These figures suggest that certain groups of Afro-Caribbeans clearly held deep reservations about ballot-box-style political participation; such reservations were not so widely shared by their Asian counterparts. Of course, part of this difference should be seen in terms of Asians' generally much greater willingness to vote: indeed, the CRE's detailed examination of 20 selected constituencies in 1983 showed that Asian turnout outstripped that of white registered electors in no less than 18 seats (Anwar, 1984: 8).

The June 1987 General Election

The level of Afro-Caribbean defection from the Labour Party remained remarkably small during the 1983 General Election (from 88 per cent in 1983 to 86 per cent in 1987). The breakthrough of sorts that did occur was the substantial drop in Labour's share of the Asian vote (down from 82 per cent in 1983 to 67 per cent in

1987). Non-Labour voting among the black electorate as a whole now reached 28 per cent, up considerably since 1983 despite the high loyalty of Afro-Caribbeans to Labour. The much heralded mushrooming of Asian support for the Conservatives was partially reflected in the only large-scale survey of black voting intentions carried out in 1987. This survey was conducted by the Harris Research Centre for Hansib Publications, an Asian-owned publisher. As Table 6.5 illustrates, barely two-thirds of Asians said that they intended to vote for Labour whilst almost a quarter signalled their intention to back the incumbent Conservative Government.

Table 6.5 Voting intentions among the black electorate in 1987, by ethnic background

Party	*Asian voters*	*Afro-Caribbean voters*	*All black voters*
Conservative	23	6	18
Labour	67	86	72
Alliance	10	7	10

Source: Harris Research Centre (1987).

Behind this data about the overall level of support for the major parties there exists more revealing evidence concerning the contrasts between Asian and Afro-Caribbean voters. For example, the Harris survey reported that 74 per cent of the former group stated that they were 'absolutely certain' to vote on polling day as compared with just 51 per cent of the latter group.

Another interesting contrast, between black voters in areas of 'high' and 'low' ethnic concentrations, was revealed in the Harris data. The intention to vote for the Conservatives rose from 15 per cent in areas containing significant numbers of black people to 39 per cent in areas of low concentrations. Conversely, Labour support fell off dramatically from 77 to 43 per cent respectively. Two possible explanations can be put forward for this phenomenon. First, it may be that black voting intentions are in some way affected by the *level* of ethnic minority settlement, with the effect largely working to the benefit of the Labour Party as the racial character of the area in question becomes less exclusively white and more plural. Accordingly, we may postulate that significant levels of black settlement have a reinforcing influence upon black voters who are already predisposed to voting Labour and that the influence is one that helps to counter the forces of defection. The second explanation focuses on the *effects* of economic geography. This view simply links 'high' ethnic concentrations with areas of relative economic deprivation such as the inner cities. Thus, relatively high levels of black settlement are associated with areas of strong Labour support in general; in such areas the forces of deprivation play a greater role in shaping black voting intentions than factors to do with the racial plurality of the area in question.

A profile of black electoral behaviour

The one thing that is abundantly clear from all of the major surveys of black voting behaviour is that the Labour Party has been the major beneficiary of the black vote. The evidence from 1987 might suggest a growth in support for the Conservatives to almost 1 in 5 of all black votes, but it is far from clear whether this rise has been the result of defections from Labour or the consequence of much higher levels of non-Labour voting among either new young voters entering the electorate for the first time and/or black voters previously unregistered or who failed to turn out. Moreover, the influence of social class upon black voting patterns appears to be remarkably limited and even the younger cohorts of upwardly mobile black voters seem cautious about backing the Conservatives in noticeably larger numbers than their older and less socially mobile counterparts. To shed light on the nature of black voting patterns we must turn to survey evidence on generational, social class and religious variance as well as evidence concerning the political perceptions and attitudes of black people.

Generation

Among the electorate as a whole, psephologists have commonly found that generational factors play a part in shaping the vote, usually to the benefit of the Conservatives from younger cohorts of voters to older ones (see, for example, Denver, 1989: 33–34). Table

6.6 describes the impact of the generational pull towards the Labour Party in the 1983 and 1987 General Elections. It is quite apparent that generational factors play a small part in shaping black voting patterns, but where they do, it is to the slight benefit of Labour comparing younger to older voters. Indeed, in 1983 more than 9 in 10 of all middle-aged and older black voters backed Labour compared with around 8 in 10 of young black voters. The influence that age has upon black voting behaviour is therefore more or less minimal.

Table 6.6 Percentage of black electorate intending to vote Labour in 1983 and 1987, by age cohort

General election	*Age cohort*			
1983	18–24	25–34	35–44	45 plus
	83	80	85	91
1987	18–24	25–44	45–64	65 plus
	73	68	78	86

Source: Harris Research Centre (1983 and 1987).

Two factors seem likely to be at play here. To begin with, these data seem to suggest that as black voters get older, they are *marginally* more likely to support Labour, thereby largely reversing the pattern of generation pull towards the Conservatives seen throughout the electorate as a whole. This explanation is usually called the 'life-cycle' effect by which younger voters' political perceptions and behaviour are markedly different from those of older voters. In the case of black voters, the effect is largely absent in that little can be put between levels of Labour support among the 18–24 group versus the 45–64 or 65+ groups.

In addition, there may be a specific generational or 'period' effect which has had a disproportionate impact on certain age cohorts. According to Denver (1989: 33–34), 'it is not so much a person's age that is important as when he or she was young and beginning to experience politics'. For example, it is easy to see how the experience of migration from South Asia, Africa and the Caribbean would have uniquely affected black voters presently over the age of 45 years who would have been young settlers in Britain in the 1950s and 1960s. This experience cannot by definition have been shared by younger black voters. The present 25–34 age group, for example, would have reached maturity during the late 1970s to mid-1980s at about the time when successive inner-city riots dominated the agenda of domestic politics; they are likely, therefore, to have been disproportionately influenced by these events. Again, whilst this effect may have taken place across the black electorate, there is very little evidence to suggest that it made enough difference to alter *substantially* voting patterns or loyalties.

Social class

A substantial volume of research has built up which shows that voting patterns are shaped by – or at least associated with – social class membership (see Denver, 1989: 30–32 for an overview of this research). Since the 1970s a certain degree of class dealignment has been widely documented in several studies of British electoral behaviour (see for example Crewe *et al.* 1977 and Sarlvik and Crewe, 1983). However, the premise that class forms the basis of party politics still remains a powerful and far-reaching assumption in British psephology which, in the 1950–70 era at least, reported a steady correlation between class and voting. The middle-class vote belonged to the Conservatives and that of the working class to Labour. What then of the influence of class upon the votes of black people?

Data from the pooled Gallup pre-election survey in 1979 are given in Table 6.7. These data make a direct comparison between class breakdowns of the white, Asian and Afro-Caribbean vote. In all three cases, Labour voting was stronger among lower-ranked social class categories. However, in the case of Asian and Afro-Caribbean voters two clear deviations from this basic pattern are apparent: first, the overall *level* of Labour support among black voters was considerably higher than among white voters; and second, the rise in Labour support among black voters belonging to lower social class categories was of a smaller *magnitude* than among white voters. Under ten percentage points separated black support for Labour among the highest and lowest social classes; in contrast, white support for Labour almost doubled across the span of social class.

Table 6.7 Voting intentions among ethnic groups in 1979, by social class

Party	*White*			*Asian*			*Afro-Caribbean*		
	A/B/ C1	*C2*	*D/E*	*A/B/ C1*	*C2*	*D/E*	*A/B/ C1*	*C2*	*D/E*
Labour	20	35	38	42	50	50	41	49	48
Conservative	57	40	32	25	28	25	17	11	15
Liberal	9	5	5	6	3	0	5	8	3
Non-voter	15	20	25	28	19	25	35	32	35

Source: BBC/Gallup (1979).

Data collected by the 1987 British Election Study (Heath *et al.*, 1991: 112) also shows that ethnicity has a large effect on voting within the working class: 76 per cent voted for Labour against 46 per cent of white respondents within the same social class. The authors note, however, that the explanation for this disparity remains unclear. Data from previous general elections suggest that the reasons proffered by black voters themselves tended to be couched in non-ethnic terms. In 1983, for example, 64 per cent of Asian and 76 per cent of Afro-Caribbean Labour voters justified their choice by citing that 'they [Labour] support the working class' (Saggar, 1984: 41). The level of class-consistent voting among the black working class far outstrips that of their white counterparts. Heath *et al.* (1991: 112–13) contend that the individual social characteristics of black voters *cannot* fully explain this difference. Statistical measures of the force of ethnicity on voting reveal that it is a highly significant relationship, even after controlling for the effect of factors such as social origin, housing tenure, trade union membership and income. They conclude:

> The political behaviour of blacks is not to be explained by their class situation, however broadly defined. They are much more inclined to the Labour Party than white voters in similar class situations, housing, local milieux, and so on. Individual economic and social factors do not seem to be the answer. Perceptions of group interests or processes of group identification are more plausible explanations.
> (Heath *et al.*, 1991: 113)

Religion

In the main, survey research has not sought to analyse the effect of religion on black voting behaviour. This omission is a little surprising given that, in the long era of class–party alignment between 1950–70 at least, religion consistently ranked among the top five variables influencing British voters at large (Denver, 1989: 39). Its force may not have been of the same order as that commonly observed in continental European political systems, but it was nonetheless a fairly important background variable in British electoral patterns. More recently, the influence of religion is said to have waned considerably and this has often been linked to a gradual decline in religious affiliation and regular acts of formal worship (Heath *et al.*, 1991: 203–4). The omission is more puzzling in the light of the growth of new minority faiths in British society following large-scale immigration, particularly from South Asia and East Africa. Brierley (1988) reports that in 1985 Hindus, Sikhs, Muslims and Jews made up 2.8 per cent of the population; with membership of religious groups much lower among the white population as a whole, followers of these four faiths constituted almost 17 per cent of all those who belonged to one faith or another.

The data that do exist in this area confirm that certainly Hindus, Sikhs and Muslims all share a high propensity to support Labour (Heath *et al.*, 1991: 86). Few significant variations in this general pattern can be detected between these three religious groups though a recent Harris poll for BBC Television did uncover some limited evidence of stronger pro-Conservative support among Muslims and Hindus compared with Sikhs (Harris Research Centre, 1991). At this stage, the paucity of reliable data on religion and voting among black voters must mean that new data should be interpreted with caution. That said, the reasons why Hindus, Sikhs, Muslims, Christians and others within the black electorate in general favour Labour still remain unclear. On the face of it, a superficial interpretation might seek to argue that membership of these religious categories itself influences voting behaviour. This, however, would be a rash conclusion since religion may merely be an associated – though not causal – link between race and voting. In other words, strong Labour support can be explained in terms of reasons to do with the forces of ethnicity and group socialisation, of which religion is one factor among many.

Black voters and the Labour Party

FitzGerald (1988) has argued that the high levels of Labour

support among black electors in the 1987 General Election were the product of the lack of an alternative party. Black voting behaviour in that year had ensured that 'the myth of "the black vote" had been laid' (FitzGerald, 1988: 22). Two thing were clear: first, the numbers of marginal seats in which supposedly floating black voters could make a difference were very few in number; and second, even where black voters were sufficient in number, it was hard to see evidence of them turning their backs on the Labour Party. Change has occurred in black voting patterns over the past four or five general elections, but it has been very modest in comparison with the steady and predictable strength of support for Labour. The much heralded rise in support for the Conservatives – particularly among middle-class Asians – has largely failed to materialise on the scale predicted by certain commentators.

Between 1974–83 support for the Labour Party among black voters regularly exceeded 80 per cent, with Afro-Caribbean electors slightly more likely to back Labour than their Asian counterparts. Virtually no trend could be detected over this period which indicated that the black electorate were deserting Labour. An interesting, though modest, dip in Labour support was, however, detected at the 1987 General Election: 72 per cent supported Labour, 18 per cent supported the Conservatives, whilst 10 per cent supported the Liberal/SDP Alliance. Reading these data more closely reveals a fairly sharp variation between Asians and Afro-Caribbeans, with one in three of the former opting to support parties other than Labour compared with around one in eight of the latter. To those who held an interest in an early collapse of Labour's following among black voters, these figures were seen as something of a breakthrough. Whether or not this dip is extended into a trend at the next general election remains to be seen, though a recent Harris poll of voting intentions does *not* confirm any loosening of Labour's support among Asians (Harris Research Centre, 1991).

The evidence shows that there is very little that is new in the overwhelming lead enjoyed by the Labour Party among black voters, but, at the same time, key changes in the political outlook of certain groups of black voters are beginning to show signs of loosening their traditional Labour moorings. To arrive at any tentative predictions about the future course of black electoral support for Labour, it is necessary to examine the figures behind the headline opinion polls. For instance, it is interesting to note the reasons advanced by black voters for their own voting behaviour. Class membership and the sense of Labour as the party best suited to their class membership has frequently topped the list of responses. This type of reason suggests certain forms of positive bonding between working-class black voters, their social class and the party said to speak for that class. If, however, the class-related image of the Labour Party were downgraded or altered in some way, it is likely that this would have a negative impact on its black support. Equally, changes in the class composition of the black electorate, whereby the working class contracts in size, are also likely to reduce Labour's share of the black vote. Processes not dissimilar to these are already said to affect the modern Labour Party and the working class, and it would be surprising if sooner or later they failed to impact upon black voting behaviour.

Other non-class-related factors commonly cited to explain Labour voting usually fall into two categories. The first of these may be described as ethnic-related reasons and encompass a range of sentiments about Labour being best suited to represent the interests of black people. In 1983 for instance, a large minority of Asians (31 per cent) said that they intended to vote for Labour on the grounds that 'they [Labour] support blacks and Asians'; among Afro-Caribbeans there was much less enthusiasm for this perspective (7 per cent).

The second category appears to be less overtly oriented to race or ethnicity but may indirectly encompass these reasons. Psephologists would describe Labour voting based on an aversion to supporting the Conservative Party as a form of negative partisanship; in other words, it is not so much that these voters are keen on supporting one party, but more that they do not want to support its main rival. Again, in 1983 some 8 per cent of Asian and 9 per cent of Afro-Caribbean Labour voters cited that 'they did not want to support the Conservatives' as the principal reason for their party choice. This sentiment may be interpreted as an indirect cover for some degree of racial consciousness about the Conservatives' aims and policies. Indeed, we may speculate that these black Labour voters were in fact expressing their doubts and worries about the hard Right of the Conservative Party. The legacy of Powell, it would seem, still lives on and prevents some black electors from making as wide a party choice as they might wish.

Academic opinion therefore appears to be rather divided about the future course of the Labour Party's relationship with the black electorate. Certainly, with around three-quarters of all black voters continuing to support Labour at the polls, there seems little prospect of any early major breakthrough by the Conservatives or others eager to attract black support. Moreover, as the broad thrust of the past four general elections seem to confirm, claims about the black vote being a floating vote have been firmly put to rest. The incentives of building an electoral strategy around the black floating vote premise have become less clear cut. The Conservatives and others have slowly realised that the task of snatching so-called ethnic marginals from Labour has been more difficult than first thought.

On the other hand, data has been published showing newly identified pockets of non-Labour support. A 1984 survey for the Greater London Council highlighted a clear contrast between East African Asians and those from the Indian subcontinent, the former being noticeably more likely to support the Conservative Party (FitzGerald, 1987). Further, the 1987 Harris survey measured black voting intentions by the level of the ethnic concentration of the respondent's neighbourhood: this interesting form of enumeration showed that in areas of 'high' ethnic concentration the non-Labour share of the vote was just 23 per cent, whereas in 'low' concentration areas this figure rose to an astonishing 56 per cent (Harris Research Centre, 1987). The so-called neighbourhood effect is clearly at work shaping black people's political perceptions, reinforcng pro-Labour attitudes through close and regular association with others from the same ethnic community.

Finally, at least one safe conclusion can be drawn about the recent history of black electoral support for Labour. Namely, whilst black voters have not made a decisive breakthrough in terms of election outcomes (as implied by the 'ethnic marginals' thesis), it is fair to say that they have played their part in preventing Labour suffering a greater rout than it did in the 1979, 1983 and 1987 General Elections. The resilience of black loyalties to Labour in the barren years since 1979 has been particularly significant given the widespread electoral haemorrhaging suffered by the party over this period. The result has been that Labour managed to hold onto some previously safe seats in 1983 and 1987 which it might have expected to surrender to the pro-Conservative swings of those years. Therefore, with the assistance of loyal black supporters, the task of fighting its way back into office has been made a little easier for Labour than it might otherwise have been.

The routes to representation

The ability of black people to influence politics is usually seen in terms of the evidence of black political participation itself. A conspicuous omission from most analyses is the question of the features of the established British political system. That is to say, the British electoral and party systems serve to promote certain forms of black participation over others. Over the past twenty years black support for mainstream electoral politics has tended to outstrip even the most optimistic assessment of the efficacy of this route to representation. The dividends of this broad strategy have, by most standards, been exceptionally modest. One of the chief reasons for this state of affairs has been the highly limited points of access and potential spoils available to discrete minorities. Against this must be set some form of explanation for the persistence of black mainstream participation. An important factor has been the seductive logic of the 'ethnic marginals' thesis which has tended to portray potential dividends out of all proportion to their true scale. Behind such evaluative analyses of the various forms of black participation lies a long-running debate concerning the relationship between race, class and ethnicity in shaping black political activism. Each of these themes are explored in this section.

Seeking representation in the British system

Any assessment of different strategies for black political influence must be prefaced by consideration of the nature of the political system in which black people are located. According to one psephological commentator, 'it is hard to imagine a political system more ill-equipped to represent the specific concerns of small and unpopular ethnic minorities' (Crewe, 1983a: 260).

Crewe's (1983a) sober message is based on the implications of six key features of British party competition, the electoral system, and the electoral impact of the issues of race and immigration. First, the present electoral system benefits larger parties over smaller ones. Thus, prospects for any separate party holding the support of black voters, but without white supporters, would be very bleak. This anti-third/fourth/fifth party discriminatory effect is already widely experienced by the Liberal Democrats. The result of this constraint has been that remarkably few attempts have been made to launch distinctive ethnic political parties. A recent exception however was the establishment in 1989 of the Islamic Party of Great Britain under the leadership of Daud Musa Pidcock. The paltry showing of the Party at its one and only parliamentary outing at the Bradford North by-election in October 1990 was entirely consistent with the level of support enjoyed by previous ethnic party candidates (Crewe, 1983a: 266–67). Consequently, most initiatives in this field have been restricted to national umbrella pressure-group-type ethnic bodies such as the Confederation of Indian Organisations which only issue advice as to how their membership should vote. Ethnic parties prepared to field candidates are conspicuous by their absence, perhaps largely because of the strong likelihood of failure.

Second, the system itself offers a restricted number of electoral spoils in the way of seats and appointments. Britain boasts only a tiny number of elected public offices – just 650 at national level which only come up for election every four or five years. This problem is compounded by the lack of vacancies for safe seats; few serving MPs fail to be reselected in any of the major parties (inspite of the mandatory reselection required of Labour members). At any one general election, vacancies created through retirement of sitting MPs and deselection are likely to be few and far between; in 1987, 87 such seats were vacated. With the absence of more elected offices, a bicameral legislature and rolling elections in the British political system, all of the pressure for black representation must be directed at this small number of seats contested between long intervals.

The example of the four black candidates who were successfully elected in 1987 is instructive here. Two of the four had served apprenticeships as Labour candidates in a previous general election and their chances of selection in safe Labour seats were enhanced by this experience. Moreover, it is significant that the 1987 election also witnessed a further 25 'also-ran' unsuccessful black candidates. The lesson for black representation must be that even by joining mainstream political parties – and thus rejecting separatist strategies such as ethnic parties – black politicians cannot count on shortening the route to elected office. Indeed, the long struggle endured by John Taylor, the Conservative Party's only realistic hope for a first black MP, in the race for selection in the safe seat of Cheltenham, seems to be illustrative of the wider picture. His experience might imply that, for many other would-be black candidates, the costs of chasing after so few spoils are thought to be prohibitive. Added to this is the claim that black parliamentary candidates are discriminated against by white voters, though academic opinion appears to be divided on this point (compare, for example, the assessment of FitzGerald, 1983, with that of Le Lohé, 1989, and Bald, 1989).

Third, minority interests tend to slip between the cracks of two-party competition. A number of writers have operationalised the theory of party strategy based on rationality originally advanced by Downs (1957). Pressure exists for the two major parties to broaden their appeal as far as possible and not to make overt the interests of any single social group, especially if there is reliable evidence to suggest that the group is an unpopular one among the electorate as a whole. Minority groups, then, have no alternative except to allow their interests to be aggregated into the broad platform of one party or the other. The historical experience of black support for Labour closely approximates this dilemma for black voters (FitzGerald, 1988). Ironically, the black electorate's weakness lies in the fact that not only has it been a safe constituency of loyal Labour support, but it has also been seen as such by Labour opponents. The Conservatives' attempts to woo black voters after 1976 appeared to be a political initiative that occurred in spite, rather than because of, the evidence of black voting behaviour. Labour, therefore, can easily afford to pay lip service to the interests of black voters, safe as it is in the knowledge that there are no real alternative parties which these voters are prepared to back. In fact, it is unlikely that the black electorate will enjoy any real political influence until the distribution of black party support is more evenly balanced than it is at present (Messina, 1989: 157).

Fourth, parties have to be extremely responsive to the marginal voter because, in the British system, government can change hands between parties following the shift of only a small number of votes. Far from pushing parties to compete more actively for the floating black voter, as implied by many commentators, the parties in fact have a better chance of winning office by chasing after the much larger and more volatile reservoir of white floating voters. In fact, as we have seen, the vast bulk of black voters have *never* been floating voters to the same extent as white voters. If anything, by moving to respond to popular opinion on issues such as immigration, the parties cannot avoid endorsing policy positions that are opposed by black voters. Fortunately for black voters there have been few occasions when any of the major parties sought to attract popular, anti-immigrant opinion (the exceptions being the Conservative Party between 1968–70 without the deliberate support of the leadership and 1978–79 with such support). With the strong inducement of exploiting such an issue in the search for as many wavering voters as possible, the wonder then must surely be that immigration has not been a major general election issue more often.

Fifth, there are simply more votes to be won by a party pursuing the support of racist, anti-black voters than by courting black voters. The only difficulty for both major parties to date has been coping with the internal conflicts that would arise from such a racist strategy. Black activists in all the major parties consequently have to operate against a background in which they must rely upon the (white-dominated) leadership not to play the anti-black card. Inevitably, this factor creates internal tensions between liberal and illiberal factions, and a variety of compromises and codes of management have been devised within the parties to handle this problem on a day-to-day basis. In the Labour Party the recent rows over black sections have been illustrative of the obvious contradictions that underlie a major party's strength of support from a minority group whose rights remain deeply unpopular among the electorate as a whole (Husbands, 1983). It is for this reason perhaps, that sceptics have doubted the credibility of the Labour Party's commitment to repeal the controversial, though popularly backed, 1981 Nationality Act.

Finally, the blunt truth is that if a major political party were to decide to play the so-called race card and become overtly hostile to the rights of black people in Britain, it would probably be rewarded by white voters resentful of the creation of a multiracial society. The Powell affair more than twenty years ago demonstrated the potential spoils of such a strategy, though in the period since it would be hard to argue that any major party has in fact pursued a sustained anti-black campaign. The fact that the card has not been played overtly can be partly attributed to the bipartisan race consensus that allowed politicians to bury the issue for the best part of a decade. The closest any party came to such a strategy was undoubtedly seen in the inflammatory language used by Mrs Thatcher in 1978 to denounce the 'swamping' of Britain by black immigrants. Certainly, for Labour, the historical association the party has had with the black electorate has not enhanced its general 'electability', and for this reason the fear of being tainted as the party of black interests has been very real for party leaders in the 1980s. In London in particular, it has been suggested that the activities of the party's urban Left on race equality issues have cost it considerable electoral support (Saggar, 1987b; Le Lohé, 1989; Lansley *et al.*, 1989; Nanton and FitzGerald, 1990).

In the light of this assessment, Crewe (1983a) not surprisingly concludes that, for the foreseeable future at least, the political rights and social opportunities enjoyed by black Britons be will be contingent on the support of liberal opinion among white politicians:

> The stark truth is that the ethnic minorities must very largely rely on the commitment and goodwill of whites to dissolve prejudice, eliminate discrimination, guarantee legal and civil rights and abolish poverty.
>
> (Crewe, 1983a: 280)

Doubtless such a bleak outlook may not be the message that many black voters and activists would want to hear. That said, its content should nonetheless inform discussion about future strategies for political representation.

The 'ethnic marginals' controversy revisited

In an article published in *New Society* just before the 1979 General Election, Crewe (1979) sought to explode the myth of the so-called ethnic marginals. In this article and another published in 1983, he argued that previous commentators – undoubtedly the authors of the 1975 CRC study – had rather over-egged the pudding by claiming that: (a) such marginals existed in larger numbers than was probably the case; (b) the Conservatives' second 1974 defeat was the consequence of the loss of such seats to Labour; and (c) the whole notion of 'ethnic marginals' had become muddled. Taking the last of the criticisms first, a more rigorous test was put forward to identify an ethnic marginal seat, requiring it to satisfy three critieria: it had to be very marginal, have a substantial proportion of black electors, and display a high differential swing between black and white voters.

The debate has also been joined by researchers who have sought to quantify the true scale of 'ethnic marginals'. According to Layton-Henry (1983: 16), Crewe's criteria produced just 14 cases in 1983, and any hoped-for gains for Labour failed to materialise. Rather, it may well have been the case that, by remaining largely loyal to Labour, black voters in some of these seats in fact prevented Labour defeats. Studlar (1983: 93) noted that while the Conservatives performed well in the Labour 'ethnic marginals', there is no evidence to link these results with any shifts in black voting. In fact, he notes, most post-election reports showed that black voters, along with council tenants, remained among the most loyal groups to Labour in an election which saw sustained defections from virtually all other social categories of Labour supporters (Lipsey, 1983). The difficulty for Labour lay not so much in holding on to black support but rather in translating it into sufficiently high turnout rates. According to the Harris 1983 pre-election survey, Afro-Caribbean Labour supporters showed a marked reluctance to turn out on polling day and this factor, more than any other, may have played a part in Labour's defence of some of its marginal inner-city seats (Harris Research Centre, 1983).

Black parliamentary candidates

An important watershed in British political history was passed at the June 1987 General Election. For the first time since the 1920s, when Shapurji Saklatvala, a Communist, represented the voters of Battersea North, a black MP was successfully elected to Westminster. In fact, four such MPs entered the House of Commons: Diana Abbott (Hackney South and Stoke Newington), Paul Boateng (Brent South), Bernie Grant (Tottenham), and Keith Vaz (Leicester East). It is significant that all but the last of these MPs were returned for inner-city seats in London. Behind these headline developments, however, were the much larger number of black parliamentary candidates who failed to be elected.

Indeed, contemporary interest in the question of black representatives was revived by the case of Dr David Pitt, who in the 1970 General Election became the best known victim of white racist electoral power. In the elections since, the wastage rate of black 'also-rans' has been, by any standards, extremely high indeed. In addition, recent debates by black representatives have tended to be conducted against the backdrop of microcosm politics; that is, a renewed interest in the social composition of Parliament to reflect the social make-up of contemporary society. The 300 Group, committed to boosting the female composition of the House of Commons, has been an example of one of the better organised pressure groups engaged in this form of new politics. Applying the same principle to the case of black people, at just under 5 per cent of the population the expectation has been to see something of the order of 32 black MPs.

Black parliamentary candidacies have included numerous cases of black activists standing on behalf of various 'fringe' parties ranging from several Trotskyist groups to a number of Independents. Between 1964–79, Crewe (1983a: 266) counted no less than 18 such cases, with no less than three clustered at a particularly sensitive by-election in Birmingham Ladywood in 1977. For the purposes of our discussion, the analysis will be limited to major party candidates.

Two central themes have preoccupied researchers in this area: the performance of black candidates and the implications for the future selection of black candidates in winnable seats. The 1983 contest was something of a breakthrough in terms of the scale of black candidacies: a significantly greater number of black candidates were fielded by the major parties than ever before (18 compared to a previous high of 5). Since 1970 some 29 black candidates had been fielded by the major parties. In 1987 the total rose again to 29. The parties of the Liberal/SDP Alliance led the way in 1983 with 8 candidates, followed by 6 for Labour and 4 for the Conservatives.

However, all of them, bar one, stood virtually no chance of being elected. Even the sole candidate with reason to be hopeful – Paul Boateng in Hertfordshire West – suffered a massive swing against him, turning a (notional) majority of 700 into a deficit of almost 10,000 votes. One study of the performance of these candidates by FitzGerald (1983) argued that, taken as a whole, their seemingly poor performance could be attributed to a number of factors other than their colour. She noted that several in fact had bucked the regional trend in the respective party's support and had done better than anticipated.

The lessons from 1983 were far from pessimistic and showed that the biggest difficulty facing black parliamentary hopefuls was not the fear of suffering a racist swing against them but rather in getting selected for winnable seats. FitzGerald was undoubtedly right to signal that selection as opposed to election was the key hurdle and attention should accordingly shift to the selection conferences of the major parties (Bochel and Denver, 1983). However, the analysis was based on merely comparing black candidates' performance with the regional performance of their parties and revealed that four candidates had performed better than their white counterparts within the same region; a further four had performed marginally worse (less than 2 per cent of vote share down) and the remaining had performed much worse. However, by using this crude regional comparison the analysis made no attempt to try to compare black candidates' performance with those of white candidates of the same party in similar types of seats. For this reason its ability to measure the true extent of racially inspired swings was compromised.

A second analysis by Le Lohé (1983) reported that black candidates were indeed the electoral liabilities that political folklore assumed they were. In quantified terms, he concluded on average about 3 per cent of a party's share of the vote was eroded, though of course such an average figure concealed enormous variance. Taken literally this figure appeared to be most discouraging and gave the major parties little incentive to adopt *any* black candidates let alone more than they had in 1983. However, Le Lohé qualified this figure, taking note of the possibility that if the 3 per cent loss was evenly distributed between two or more rival parties, the actual negative swing would be much lower. Moreover, he argued that in the vast majority of seats the alleged liability of a black candidate was not, and was unlikely to be, an issue at all. It was only in marginal seats that the ethnic origin of candidates might lead to difficulties, though he conceded that it was in these seats that selectors might choose to exert greater caution.

Finally, comparison of the differential performance of black candidates in each of the three main parties reveals some interesting evidence. By comparing black candidates' performance with their respective party's national performance, we can take some account of the effect of party label. This control is important since the greatest influence on black candidates' performance – like all candidates – are the fortunes of their respective parties (Saggar, 1984). In 1983, black Labour candidates suffered an even worse fall in vote share than their heavily defeated party (–2.25 per cent in excess of Labour's heavily reduced share of the national vote). For black Conservatives a similar outcome was seen (–2.48 per cent) though this was chiefly due to their failure to match the unchanged strong performance of the party nationally. The worst outcome was perhaps unexpectedly experienced by black Alliance candidates (–6.6 per cent) though this was caused by their average rise in vote share falling below the mammoth leap in support won by the buoyant Alliance.

The conclusion of the last two pieces of research confirm the view that black candidates suffer some degree of handicap that is not explained by other likely factors. That said, the political circumstances in which negative racist voting might result in a major party losing or failing to capture a marginal seat without the possibility of some degree of compensatory black support are fairly remote. Political parties may therefore continue to exhibit considerable conservativism about adopting black candidates. With the exception of a limited number of very marginal seats, there is little reason for the party selectors to worry too much about the electoral consequences of adopting a black candidate. In marginal seats, however, the evidence suggests that continued caution will be exerted by selectors and on a rational basis.

Overview and conclusion

The relationship between black ethnic minorities and the electoral process is arguably the most widely documented area of research on race and politics in Britain. Even the most casual glance at the library shelves will reveal that from the mid-1960s onwards the business of voters, candidates and policies has preoccupied academic researchers. In particular, studies of the impact of race factors upon the voting patterns of minorities themselves has been extensively documented. In a sense, of course, this tendency to focus upon electoral behaviour and party competition reflects a more general preoccupation with these themes within political studies since the 1960s. The behavioural revolution, as this largely distinctive approach became known, remains a familiar tradition of the discipline and for that reason it would be rash to think that the academic study of race and party politics is in any way particularly unique or novel. It is not and, as the final chapter of this volume argues, our survey of race and politics in Britain is necessarily constrained by the behaviourial tradition (Saggar, 1990).

That said, the constraints of behavioural research have not dented by any means our by now quite considerable knowledge of black participation in formal politics. Important research has emerged to show *inter alia* that: the black electorate has remained largely loyal to the Labour Party over several elections; the social class, non-ethnic reasons for alignment with the Left have been uppermost in the minds of black voters; the black vote appears to be heavily shaped by the forces of race and ethnicity as it is poorly correlated with variance in social class and generation; the Conservatives and the centre parties have pursued vigorous, though largely unsuccessful, campaigns to attract black votes; black parliamentary candidates as a whole continue to represent electoral liabilities to the parties, though rarely in circumstances that are likely to make sufficient difference to the outcome of an election; and the claims made about the pivotal role played by black voters in marginal seats have usually been exaggerated.

We have seen in the course of this chapter that many of these studies have made great play of the notion that black voters made up a sizeable part of the population of floating voters. Such a conclusion was often drawn in spite of the findings revealed by empirical evidence. The persistence of black electoral loyalty has confounded various commentators who have prematurely declared the black vote as no longer safe for Labour to count upon. In fact, the evidence points to a rather different message, namely that there is no viable alternative to Labour for most black voters and, for that reason, the interests of black people can be easily neglected by the parties.

Labour policy-makers are able to shift black interests onto the back burner, safe in the knowledge that black votes will generally require less effort to attract than those voters who really matter, namely marginal voters. Conservative strategists, meanwhile, have little incentive in courting the interests of a group whose votes are extremely unlikely to shift *en masse* to the Right. The upshot of this is that black voters are strategically poorly located in British electoral politics; moreover, some of the features of party competition and the electoral process further minimise the chances for effective representation of black people. The work of Messina (1989) has been most interesting in this regard, arguing that competitive 'two-partyism' is likely to let black political interests slip between the cracks of the democratic process.

Studies of black voting behaviour have dwelt on the factors underlying the black electorate's skewed support for the Left. The influence of various social background variables in explaining black voting distribution has been minimal. But underscoring this discussion have been three principal interpretations of trends in black voting behaviour. The first view approximates closely to the familiar social class explanation of voting behaviour based on a *socio-economic model* of political change. It has contended that black support for Labour has been based on class since black people are disproportionately members of the working class and have hitherto voted for the party said to represent their class interests. As economic prosperity and social mobility are more widely enjoyed by the black population, the strength of black identification with the working class will diminish. The rise of middle-class social identity among sections of the Asian community has been commented upon as an early sign of the process of embourgeoisement that will lead to a more even distribution of the voting preferences of the black electorate.

The second view may be described as the *rational model* which attaches a premium to analysis based on the issue preferences of black voters. It emphasises the ability of black voters to draw their own conclusions about, say, the record of both parties on immigration policy. By observing that little has actually distinguished Labour and Conservative governments' policies, black voters will, the argument runs, choose to reward and punish the parties accordingly. Of course, on immigration the choice has been rather slim between two unappealing options, but it could be argued that Labour's wider distance between policy and practice has given cause for greater disillusionment among its black supporters. Certainly Conservatives have been at pains to remind black voters that the 1972 treatment of Ugandan Asians compared favourably with the rather tardier response given to Kenyan Asians under Labour in 1968. Issue-voting may work to the advantage of different parties over different issues but its real significance lies in burying forever the assumption that black voters are in the 'natural' constituency of any of the parties.

Finally, the third perspective, which can be described as the *cultural model* and is based on rather more speculative thought about sections of the black electorate. This approach relies on a particular reading of cultural values of the Asian community, arguing that it possesses an inherent conservatism over questions of family values, tradition, education and even social stability. The Conservative Party, the argument runs, has a long-term 'natural' advantage over Labour in attracting and holding on to Asian votes. The argument is bolstered by the case of the Jewish community that is often cited in this connection as an illustration of the steady rightward drift of a once impoverished immigrant group. Of course, it must be said that the empirical evidence to support this particular perspective is highly sketchy and impressionistic. The argument's lack of solid grounding in verifiable empirical data has nonetheless not inhibited its wide and regular exposure in the media where in recent years topics pertaining to 'Asian community values' have become extremely fashionable.

7

The Politics of Race, Nation and Culture

Introduction

The intervention of Enoch Powell in 1968 in the row over continued non-white immigration exposed dramatically the weak basis of the two-party consensus on race. The impact of his remarks also demonstrated the extent to which political conflict was underscored by racialised political ideology. Put another way, British politics is not merely about the actions and reactions of politicians. It is also about the ebb and flow of ideas, values and assumptions. With this in mind, this chapter turns to explore the ways in which ideas about race have a bearing on thinking about nationhood and national identity. This theme was initially brought to prominence by the fallout from the Powell controversy almost a generation ago, though concerned opinion had been voiced on the matter by the traditional Conservative Right since the dismantling of the British Empire.

At its heart, the race/nation theme is concerned with whether accepted notions of 'being British' are compatible with racial and ethnic pluralism. In the 1970s the questions posed by Powell were translated into the hardline confrontational politics of the far Right. In more recent times this theme has been returned to by a variety of commentators, not always, though mostly, linked to the Right of the Conservative Party. More particularly, the ascendancy of the New Right in Britain and other industrial democracies has provided a further boost to fundamental rethinking about the cultural fabric said to bind together modern societies.

In Chapter 5 we examined the development of the issue of race and immigration in party politics in the post-war period. The parties played a key role in the racialisation of many areas of British political life. Moreover, issues pertaining to race themselves led to divisions and conflicts within the parties. That earlier chapter did not, however, seek to explore the manner in which race issues and concerns were closely entwined in the broader development of political discourse in Britain. The role of racial ideologies was touched upon in Chapter 2 where it was noted that racial ideas had been a long-established feature of British social and political history. The colonial era in particular has been closely associated with the development of systematic theories of racial classification and ordering. By providing an account of the contemporary picture, we should take care not merely to offer an historical review that traces racialised ideologies from the Victorians to the present. It is vital to ensure that changing ideological constructions of race are appreciated. Where once ideological messages emphasised abstract concepts of racial ordering, in more recent times questions relating to common social consciousness and the 'British character' have taken greater prominence.

Contemporary British politics is home to an important debate about what constitutes 'Britishness'. In this chapter we shall survey the features of this debate and its impact upon public policy choices. We shall begin by tracing the origins of the debate within the political discourse of Powellism. The chapter will then look briefly at the explicitly racist politics of the far Right and chart the rise and fall of the National Front in recent British electoral history. The third part of the chapter will be devoted to an extended review of the arguments of the New Right, especially in relation to contemporary policy debates about state education.

The Powell legacy

In Chapter 4 we reviewed the political controversy caused by Powell's famous April 1968 speech. In it he had outlined a vision of the future of Britain following sustained non-white immigration. He then followed it with a series of speeches up and down the country which he used to set out the basis of his alternative policies. These policies, he argued, would avert the threat of racial strife spilling over into the streets of Britain. Instead, a policy of immediately halting all black immigration – including secondary immigration involving dependants – was proposed; following that, a phased policy of non-voluntary repatriation of black immigrants would be introduced. Powell's policy prescription, of course, was not implemented. But, in the course of the 1970s and 1980s, large aspects of the rationale that underlay his recommendations were implicitly endorsed by governments of both parties (Layton-Henry, 1984: 75–86). The real change marked by Powell's intervention, however, was the distinctly social and cultural terms in which he couched his argument. Black immigration had to be opposed, he contended, because of the fundamental threat it posed to the British way of life. It is this socio-cultural core that represents the most far-reaching and contestable of Powell's claims.

Powellism as an ideological force

Powell had posed two central questions to British political elites: first, whether as elites they had been sufficiently responsive to grass-roots opinion of the immigration issue (they had not, he claimed, and supported his claim by the extraordinary popular support he had received); and second, whether living and working in a country of itself made a discrete ethnic group think of themselves as 'belonging' to that country. Let us examine each of these questions in turn.

This first claim rested on Powell's belief that senior politicians of both major parties had effectively betrayed the electorate on the immigration issue. His remarks immediately tapped widespread frustration with the bipartisan race consensus (Schoen, 1977). From the late 1950s onwards it had been apparent that the influx of significant numbers of black immigrants was deeply resented by the white population (Studlar, 1978). Citing this observation, Powell argued that a virtual conspiracy had taken place whereby politicians refused even to discuss the scale of immigration let alone its long-term impact upon the British nation. His own fairly prominent role in official sponsorship of black immigration required to fill gaps in the 1950s' labour market was of course conveniently set aside, though Powell himself claimed that it had never been anticipated that the labour migrants would come in very large numbers nor stay permanently (Powell, 1969).

Ultimately, it was Powell's virulent criticism of his own parliamentary colleagues that so alienated him from the political establishment. By denouncing their collective actions as a betrayal of the representative sovereignty placed in Parliament by the electorate, Powell effectively called into question the whole basis of British parliamentary democracy. Or to put it more accurately, he chose to make political capital out of a distinction he drew between how the parliamentary system ought to work and how he claimed it had worked (Smithies and Fiddick, 1969). The irony of this criticism was that Powell had seen himself as a long-standing champion of the rights of Parliament over the executive and his argument therefore condemned the whole of Parliament as unresponsive to public opinion, a view he rarely took or felt required to take on virtually any other issue.

The logic of Powell's argument that the parties had betrayed the electorate did not stand up for long. In fact, as we have seen, since the mid-1960s both major parties had gradually shifted to adopt a restrictionist line on immigration (Dummet and Dummet, 1982). Elite politicians had shown themselves to be responsive to popular feeling, though their actions often fuelled the desire to curb immigration yet further. By creating a 'race-immigration problem', politicians had conceded that race relations could not be improved without the continual reduction of immigration. Therefore, it could be argued that elite responsiveness on the issue did not so much follow popular sentiment as actually precede and create it.

To that end, it could also be argued that Powell's intervention in 1968–70 merely constituted an explicit statement of hostility towards black immigrants based on a premise which had already found its way into the heart of official party policies. That black immigrants were generally unpopular and an electoral liability was not in dispute prior to Powell's interjection into the debate; the dispute that did arise following his remarks centred on whether such explicit anti-black sentiment could be tolerated at the heart of government. Powell therefore merely played on the latent hostility to black people that already existed, only adding his own touch to the grim warning repeated so often both before and since. In June 1969 he stated:

> The immigrants here are still in large numbers integral members of the communities from whence they came. Let another decade or so

> elapse, and this will no longer be so. The tragedy of a growing minority, *alien here* and yet homeless elsewhere, will have been fastened on them and us forever. (Quoted in Dummet and Dummet, 1982: 123) [author's emphasis]

The second claim went to the heart of Powell's critique of the development of a multiracial society. His concern was rooted in the belief that the nation and nationhood could only be defined meaningfully in cultural and ethnic terms. Powell viewed legalistic notions of nationality as ultimately baseless since, he contended, the nation required the common allegiance of its citizens, a form of allegiance and bonding it was argued that could only stem from a common ancestry and shared past. The presence of large numbers of black immigrants in Britain was therefore viewed as a threat to the stability and social cohesion of society. The British 'national character' had been diluted and fundamentally altered. It could no longer claim to be of the same mould that was once recognised by Powell and his supporters.

Powell's views on the undermining affect of racial pluralism upon the British nation were arguably the most enduring of all his arguments. Throughout the 1970s and 1980s both he and his supporters returned to this theme, using a style of language that mourned the passing of a golden age of 'Britishness'. For example, in late 1981, in the wake of rioting that had occurred across urban Britain, he wrote:

> The spectacle which I cannot help seeing . . . is that of a Britain which has lost, quite suddenly, in the space of less than a generation, all consciousness and conviction of being a nation: the web which binds it to its past has been torn asunder, and what has made the spectacle the more impressive has been the indifference, not to say levity, with which the change has been greeted.
>
> (*The Guardian*, 9 November 1981)

These ideas have had a considerable impact upon recent debates about the cultural basis of British nationality. As Seidel (1986: 129) observes, the neo-conservative New Right has shown great interest in what are sometimes described as 'alien cultures' within Britain. The result, she argues, has been the development of a more pernicious form of racism which has been coated in the acceptable language of cultural norms and expectations. Seidel claims that an example of this racism was the 'swamping' imagery contained in

Mrs Thatcher's controversial 1978 television interview. These remarks served to construct an ideological message whereby notions of 'British' and 'British character' became metaphors for cultural and ethnic homogeneity. Black immigrants who now 'swamped' Britain were therefore threats to familar ideas of the national character which, Mrs Thatcher reminded her audience, 'had done so much for the world' (Granada Television, 1978).

According to the terms of this argument, the long-term claims of black immigrants and their descendants to 'Britishness' would be subject to dispute (Smithies and Fiddick, 1969). The problem they posed was not merely limited to their obvious cultural differences from white British society. Rather, the cause for worry, according to Powell, was the long-term impact of their culture upon white society. Powell and others may have regretted the passing of a narrowly defined and partial recollection of British society prior to mass non-white immigration. But they also denied that there was the remotest chance for a successful multiracial society to be created in its place. The young offspring of black immigrants would not necessarily show any greater allegiance to the dominant cultural norms of white society, argued Powell. The fact that they had been born and raised in Britain made little difference, either to their own sense of cultural identity or to the view held of them by white Britons. They would remain alien to the cultural fabric of a society which was and would remain oriented to a past shared specifically and exclusively by white people. This critique contained an important message regarding the rearguard defence of white society in cultural, rather than overtly racial, terms. It was a message that was embraced by both Conservative populists and extreme Right activists alike.

'Kittens and kippers'

In an important article published in 1981 Behrens and Edmonds described the approach taken in the 1970s by Conservative populists on the issues of race and immigration. They noted that the question of immigration policy *per se* was less important to the Right of the party by the late 1970s. Instead attention had begun to shift to the question of the Conservatives' future policies towards race. Whilst many populists still hankered after repatriationist fantasies, for the most part the hardline campaigners on immigration had recognised that more immediate problems lay ahead. These problems were likely to be topped by the pressing demands of alienated and frustrated white people who felt threatened by the black presence in Britain. Conservative race populists at this time therefore found common ground with traditional neo-conservative thinkers who had begun to develop a critique of the multiracial society which Britain had become. Together, populists and neo-conservatives formed the basis of the New Right alliance of forces which rejected Britain's multiracial character. The black minority population they contended were rather similar to the hypothetical example of a kitten which, although placed and raised in a kipper box, indubitably continued to be, and be seen as, a kitten; a kipper it was not and nor could it ever be seen as such.

The analogy adopted makes great play of the immutable identity of a given species, though critics have retorted that the biological basis of the illustration has little resemblance to the case of the socially constructed identity of different ethnic groups. Whereas the hypothetical kitten has a naturally conceived identity and our understanding of what makes it a kitten is based on observation and classification, the same cannot be said of a member of a particular ethnic group. In the latter case it is essentially the features of the group's shared social character that form the basis of its ethnicity as well as our understanding of its distinctiveness. There is, therefore, little need to search for Aristotelian essences when describing or analysing the member of an ethnic group in the way that human understanding of a particular animal species requires. Instead, the requirement is merely one which acknowledges the distinctive characteristics of a social group along the familiar lines of comparisons of *inter alia* language, diet, heritage, kinship and social mores.

If it is accepted that these features are essentially fluid and subject to social and ideological construction – however rigid the characteristics of an ethnic group may appear – then it follows that the kitten/kipper analogy has no basis whatsoever. On the other hand, if a political ideology seeks to base its defining foundations upon the claim that social relations stem from some form of racial ordering, the argument can be sustained. In the end, the applicability of the analogy stands or falls on our understanding of ethnicity as a force shaping human relations. A deterministic view, based on an acceptance of the existence of discrete racial groups, would lead us to endorse its applicability. A view which emphasised the social construction of the dynamics of ethnicity would, by contrast, lead us to reject both the premise and conclusions of the analogy.

Needless to say, the premise and conclusions of the argument were embraced wholeheartedly by race populists active within and on the fringes of the Conservative Party. Moreover, the argument also found favour among sections of the intellectual, neo-conservative Right, many of whom made no great claims about fundamental differences between racial groups. Their 7interest stemmed more from a broader critique that was developed from the late-1960s onwards concerning the moral and social cohesion of mature liberal democracies. The role of race within this broader picture was aligned to aspects of the economy and moral order, all of which were said to be in decline in Britain. The New Right racialised critique of the changing national character and a variety of counter-arguments will be returned to later in the chapter.

The rise and fall of the extreme Right

One of the most pertinent features of racialised politics in Britain since the 1960s was the rise – and subsequent fall – of organised extreme Right political movements. These movements were spearheaded by the National Front and all shared a common purpose of both political and physical attacks upon the black immigrant population. By the early 1980s the National Front had emerged as a spent electoral force but many of its ideas and campaigns had been transmuted into mainstream party competition. Indeed, it has been suggested that competitive two-party systems are often *structurally* incapable of articulating the interests of single-issue protest groups. In the British context, one commentator (Messina, 1985 and 1989) has contended that the rise of the National Front during the 1970s can be attributed to the suffocating impact of the bipartisan race consensus which prevented an open expression of popular feeling about black immigration.

Neo-fascists, Empire Loyalists and others

The rise of the National Front during the 1970s resulted in a number of studies of history, organisation, philosophy and electoral impact (Walker, 1977; Billig and Bell, 1980; Fielding, 1981; Taylor, 1982; Husbands, 1983). The political party itself was the result of a decision taken in 1967 to merge the League of Empire Loyalists and the British National Party (Walker, 1977: 67). As Layton-Henry (1984: 91) reports, the merger also involved a number of fringe far-Right groups whose members were urged to support the new party. The party's foundation occurred against the backdrop of the liberal hour in British race relations when considerable attempts were made by the parties, firstly, to defuse the race issue and, secondly, to adopt progressive measures to foster integration. However, not long afterwards the atmosphere of liberal optimism became soured and the party received an important fillip through Powell's outspoken attack on immigration in 1968.

Black immigration, however, was not the only platform of the party. In fact, many of its predecessor organisations had been closely involved in rearguard campaigns to undermine Britain's decolonisation policies since the 1950s (the League of Empire Loyalists). Others had been linked with various anti-Semitic campaigns going back to the 1930s (the British National Party), and some had had strong associations with neo-fascist ideologies (the National Socialist Movement). Furthermore, sections of the National Front's leadership also began developing a more rigorous critique of the alleged moral and social decline of Britain for which they argued black immigrants were to be held responsible. But in the short term at least, the party was committed to campaigning against black immigration and for a policy of non-voluntary repatriation. The party's birth had owed a lot to the spontaneous growth in the early and mid-1960s of local anti-immigration pressure groups such as the Southall Residents Association and the Birmigham Immigration Control Association. In the context of the Powellite whirlwind of the late 1960s, the party soon gathered significant levels of popular support. By 1969, the party's newspaper, *Spearhead*, claimed that membership enquiries had reached 180 per week. By 1972 its mass membership peaked at an estimated 20,000 individuals (Taylor, 1982).

Despite its early strong following, the 1970 General Election proved to be a disappointment to the National Front. It only secured 3.5 per cent of the vote in the seats it fought. Steed (1978) has sought to explain this poor showing by noting that the party's electoral strength was largely made up of a core of committed supporters. Consequently the higher turnout rates of general as opposed to local elections tended to reduce the party's share of the vote in general elections. It is also likely that the 1970 poll was an unsuitable initial electoral test for the party given that the focus of media attention was squarely on Powell who made his continued support for the Conservatives, rather than another fringe party, abundantly clear. To be sure, the National Front's relationship with the Conservative Party has always tended to produce both opportunities and constraints. On the one hand, the party has often relied upon outspoken Conservative politicians such as Enoch Powell and Margaret Thatcher to raise the overall saliency of race and immigration in British politics. On the other hand, both parties have periodically competed for the same voters who often share not just a fierce opposition to black immigration but also a more generalised enthusiasm for the symbols of patriotism, British parliamentary sovereignty and an authoritarian moral code.

The basis of National Front support

The question of surges and declines in support for the extreme Right has been the subject of immense sociological and political research (Steed, 1978; Harrop and Zimmerman, 1977; Nugent and King, 1977 and 1979; Husbands, 1979 and 1983). Several commentators have observed varieties of the same pattern, namely an association with the local or neighbouring presence of significant black minority populations. In addition, the experience of unemployment and/or social deprivation has been linked with support for the National Front. Phizacklea and Miles's (1980) empirical study of Harlesden in north-west London indicated that working-class racialised antipathy towards the local black presence was grounded in a more general set of social and economic beliefs about the decline of inner city areas. The National Front's appeal in this context was far from exclusively racial and relied little on ideological abstractions concerning racial superiority and inferiority. Survey data from 1978 reported by Harrop *et al.* (1980) revealed that the belief that the National Front stood for 'ordinary working people' was endorsed by one in four of all respondents.

A more psephologically oriented explanation has been advanced in the work of Husbands (1979 and 1983) who has emphasised the role played by white perceptions of the growth of the black population. This view, dubbed the 'threat hypothesis', has contended that it is not so much the actual presence of black people which fuels white racist fears but rather the prospect, however ill-founded, of imminent increases in the black population. White voters, alarmed by the perception of anticipated rapid and unwelcome social change, respond by endorsing a political movement which seeks to address and explain these concerns. Citing evidence from the 1977 Greater London Council local election, Husbands observed that amongst the largest swings secured by the National Front were in wards that bordered upon – though did not include – the areas of highest black settlement, the bulk of which were geographically clustered in a north-eastern arc around outer London. Moreover, the momentum built up by campaigning in economically declining inner-city areas has often been boosted by a general lack of faith in the established parties. It is interesting to note that the high-water mark of support for the National Front probably occurred between 1976–78, at a time when disillusionment with the Labour Government had reached a peak and the Conservatives under Mrs Thatcher had yet to launch their populist campaign on immigration.

A rather different explanation has been proffered by Taylor (1979) who notes that, despite limited electoral success, the National Front was never able to mount a serious attempt for representation let alone power. The impact of the party instead lay in ensuring important changes in the values and assumptions of the British political system. These changes have centred on forcing established parties to end their self-enforced reluctance to discuss the immigration issue. To that end, the National Front amounted to a catalyst for greater elite responsiveness to grass-roots anti-black, anti-immigrant sentiment. This form of political change, argues Taylor (1979: 145), has been entirely consistent with the 'strain of hostility to black people . . . which has been fairly constant in level and magnitude'. The basis of the party's appeal therefore can be linked to, and is a by-product of, this pernicious aspect of British political and social culture. Its more precise electoral strength, however, has ebbed and flowed as a consequence of the race and immigration strategies of the major parties. The major party strategies on the issue in turn changed fundamentally in the late 1970s when the consensus to de-politicise the issue was terminated by the unilateral actions of the Conservatives.

This thesis is also echoed by Messina (1985 and 1989) who has focused on the increased inability of the consensus to deliver. The reluctance of the major parties to tackle the issue provided fertile ground for a third force, the National Front. The rapid rise in the National Front's activities and strength served to repoliticise race in an abrupt and volatile fashion. The forced return of the race issue to the centre of the political stage was met with, and further encouraged by, the growth of the organised anti-racist movement. Together, the National Front and its organised opponents represented an extra-party mode of articulating political interests which had been largely smothered by the major parties. The development of the politics of single-issue protest movements during the 1970s is considered below.

The Anti-Nazi League

Following and largely as a result of the rise in electoral support for the National Front in the mid-1970s, a number of activists on the far Left took the initiative to tackle directly the Front's message of anti-immigrant hostility. The Socialist Workers' Party (SWP), a far Left Trotskyist group, had previously been highly critical of the effective abandonment of black interests by the major parties. Working in conjunction with sympathetic politicians in the Labour and Liberal parties, the SWP founded in November 1977 a new body, the Anti-Nazi League, aimed at combating the National Front. The League was initially intended to be a non-party body aimed at bringing together under one banner a variety of anti-racist and anti-fascist groups. Messina (1989: 10) notes that, despite the intention to create a broad-based pressure group, in practice the League was dominated by the continuing anti-National Front activities of the SWP. The League grew impressively in its early months and within a year had attracted considerable popular support, particularly among the young who were at least partially recruited to its message through bodies such as Rock Against Racism and SKAN (School Kids Against the Nazis). The former of these bodies had in fact pre-dated the League's own foundation; it was set up in August 1976 by several SWP activists partly in response to questionable sub-Powellite remarks made by two giants of the popular music industry, Eric Clapton and David Bowie (Gilroy, 1987: 120).

During the course of 1977–78 the League organised numerous protest marches, public meetings and even two well-attended rock music concerts in London parks (Widgery, 1986). The League represented an important development in the politics of race because its *raison d'être* centred on street politics and mass activism. It placed little faith in the established parties' record of campaigning for the interests of black people. League activists felt that the major parties had preferred instead to distance themselves as far as possible from black people, a group whose interests were perceived to be unpopular and an electoral liability. Extra-parliamentary action was therefore required according to the League's leadership, and this often involved direct confrontation with the National Front on the streets. Moreover, the League emphasised the underlying fascist ideology which it perceived lay at the heart of the National Front.

This approach to the race issue was considerably more ideologically based and action-oriented than had hitherto been seen in British politics. For example, in April 1979 League activists were in the vanguard of public demonstrations against a National Front election rally in Southall. The League-organised protest rally ended in violence, involving street clashes between demonstrators and the police, mass – often arbitrary – arrests of Asians in Southall, and the death of one demonstrator allegedly at the hands of the Special Patrol Group. The episode undoubtedly marked for many League activists an illustration of the State's apparent protection of and cover for Nazi ideology.

The League's support eventually declined and it fell from prominence shortly after the 1979 General Election. At least one of the reasons for its demise was the growth of factional infighting in its ranks. As mentioned previously, it had become dominated by the SWP not long after its inception and this factor had led to considerable resentment among its non-Trotskyist activists and supporters. For their part, SWP activists among the League's leadership began to see the extra-parliamentary route of opposition to the National Front as the only credible option; thus they were reluctant to ally the League too closely with the major parties, a sentiment ironically shared by important sections of the Labour and Conservative party leaderships.

However, the most important factor behind the League's collapse after 1979 was the decline in the National Front's popular support. The League had largely been set up to combat the Front in direct and blunt terms. By all accounts, during 1977–78 it had done just that. However, by mid-1978, as the Conservatives' hardline immigration stance became more widely projected, much of the wavering, loosely committed support for the National Front began to evaporate. The Front had been strategically outmanoeuvred by Conservative populists and found the basis of its support – frustration overthe major parties' neglect of the immigration issue – severely eroded. In May 1979, despite having fielded a record number of parliamentary candidates (303), the National Front's average share of the popular vote plummeted to just 1.4 per cent (3.1 per cent in October 1974). With its central political message and most popular policies stolen by the respectable Right, the Front faced electoral disaster. The League had achieved its aims – though not directly through its own actions – and, like the Front, faced a bleak future. According to Messina:

> The preoccupation of the Anti-Nazi League with the National Front, the key to the meteoric rise of the movement, was responsible for its decline after the NF's electoral support collapsed . . . . Like the NF, the future of the ANL was linked to the parties' posture on race in that its survival depended on the continued unwillingness and/or inability of the Labour party to assume an anti-racist posture.
>
> (Messina, 1989: 123)

The New Right agenda

In this section we shall turn to examine the various critiques of multiracial British society developed by leading thinkers of the New Right. Having traced the major component elements that make up the collective New Right school, we shall explore the question of cultural pluralism and its relationship to the cohesion and integrity of the nation-state. Thereafter, some of the key public policy implications of New Right thought will be discussed, with close attention paid to the area of state education, a policy sphere which has frequently been seen by the supporters and critics of the New Right as a litmus test for contemporary debates about a multiracial society.

Variations on New Right themes

Gordon and Klug (1986) stress that any discussion of the New Right should distinguish between two important sets of thinkers and approaches. One group can be termed New Right libertarians who are largely motivated by the doctrine of economic liberalism. Viewing social relations in largely economic terms, the origins of the libertarians lie in the heyday of nineteenth-century British capitalism. Their view of racial discrimination is somewhat detached, regarding it as the outcome of non-prejudicial market forces; if the market discriminated in favour of one set of outcomes over another, it was said to do so through colourblind eyes.

Indeed, discrimination in and of itself remains at the core of the market principle, and the allocation of scarce goods and resources requires there to be an *uneven* outcome of winners and losers. For economic liberals there can be no force more responsive and effective than Adam Smith's 'invisible hand of the market'; consequently all anti-discrimination laws are viewed with grave suspicion as unwarranted interferences in the regulation of market forces.

Significantly, libertarians appear to have few decisive views on black immigration or its social consequences. Some have observed that the process has created localised difficulties, but in the main the settlement of large numbers of black immigrants since the Second World War has been seen as a source of opportunity and revitalisation for the ailing British economy. Certain libertarian writers have in recent times expressed great enthusiasm for the prospect of a more liberal immigration regime, arguing that tighter European regulation of immigration policy will merely serve to create a protected and inefficient labour market. Examples of libertarian pressure groups include the following: the Institute of Economic Affairs, Aims of Industry, the Centre for Policy Studies, the Freedom Association, the Social Affairs Unit, the Adam Smith Institute, and the Libertarian Alliance (Gordon and Klug, 1986).

Alongside this approach is that of a second group known as New Right social authoritarians. According to Gordon and Klug (1986) this group represents the bulk of recent New Right commentary on racial and cultural themes. Social authoritarians have been closely involved in debates about race in Britain largely because their interest lies in the question of the social cohesion of modern society. In order to evaluate the prospects for such cohesion, emphasis is placed on social actors and forces in shaping the cultural map of a nation. Whereas 'the economic consumer' may serve as the central unit of analysis for libertarians, 'the social group' is seen in these terms by social authoritarians. The golden age of the nineteenth century holds no special attraction for social authoritarians other than in the form of the often mythologised reverence for Victorian codes of public morality and social immobility.

Social authoritarians tend to take a universally hard line on most social issues especially concerning law and order, sexuality and the family. A close link is maintained by many commentators with an active Christian morality lobby. Significantly, social authoritarians have been motivated by a concern for the moral integrity of a nation at risk from (a) black immigration, (b) black reproduction, and (c) black social behaviour. (We shall inspect the nature of some of these claims more closely below.) Examples of pressure groups coming under this heading include: the Monday Club, the London Swinton Circle, the Salisbury Group, Tory Action, WISE (Welsh, Irish, Scots and English), and the Focus Policy Group (Gordon and Klug, 1986).

It is important to note three points about the two groups that comprise the New Right. First, the various debates in which the New Right have been associated have not necessarily involved both these traditions. Indeed, on most of the issues discussed in this section, it has been social authoritarians who have set the pace. Libertarian interest has usually extended no further than generalised support for the economic consequences of immigration and micro-level analysis of market behaviour.

Second, both approaches have found a receptive home in the Conservative Party and, in fact, are closely entwined in the main traditions that have formed the party since the 1840s. This tacit alliance has sometimes led to uneasy relations between the respective camps and in recent years has undoubtedly been the source of severe conflict over the conduct of economic policy in particular. However, it should be remembered that the endurance of the Conservative Party has often been based on its successful fusion of these two traditions. To be sure, even the best-known champions of economic liberalism have also laid great importance on the role of a strong state in the social realm – a characterisation made by Gamble (1988) about the logic of Thatcherism.

Finally, the New Right should not be confused with identifiable political movements or groups. At most it amounts to a political tendency which has placed greater emphasis on developing a critique of the post-war Keynesian settlement than on campaigning or political mobilisation. That said, key New Right thinkers have had a far-reaching influence upon policy debates in recent years. Gordon and Klug (1986) are at pains to point out that New Right contributions to policy debates have operated through a hidden racial code. However, the absence of overt references to race has not made these contributions any less racialised in their relevance to policy questions. Indeed, these authors contend that the arguments of the New Right often amount to a new racism, absent of racial explicitness and shrouded in the language of social responsibility.

Moral and social 'threats' to nationhood

As early as 1969, Powell rebuked the allegation that his argument was based on racist assumptions: he did not despise any other human being on the grounds of race and nor did he believe that one race was inherently superior to another (Seidel, 1986: 114). By 1981 the argument had developed into a fundamental attack upon the 'alien wedge' that resided in – but did not belong to – England. In a widely reported speech Powell asserted:

> The presence of a common status where there was no common nationhood had produced in the cities of England a concentration of other nationals who asserted the contradictory claim to belong – and not belong – to this nation . . .. A nation which . . . deliberately denies its continuity with its past and its rootedness in its homeland is on the way to repudiate its existence.
>
> (quoted in *The Guardian*, 9 November 1981)

New Right thinkers have generally not concerned themselves with a close examination of minority cultures and values. Instead, the focus of their attention has usually been to describe the features of the dominant shared culture of British society and to note alleged irreconcilable differences with the cultures of black minority communities. In doing so, New Right polemicists have taken their cue from the legacy of Powellism which had by the 1980s evolved into an account of English or British national identity.

Powell, as we observed earlier, had been keen to signal his view that the objectives of liberal integrationists were ultimately unachievable. These aims, he suggested, would not only be undermined by the failure of white people to accept black people as 'British' but they would also be frustrated by the refusal of black people to readjust their cultural values and ties. Having accepted that earlier waves of ethnically distinct immigrants had 'contributed to the gene pool of the English people' (1981), for Powell the influx of large numbers of black immigrants posed a rather different and unresolvable problem. Powell loosely justified his claims by reference to the cultural heritage of Asian and Afro-Caribbean immigrants who, he argued, held no close association with the shared cultural heritage of the 'four white nations' of the British Isles. This reference to the cultural heritage of black immigrants was not explored further by Powell himself though it has become a key theme of New Right interest in recent years.

Recent New Right-inspired writers have returned to the question of black people in Britain and portrayed their presence in negative terms. For cultural and other reasons the black presence is fundamentally at odds with the New Right's normative conception of English society. In 1982 John Casey, a Cambridge don, published an essay in *The Salisbury Review*, the house journal of much neo-conservative writing, which outlined the argument. To begin with, British history was defined in cultural terms that are exclusionary towards black minorities:

> There is no way of understanding British and English history that does not take seriously the sentiments of patriotism that go with a continuity of institutions, shared experiences, language, customs, [and] kinship . . . English patriotism has at its centre a feeling for persons of one's own kind.
>
> (quoted in Seidel, 1986: 112)

Secondly, certain minority communities such as West Indians are seen as a 'problem' whose behaviour is in essence alien to the 'British way of life':

> The West Indian community is *structurally* likely to be at odds with English civilisation. . . . The family structure . . . is markedly unlike our own: educational standards that are below those of all other racial groups . . . and the involvement of West Indians in a vastly disproportionate amount of violent crime.
>
> (quoted in Seidel, 1986: 112)

Nor are Asians immune from attack, for their cultural traditions present an obstacle to their successful integration into British society:

> By their large numbers, their *profound* difference in culture, they are most unlikely to identify themselves with the traditions and loyalties of the host nation.
>
> (quoted in Seidel, 1986: 113)

Casey concludes that 'the great English cities are now becoming alienated from national life' and that 'black and brown communities will turn Britain into a different sort of place'.

In a collection of papers entitled *The New Right: Image and Reality* published by the Runnymede Trust, Parekh (1986: 38–43) contends that the assumptions upon which such an argument is built are riddled with contradictions and half-truths. Casey's argument can be dismissed on four principal counts. First, asserts Parekh, the viability of the State is simply not conditional on a sense of unified nationality as claimed by Casey. The example of the United States is cited to illustrate a diversity of nationalities under a single coherent state.

Second, Parekh challenges Casey's claim that the unity of the nation depends on a shared sense of kinship. Indeed, no such common bonding or kinship is required to build a sense of nationality and the cases of the 'Americanisation' of different groups that settled in the United States is cited. Moreover, notes Parekh, it is simply not true to claim that the English are a homogenous ethnic group; they are not, and instead have strong Scottish and Welsh links which have gradually developed a sense of British nationality.

Third, the view that black minorities cannot or will not develop a sense of shared nationality with the white majority is rebutted directly. Parekh sees no evidence for such a view, noting that all previous immigrant groups have eventually rid themselves of their 'alien' identity. There is no reason to think that Afro-Caribbeans and Asians, peacefully settled in Britain, will not also strive to identify with a sense of Britishness so long as it does not exclude them. Furthermore, Parekh (1986: 41) stresses that 'their colour acquired importance only later and largely because British society used it to identify and discriminate against them.' The problem therefore lies not so much with black minorities who did not want to think of themselves as British but rather with a dominant white society which continues to view them as a threatening 'alien wedge'.

Finally, Parekh refutes Casey's view that extreme and morally contentious policies such as enforced repatriation of black people can be justified on the grounds that it serves the higher goal of preserving British nationhood. Nothing could be further from the case; Parekh observes that such a policy cannot be reconciled with another putative aspect of the British character, namely, the tradition of liberal tolerance towards minority faiths and ethnic groups.

The New Right questioning of the compatibility of black minority groups with British nationhood has been a key dimension of the onslaught against a multiracial society. It has been based on a discourse which is not as overtly racist or xenophobic as that of the extreme Right. In sum, observes Seidel (1986: 113), it is different in style: 'Casey's arguments are couched in restrained and seemingly detached academic language, which lends them legitimacy.' As Barker (1981) has argued, the racism of the New Right does not depend on outdated modes of thinking about racial superiority; rather, it is an ideological force which merely requires the articulation of cultural codes of behaviour and expectations which are exclusionary towards the claims of black people.

Education and the New Right

The educational policy sphere has emerged in recent years as something of a battle ground between enthusiasts and critics of New Right ideas about the politics of race and nation. As the Dewsbury (white parents' opposition to the multicultural curriculum) and Bradford (Ray Honeyford's censure by his local education authority) episodes have shown, the issue has been at the centre of enormous controversy. There are three chief reasons for this (see also Saggar, 1991a: 104–6). First, education has become the symbolic focus of localised tensions over race. In a sense educational policy has emerged as the litmus test for the impact of all local public services on discrete social groups. To that end, the measurement of 'successful' policy is judged in terms of 'acceptable' policy and it is not surprising to note that virtually all policies have often tended to be compromises between conflicting priorities.

Second, the educational sphere illustrates the differential policy responses of local policy-makers to statutory obligations. Since the 1950s and 1960s even the most conservative illiberal local education authorities have found that they could not deny black minorities access to this category of public services. However, in many cases they have succeeded in providing different standards or qualities of service. For instance, by utilising school catchment areas, educational policy-makers have justified differential quality on the grounds of the often unfounded fears of white parents about educational standards. Thus, certain schools have become ghettoised in the quality of service they are able to provide. This state of play has in turn resulted in considerable resentment by groups of white and black parents alike, many of whom have been prepared to make the education of their children tests of principle about race relations in general. School busing policy operated in Ealing in west London during the 1960s and 1970s was an illustration of such differential public service delivery (Saggar, 1991a: 81–111).

Finally, in recent years we have begun to see a transformation in debates about education policy by which integrated stable schools are viewed as a measure of the success of liberal approaches to race policy. Thus, liberal integrationists may have won strategic battles in the past against segregation in schools, but more recently this assumption has been under threat (Saggar, 1991a: 82–91). What some may view as an unholy alliance has emerged between groups of white parents opposed to multicultural curricula and groups of black parents keen to foster separatism on grounds of religion. For example, it is interesting to note that a leading right-wing pressure group, PACE (the Parental Alliance for Choice in Education), headed by Baroness Cox, has recently advised and supported the local campaigns of white Christian parents *and* black Muslim parents opposed to what they see as the forced exposure of their children to the 'mishmash' of a multi-faith religious curriculum.

By a curious twist of logic, religious separatists from black minority communities have found common cause with white neo-conservatives opposed to the multi-faith, multicultural ethic of contemporary state education. Such an alliance would have been unthinkable only a few years ago. Its recent emergence is a measure of the intolerable pressure which the liberal code of management of race policy has come under. For many years the sole source of criticism of liberal values in race policy affairs was that of repatriationists such as Powell. Recent developments have highlighted the extent to which scepticism is also shared by sections of the black minority population as well (see also Saggar, 1991a: 166–67).

The main bone of contention between liberal educationalists and their critics has been the issue of multicultural education policy. Liberal multiculturalists have long argued that a white bias characterised western education curricula and that reform was needed which would benefit minority pupils' educational standards, raise black self-respect, and promote positive images of equality. Consequently, since the 1970s many educationalists and local education authorities (LEAs) have been working on the introduction of detailed new curricula which attempt to advance these goals. However, at the same time many of their efforts have been the subject of intense criticism from New Right-inspired circles. These critics have charged that, at best, multiculturalism has produced a 'rag-bag' of half-truths which have equipped pupils with no particular knowledge, and, at worse, the use of the curriculum as a means of averting conflict in schools has produced the opposite result.

The more scathing attacks on multiculturalism have been reserved for progressive LEAs which have been at the forefront of innovation and reform. The now-abolished Inner London Education Authority was a major target of criticism during the 1980s from those who saw its activities as tantamount to the political indoctrination of black and white pupils alike. Moreover, critics have alleged that history syllabuses have denied the positive aspects of Britain's colonial past and that multiculturalism has been transformed into a vehicle espousing a 'mania' against white society (Scruton, 1984a and 1984b).

Writing in *The Salisbury Review*, Ray Honeyford (1983), then a serving head teacher, launched an attack on the whole approach taken by the multiculturalists. His first objection was directed towards mother-tongue teaching described as 'a prescription for linguistic chaos'. Secondly, he condemned the practice of legitimising 'anti-British prejudice' which he saw in the work of educationalists determined to expose the impact of British imperialism upon black people. But his most damning words were reserved for the new army of 'race experts' which he claimed had not only taken over educational policy-making but had also built a new 'race-speak' to filter out legitimate criticism. Consequently, he argued, any challenge to the new orthodoxy was immediately and invariably branded as 'racist'; the outcome was a form of 'inverted McCarthyism' which effectively censored all dissent. Honeyford's argument did not stop there but was extended in a second article (1984) in which he challenged the 'the multiracial zealots' in more strident terms. This contribution repeated the widely circulated claim of New Right voices that racism had little to do with black education failure, the causes of which he claimed were 'located in West Indian family structure and values'. In addition, Honeyford returned to and expanded on an earlier theme concerning the cultural superiority of the English language:

> We in the schools are also enjoined to believe that creole, pidgin and other non-standard variants have the same power, subtlety and capacity for expressing fine shades of meaning, and for tolerating uncertainty, ambiguity and irony as standard English.
>
> (quoted in Seidel, 1986: 121)

Gordon and Klug (1986: 29) have described the debate over multicultural education as 'the battle for hearts and minds'. Indeed, at its core it has been a battle of ideas in which vastly different – and often contradictory – meanings are attached to apparently accepted terms. But it is a debate which is not merely about the relationship between race and educational practice; it also pertains to our broader understanding of race and racism in contemporary British society. The significance of the New Right in this area lies in its seemingly non-racial language and style, rendering charges of overt racism virtually meaningless. Nonetheless, the agenda of the New Right may constitute a 'new racism' by which cultural and social divisions are reinforced within a reformulated concept of nationhood. In short, the cultural characteristics and traits of black people may be used to exclude them from New Right interpretations of 'Britishness'. In doing so, their legitimacy as British subjects, on an equal footing with the majority of white people, has come under attack. This process of subtle exclusion lies at the heart of the charge that the agenda remains no less ominous than that of the Powellites of an earlier age.

Overview and conclusion

In the course of this chapter we have surveyed a variety of

responses from the Right to the emergence of a multiracial society in Britain. These responses have included the campaign against black immigration spearheaded by Powell in the 1960s and 1970s, the electoral rise and fall of extreme Right groups such as the National Front, and lastly, the development of a more sophisticated New Right discourse about the compatibility of black communities within British nationhood.

These three themes have been surveyed in an order that roughly approximates to their chronological impact upon British politics. However, underlying them all has been a continuous series of ideas relating to Britain's transformation in the space of a generation from a largely monoracial society to one hallmarked by the pluralism of race, ethnicity, faith and language. What is certain is that the Right as a whole – and occasionally joined by sections of the Left – has been sceptical about this transformation. However, whilst the unreconstructed Powellites and the neo-fascists couched their opposition in blunt and often brutal terms, the approach taken by the New Right has been altogether more subtle. Indeed, the claims made by leading neo-conservative thinkers have been met with great respectability. The discourse about race, nation and culture within which these claims are located has been incorporated into the elite circles of political parties. To be sure, the success of these ideas can be measured by the degree of resonance between influential New Right pressure groups and key Conservative politicians.

The politics of Thatcherism, particularly in its early phase up to 1983, bred an intellectual climate receptive to fundamental policy discussions about the meaning of national identity. Moreover, as Parekh (1986: 34) has noted, the ideological force of the New Right has to be located in the context of a wider analysis of the causes of Britain's social, economic and moral decline. Various economic and moral prescriptions have been advanced by the New Right's analysis of decline. On the political front it has been argued that nothing short of a redefinition of national identity, based on ethnic and cultural unity, is needed to arrest decline. As we have seen, Parekh's counter-arguments have claimed that New Right ideas are based on an ideological construction of the nation-state which is at variance with the evidence of national unity in the context of ethnic pluralism.

Finally, perhaps the most important development that has arisen from recent debates has been the determination of New Right commentators to take the fight to their liberal and radical critics. This development has involved the denial of not just racism but explicit racialised categories. Thus, scepticism about the black presence in British society is presented as a rational outcome based in 'accepted' white sentiment to be with 'one's own kind'; the potential charge of racism is effectively denied on the grounds that it is an irrational response to the black presence.

The challenge to the anti-racist movement is further extended by New Right claims that inequalities of race in society have nothing to do with racial discrimination. These inequalites are said to be rather the result of a combination of problems within the black population and the self-fulfilling prophecies of the anti-racists. The 'new racism', as critics have dubbed New Right contributions, is therefore uninterested in phenotypically-based theories of race. It is instead about the outcome of the social construction of ideological values and assumptions, in this case the categories that belong and do not belong to the nation. The black presence is therefore easily and routinely presented as the 'enemy within' threatening the social cohesion of contemporary society.

This discourse revolves around the assertion that there is nothing unusual about white people's wish not to mix with the black population. Rational consideration – not extreme reaction – are said to characterise their resistance to racial mixing, and evidence for this claim is even presented from the patterns of social kinship that mark black settlement in Britain. Solutions to this problem range from those who advocate the forced incorporation of black people into the dominant cultural norms of white British society, through to those who persist in hankering after the option of complusory repatriation. At the very least, respected figures inspired by the New Right critique, ranging from Norman Tebbitt to John Biffen, have called for what they describe as a more open and less guilt-ridden debate over the future of British race relations. A new era of fundamental questioning and re-evaluation about Britain's multiracial experience is therefore likely to characterise future political debates about race and nation.

8

Concluding Remarks

In this book we have examined two related phenomena: the political impact of race on Britain and the involvement of black people in the British political system. We have utilised a variety of approaches to these two themes, including, *inter alia*, examination of historical, demographic and psephological theory and evidence. It is not the purpose of this final chapter to provide a summary of the book – self-contained overviews can be found at the end of each of the chapters. Instead, we shall begin to draw together some of the broader arguments of the book and relate them to several key debates about the politics of race in Britain.

The chapter is composed of three themes. First, the merits and drawbacks of the established literature on race and politics will be discussed. The second section will be devoted to a discussion of the liberal framework of British race policy and will contrast this with radical and conservative perspectives. Finally, the book ends by briefly examining the future prospects for race and politics in Britain.

The political analysis of race

We have seen that race has had an important and far-reaching effect on British politics. Whilst most of the developments relating to the racialisation of British politics have occurred in the period following mass non-white immigration, it is apparent that questions of race have permeated through political history for a much longer period. Indeed, from the age of the establishment of international trading routes, through to the heyday of slavery and an imperial policy, Britain has had a close familiarity with black people. For much of this 400–500 year history, a significant minority black community existed in Britain itself. Whilst the end of slavery was associated with a fall in the community's size, a limited but influential black population continued to thrive in major cities such as London, Liverpool and Bristol. In addition, throughout the nineteenth and early twentieth centuries, a small black elite was to be found in urban centres, many of whom were active and influential in political life. Thus, the post-war migration of black Commonwealth citizens which began with the docking of the SS *Windrush* in 1948, took place against an already racialised background. Victorian England in particular had developed sophisticated psuedo-scientific theories about the non-white races and many of these ideas shaped the reception given to the post-war black settlers.

It is important to remind ourselves of the historical context in which Britain experienced mass black immigration. The circumstances of post-war immigration added a further twist to British racial discourse. The economic boom experienced by the British economy during the 1950s ensured that, for a while at least, non-racial factors occupied a role in the debate over immigration. However, as the evidence shows, the racial character of the debate was never far from the surface and by the mid-1950s politicians had begun to be concerned with the social dimensions of black immigration. There developed in British politics at that time an implicit assumption about the socially undesirable nature of continued black immigration, though several writers have stressed that this assumption was merely built on values about race already prevalent in British society. It was against this backdrop that the political parties from the 1950s onwards first defined the black population as a social 'problem' and then discovered the electoral advantage of distancing themselves from liberal immigration policies. Arguably, the evidence of the race and immigration issues in British politics in the 1960s and 1970s was testimony to the underlying hostility of British society towards its newly created multiracial character.

The importance of locating our study of the politics of race within a historical context cannot be overestimated. A great many of the more generalised accounts of the politics of race have sadly neglected the contribution of political history, choosing merely to provide a cursory examination of the post-war period. Specialist studies of the political history of slavery or of black communities in Britain have consequently become marginalised and rarely receive exposure before the more general reader. This particular illustration of the shortcomings in the literature is to be regretted and largely reflects the underdevelopment of political analyses of race.

As noted in the opening chapter, political studies as a discipline have tended to neglect the study of racial issues in British politics beyond the electoral impact of the issue of non-white immigration. Sustained empirical research has been left to a small community of specialists. These specialists have in turn been preoccupied with questions based on the political participation of black people, principally as voters and occasionally as candidates. We, therefore, have amassed a large volume of information about black voting patterns, though, in the view of the present writer at least, comparatively limited knowledge about race and electoral participation. Indeed, our knowledge about political attitudes and sources of political motivation amongst the black population remained limited. Evidence of enduring loyalty to the Labour Party is confirmed by survey research, though the reasons for such behaviour remain less clear. A more rigorous attempt to combine the findings of research on political participation with research on other themes such as urban politics and community power would greatly enhance the analytical strength of the literature as a whole.

The political analysis of race developed in this book has tried to draw upon a variety of theoretical and empirical approaches. We have, for example, considered the arguments and evidence of political historians, social demographers, political behaviouralists and political philosophers. But there remain many areas of poor coverage. In particular, the extant literature base has fought shy of a theoretical exploration of the relationship between race and political power. Whilst a large volume of empirical research has been collected demonstrating racial inequality in Britain, political scientists have conspicuously ducked questions on black access to the political agenda and policy-making process.

To take one example, Messina's (1989) recent study *Race and Party Competition in Britain* highlights the focus of writers on topics such as political parties and electoral participation. The strength of Messina's work undoubtedly comes from his willingness to examine the reasons for the breakdown of issue management and the growth of single-issue protest groups. However, in common with the behavioural traditions of the discipline in general, the approach of his work is geared towards answering the question 'who participates?' as opposed to 'who benefits?'. This behavioural orientation seems *particularly* unsuited to the analysis of race and racism since these topics are so closely interwoven into questions of bias, discrimination and inequality. Therefore, an analysis which explains as well as describes must recognise the implicit and unavoidable association between the politics of race and the politics of exclusion.

The reader will no doubt be aware of the maxim that the answers and conclusions generated by social research often depend upon the questions asked to begin with. Nowhere does this point have more relevance than in the study of the politics of race.

And yet there are grounds for worthwhile future developments in analysis. We saw earlier that political and social philosophers in particular have made a number of important contributions in recent years. Many have concentrated on countering the arguments put forward by neo-conservative analyses of race (Parekh, 1986; Seidel, 1986). Others have focused on the philosophical dilemmas that have arisen in societies characterised by diverse religious beliefs (Parekh, 1990; Jones, 1990). Attention has fallen on the role of race in state and class theory (Robinson, 1983; Omi and Winant, 1986), and on the practical problems arising from the principle of toleration (Dworkin, 1985; Mendus, 1989). These developments taken together suggest that older fixations with the stuff of 'black, brown and green votes' (Crewe, 1979) may be beginning to give way to more critical thinking about the politics of race. In any case, the pace of change within the literature will depend on the extent to which scholars are prepared to explore inter-disciplinary links in the analysis of race and racism.

Liberals and their critics

Of course the continued restriction of black immigration was not the sole feature of the parties' involvement in racial affairs. As we have seen, a series of important reforms were undertaken during the 1960s which were designed to facilitate the integration of black immigrants and their children into British society. These 'liberal hour' reforms, as they were dubbed by sympathetic commentators, consisted of a piecemeal strategy outlawing certain forms of racial discrimination and sponsoring voluntary sector initiatives to foster inter-racial understanding.

Both the general strategy and its component reforms have found their supporters and critics among academic commentators. Some perspectives have lauded the progressive goals of the reformers whilst expressing doubt over the efficacy of some of the policy instruments established to further those goals. Others have challenged the basis upon which anti-discrimination and racial harmony reforms were adopted, arguing that they betrayed a naivety about the depth and causes of racism. Moreover, it has been argued that these measures were merely designed to shroud the threat of overt racial conflict in a cloak of superficial, but ultimately unsustainable, harmony. A third view has been expressed which has been deeply sceptical about the chances of successfully integrating the black and white population. This view has encompassed several perspectives, ranging from those who perceive there to be fundamental and irreconcilable divisions between different racial groups, through to those who have opposed the role of the state in the private, self-regarding sphere. There are undoubtedly numerous riders to, and points of common ground between, these three schools of thought. However, for the sake of analytical convenience, following Banton (1987), they can be respectively described as the liberal, radical and conservative analyses of the politics of race in Britain.

These respective analyses represent not only contrasting approaches to the study of race and politics but also the different philosophical understandings of race and social theory. The scepticism of the conservatives for example can be traced to state theory in which the traditions of pluralism and the minimal, arbiter state have been influential. The benevolent role of the state and the opportunity to effect widespread social change through the democratic political process, are illustrations of the tacit assumptions shared by liberals. Equally, radicals rest part of their analysis on a lingering doubt about the ability of formal political participation to deliver worthwhile and lasting social reform. Many radicals thus prefer to invest greater faith in the politics of protest against the shackles of oppression, be it based on race, class, culture or whatever.

In all of these examples, we are reminded once again of the pertinence of theories of *political* explanation in our study of race and politics. As the opening chapter made clear, it is not sufficient to rely upon the theoretical advancements made by sociologists. In order to understand more fully the relationship between race and politics, scholars must be more prepared to integrate research and writing on 'race politics' with mainstream developments in the study of British politics and government. In order to move in this direction, a measured downgrading of familiar behavioural approaches, accompanied by a revitalisation of other approaches such as policy studies and political history, will be needed.

The liberal, radical and conservative schools of thought are important to our understanding of the politics of race because of the debate to which they inevitably lend themselves. The contrasting interpretations they each advance have been the subject of an important journal article by Banton (1987) who has compared their respective conclusions about the trajectory of the racial issue in British politics. Radical standpoints, he has argued, have tended to dominate the questions posed by recent additions to the literature and have shared 'a belief that ideology is a necessary concept for the analysis of political behaviour' (1987: 41). They have not necessarily provided many of the answers, choosing instead to concentrate on more theoretical investigations of the relationship between, *inter alia*, race and class and race and imperialism. He also notes that liberals, and to a lesser degree conservatives, have been most active in empirical research of the racial issue in British politics, with the latter in particular antipathetic to the role of theoretical models of explanation. The liberal perspective, of course, also represents the dominant approach taken by policy-makers in British politics over the past thirty years. Politicians in the main have stuck by a strategy of curbing the worst excesses of anti-black hostility, by enacting statutory rights for black people and promoting voluntary integration measures.

Whilst the liberal camp has placed great emphasis on the responsibility of elite politicians for the protection of black minority interests, conservatives by contrast have stressed that the success of integration policies remains conditional on the attitudes of the black population. These contrasts do not merely reflect different views about the routes to racial integration but also different understandings of the the state's relationship with its citizens. A form of contract theory seemingly underpins the liberals' belief in the halfway house of safeguards in exchange for integration, whereas the conservative could be expected to doubt whether such safeguards would be sufficient to combat the disintegrative tendencies of certain minority groups.

The recent contributions of neo-conservative critics are particularly pertinent to debates about the successes and failures of the dominant liberal approach. We have seen that a variety of New Right-inspired voices have joined the debate over the future prospects for Britain's multiracial society. Taking their cue from old Powellite ideas about national integrity, these commentators have argued that the rejuvenation of British society is dependent on a common ethnic 'stock'. Without such a unity of ethnic identity, it is claimed that allegiance to the British nation becomes meaningless. Thus, the 'true' sense of British nationhood is deprived from the ethnic minority groups who do not share the features of, and cannot belong to, the dominant white majority. To these commentators the creation of a *de facto* racially plural society has been tantamount to an unprecedented betrayal of the white population by unresponsive elite politicians. Moreover, the adoption of race relations laws and the establishment of a race bureaucracy has taken place in spite of the permanent 'alien' status of the black population. This population, they contend, cannot be – and never will be – 'British' in the sense described.

The technical–legal status of the black population will no doubt remain 'British' for the foreseeable future but the difficulty arises in the notion of 'black British'. For the New Right the notion has virtually no meaning. Consequently, in answer to questioning about policy solutions favoured by the New Right, several commentators have recommended in respectable terms options once disimissed as the repatriation fantasies of Powellites, neo-fascists and others. These policy choices are today not so easily dismissed, largely as a consequence of the ascendancy of New Right political ideas in general and also because of the seemingly non-racial discourse in which they are located. This option aside for a moment, many New Right commentators have endorsed a number of fully worked policy proposals in recent years. These have ranged from the 'forced incorporation' of black minorities through to the retrospective transformation of black

British citizens into guest-workers along the lines of the German case (see Messina, 1990, for a discussion of developments on the politics of labour migration policy across western Europe).

The debate between liberal perspectives on the politics of race and its critics will continue and perhaps intensify in the future. Such a development should be welcomed on two grounds. First, it will hopefully foster a climate of more fundamental re-evaluation of British approaches to race relations spanning the past thirty years. There are limited signs that politicians, policy-makers and academics are interested in nurturing such an ongoing exercise (Bonham-Carter, 1987, Benyon, 1984, and Bulpitt, 1986, respectively). That said, it is likely that the running will initially be made by students of contemporary history. The approach of the thirty-year watershed since the passage of the 1962 Commonwealth Immigrants Act will no doubt precipitate a flurry of illuminating research activity.

Second, the process of comparison and debate with conservative and radical opinion will hopefully have the effect of modernising and even improving liberal thinking on race relations. The liberal perspective of trying to build an acceptance compromise between majority expectations and minority rights can often seem like chasing after an impossible and elusive goal. Indeed, dilemmas of this sort have characterised liberal political thought on many fronts and the race question is arguably just the latest twist to this tradition. However, a number of rather naive assumptions about, for example, freedom of expression conflicts have tended to weaken the liberal case, or at the very least expose its inherent contradictions. As the Rushdie affair illustrated, the old unreconstructed liberal perspective, which dominated British approaches to racial pluralism, has come under increased strain in recent years. The perspective has consequently had to selectively discard its more untenable dimensions in order to survive as the dominant paradigm. The legacy of Roy Jenkins' post-melting-pot vision, liberal enthusiasts should be assured, can only be preserved through a more open examination of its constraints and opportunities for policy-makers.

Future prospects

Finally, we should pause to consider future developments in the politics of race in Britain. It is difficult to introduce any degree of precision in our generalisations but a number of points are undoubtedly worthy of brief discussion. Three stand out in particular.

Post-consensus race politics

A great amount of attention has been paid to the ending of the age of the de-politicisation of race. Perhaps too much. It is certainly the case that from around 1975 onwards the Conservative Party reintroduced the notion of attracting wavering voters on the appeal of the single issue of immigration control. The political gains potentially available to a party that clearly articulated a tough line on black immigration have been documented for some time (Butler and Stokes, 1974). Moreover, according to Crewe (1983a: 263) 'there are votes for the picking in fanning the flames of racial resentment'. All of this may have been instrumental in the Conservatives' strategic shift further to the Right on the issue during the late 1970s.

However, with the successsful implementation of a new Nationality Act in 1981, the Conservatives' concern with immigration policy *per se* virtually disappeared. One view of the sudden end of the salience of the issue among Conservative strategists was that this merely reflected its declining saliency amongst the electorate. Or as Crewe (1983b) put it, in the immediate aftermath of the 1983 General Election, 'immigration dropped off the bottom of the political agenda'. An alternative view has been that the locus of the race issue has shifted from matters to do with immigration statistics and towards a more subtle debate concerning ethnic identity and nationhood. The Conservative Right have been at the fore of this important change, one which has not so much ended the popular saliency of race as transformed it into a new political debate about race and nation.

The issue of race at the beginning of the 1990s has therefore taken a new guise. The debate over the pluralisms of ethnicity, culture, faith and group identity has given a new role to the centre. The ideas behind a common and united nationhood are not far removed from issues concerning the nation-state, an area in which the centre has long assumed a hegemony of sorts. However, it is interesting to note that these debates have been largely fuelled by recurring conflicts over public policy provision in a multiracial society, conflicts which by their nature are located within the context of local politics and government. For example, discussions about the range of the school curriculum, the sensitivity of public service delivery to different ethnic groups, and minority access to public services have become the regular features of the race issue in everyday politics. The outcome of these discussions however, will depend heavily on how British policy-makers interpret the ethnically related priorities of black people.

The role of progressive or 'leader' local authorities who have taken up the banner of racial equality will also be of importance. For many of these authorities the race issue has been far from depoliticised, for two chief reasons. First, several of them have forcefully argued that the cause of race equality is inseparable from broader socialist–inspired strategies for social justice and greater equality. Second, the period since 1982 has witnessed a growing escalation in New Right counter-attacks upon the anti-racism project of radical municipal socialists. As Gordon (1990: 188) has written:

> The New Right argues Britain is not racist. What exists is not institutional racism but personal racism, the behaviour of individuals who may behave in a discriminatory way. Thus, the argument continues, there is no legitimate need or basis for anti-racism.

Against this peculiarly politicised picture of race within local politics, it is hard to see how the non-political consensus can be returned to. Once the genie has been let out of the bottle, it cannot be put back in.

Changing notions of minority and group rights

Another key factor that is likely to fuel a political debate about race will be changing notions of minority and group rights. Obviously a great deal will depend upon the extent to which black communities can mobilise around a common minority or group status (see also Addendum to Chapter 3, below). The evidence to date suggests a rather mixed picture in which discrete racial categories, for example, have had only limited success in attracting the loyalties of Asians and Afro-Caribbeans. The category of 'black' or 'black minority' certainly only appears to have resonance among certain sections of these two communities, though widespread use of these labels is often more likely to reflect the analytical conveniences sought by scholars.

The results of the 1991 General Censuss will undoubtedly influence future conceptions of minority and group status. Arguably, the traditional and familiar umbrella term of 'black' is set to disappear forever through the Census' methodology, to be replaced by a variety of descriptive terms which include varieties of 'black' and 'Asian'. However, perhaps the most significant development lies in the move away from a proxy measure of ethnicity based on indirect counts of birthplace to a more flexible yet direct measure based on an ethnic origin question. It will be this question, perhaps more than anything else, which will provide clues about the future form of race politics that is likely to be forged in Britain.

Black political organisations and elites

Finally, and related to the previous point, speculation concerning the future of race politics would be incomplete without consideration of change within the political organisation and leadership of black citizens. Recent years have witnessed enormous changes. Let us note two. First, since 1986–87 in particular the electoral path to formal representation has opened dramatically. Black councillors in London alone swelled in numbers from 75 to 134 in the 1986 local elections and the growth has continued in 1990. Moreover, the successful breaching of the parliamentary route to representation by four black Labour MPs in June 1987 – followed by a fifth with Dr Kumar's Victory at the Langbourgh by-election of November 1991 – further confirmed the view that elected office will be extremely important to the future development of black politics. Needless to say, representational politics has more than its share of critics from within the world of black politics. However, the magnitude of the 1987 breakthrough should not be undermined given the peculiarly hard task of getting small, discrete and putatively unpopular minorities elected within the British electoral system.

Second, socio-demographic trends have slowly but surely begun to eat away the firm working-class character of the bulk of Britain's black population. Although still not widespread, research has outlined the early signs of dramatically improved social mobility among certain groups of Asians. This pattern may be enough to warrant a significant split in the social class allegiances of younger versus older cohorts that, one would expect, will begin to be reflected in their voting behaviour. To herald a widespread defection from Labour may be to jump the gun somewhat or to read too much into this social trend. In many other areas however, evidence confirms ever closer convergence between the social and economic profiles of black and white Britons. Therefore, future convergence in political behaviour cannot be ruled out and might even be prudently anticipated by observers of race and politics in Britain.

Guide to Further Reading

A full bibliography is to be found at the end of this volume containing references for all the sources cited in the text. The purpose of this guide therefore is to provide advice about reading material on the themes covered by the various chapters.

Besides the sources listed below, readers should find the following journals particularly useful for articles on racial and ethnic relations in general: *New Community*, *Ethnic and Racial Studies*, *Immigrants and Minorities*, *Patterns of Prejudice*, *International Migration Review*, *Race and Class*, *Critical Social Policy*, *Equal Opportunities Review*, and *The British Journal of Sociology*. In addition, several political studies journals should be consulted for their occasional though none the less useful coverage of issues pertaining to the politics of race. The most important journals in this category are: *Political Studies* (particularly good for political philosophy themes), *Policy and Politics* (useful for policy studies topics especially in relation to local politics and government), *The British Journal of Political Science* (strong on electoral and legislative behaviour), *Parliamentary Affairs*, *Political Quarterly*, *Public Administration*, *New Left Review*, and *Local Government Studies*. Finally, topical up-to-date information about developments in politics and policy-making can be found in the Runnymede Trust's monthly bulletin, *Race and Immigration*, stocked by most academic and reference libraries and also available on subscription from the Trust at reasonable rates.

Chapter 1

Rex and Mason (1986): one of the most useful reviews of the literature on the sociology and politics of race.
Ben-Tovim and Gabriel (1982): worthwhile introduction to the literature.
Cashmore and Troyna (1983): exceptionally useful for background reading on social science concepts and theories.
Solomos (1986) and Saggar (1991c): critical reviews of the literature on the political analysis of race in Britain since 1962.
Saggar (1990): draws distinctions between behavioural and policy studies approaches to the political analysis of race.
Banton (1987): short though incisive article comparing three academic perspectives – radical, liberal and conservative – on the political impact of race.

Chapter 2

Fryer (1984): best introduction to the subject, combining an appreciation of the history of the black presence in Britain and the development of racism and racial ideologies in British society.
Holmes (1988): good alternative to above.
Walvin (1984): short account based on a much richer television series.
Ramdin (1987): extremely detailed and useful study which concentrates on developing a class analysis of the black presence within the working class.
James (1938) and Williams (1944): for two contrasting theses on the development and abolition of black slavery.
Rich (1986b): scholarly account of racial ideas in the history of British imperialism.

Chapter 3

Bhat *et al.* (1988): collection of articles on various aspects of the social demography of the black population.
Robinson (1990a and 1990b): both useful for original material on the black population and component groups therein.

Bulmer (1986): handy summary of the arguments surrounding the inclusion of a direct ethnic origin question in the General Census.
Brown (1984): contains full details of the 1982 PSI survey.
Robinson (1986): impressive study of the South Asian population.
Haskey (1990): summary of up-to-date Labour Force Survey data on the black population.

Chapter 4

Katznelson (1973), Freeman (1979): important accounts of government race and immigration strategies; particularly good on the period 1945–70.
Messina (1989): as above; particularly good on the period 1970–87.
Miles and Phizacklea (1984), Layton-Henry (1984) and Banton (1985): contrasting interpretations of the politics of race in the post-war period.
Banton (1987): critical review of above.
Saggar (1991a): policy analysis of the local impact of the liberal race policy framework.
Foot (1965): thoroughly readable early account of the political impact of race and immigration.
Rose *et al.* (1969): detailed findings of an early survey of race relations carried out by the Institute of Race Relations.
Deakin (1970): abridged version of above.

Chapter 5

Carter *et al.* (1987): reports fascinating original evidence of government discussions about Commonwealth immigration during the 1950s.
Messina (1989): puts forward an account of parties' race strategies loosely derived from earlier rational choice-based theories of party competition.
Foot (1965): contains lucid descriptions of Labour and Conservative approaches to immigration policy during 1950s and 1960s.
Miles and Phizacklea (1984): polemical, though incisive, account of the politics of race since 1945 – particularly concerned with the 'drift towards repatriation' hypothesis.

Rich (1986a): interesting essay on different strands of Conservative thinking towards race.
Layton-Henry (1978): timely report on populist initiatives on immigration policy in the Conservative Party.

Chapter 6

Studlar (1985): extremely important article describing the limited pace of race issues moving up the political agenda.
Crewe (1983a): arguably the most authoritative interpretation of strategies to promote black political representation, albeit one that arrives at a rather pessimistic conclusion.
Studlar (1983): sets out a number of important pointers to the analysis of the 'ethnic vote'.
Studlar and Layton-Henry (1990): policy analysis of problems of issue recognition and agenda-setting.
FitzGerald (1987): contains interesting evidence about black political attitudes and modes of participation.
Gilroy (1987): includes stimulating writing on the politics of anti-racism.
Gouldbourne (1990): collection of essays on different aspects of black political activism.

Chapter 7

Seidel (1986): well-researched secondary analysis of New Right writing on race themes.
Levitas (1986): very helpful edited volume of essays (including the above) on social, moral, political and economic aspects of New Right thought.
Parekh (1986): brief and largely convincing article rebutting the arguments of a leading New Right thinker.
Gordon and Klug (1986): contains a timely inventory of New Right pressure groups and think-tanks.
Husbands (1983): well-researched exposition of the 'threat hypothesis' for support for extreme right political movements.
Behrens and Edmonds (1981): lively sketch of the influence of sub-Powellite ideas in the Conservative Party.

Powell (1969): outlines the 'betrayal' and 'alien wedge' theses among other more general points.
Walker (1977), Taylor (1982) and Steed (1978): all useful accounts of the organisation, policies and appeal of the National Front.

Chapter 8

Glazer and Young (1983): worthy illustration of policy analysis-oriented comparative research, containing a thoughful concluding chapter by Young.
Nanton (1989): outlines a number of important questions relating to conceptions of racial categories in public policy.
Saggar (1990): critical review of what is 'wrong' and what is 'right' about recent writing on race within political studies.
Jewson and Mason (1986): overview of three approaches to equal opportunities policy.
Banton (1991): brief discussion of sociological problems in the conceptualisation of race.

Bibliography

Abercrombie, N. and Warde, A. (1988), *Contemporary British Society*, Cambridge: Polity.

Alderman, G. (1989), *London Jewry and London Politics 1889–1986*, London: Routledge.

Anwar, M. (1980), *Votes and Policies: Ethnic minorities and the general election 1979*, London: Commission for Racial Equality.

Anwar, M. (1984), *Ethnic Minorities and the 1983 General Election: A Research Report*, London: Commission for Racial Equality.

Anwar, M. and Kohler, N. (1975), *Participation of Ethnic Minorities in the General Election of October 1974*, London: Community Relations Commission.

Bachrach, P. and Baratz, P. (1970), *Power and Poverty: Theory and practice*, London: Oxford University Press.

Bald, S. (1989), 'The South Asian presence in British electoral politics', *New Community*, 15.4, 537–48.

Ballard, R. and Ballard, C. (1977), 'The Sikhs: the development of South Asian settlements in Britain', in Watson, J. (ed.), *Between Two Cultures: Migrants and minorities in Britain*, Oxford: Blackwell.

Banton, M. (1985), *Promoting Racial Harmony*, Cambridge: Cambridge University Press.

Banton, M. (1987), 'The beginning and the end of the racial issue in British politics', *Policy and Politics*, 15.1, 39–47.

Banton, M. (1991), 'The race relations problematic', *British Journal of Sociology*, 42.1, 116–30.

Barker, M. (1981), *The New Racism*, London: Junction Books.

BBC/Gallup (1979), *General Election Exit Poll*, ESRC Data Archive, University of Essex.

BBC/Gallup (1987), *General Election Exit Poll*, ESRC Data Archive, University of Essex.

Beetham, D. (1970), *Transport and Turbans: A comparative study of local politics*, London: University Press for the Institute of Race Relations.

Behrens, R. and Edmonds, J. (1981), 'Kippers, kittens and kipper boxes: Conservative populists and race relations', *Political Quarterly*, 52, 342–47.

Ben-Tovim, G. and Gabriel, J. (1982), 'The politics of race in Britain, 1962–79: a review of the major trends and of recent debates', in Husbands, C. (ed.), *Race in Britain: Continuity and change*, London: Hutchinson.

Benyon, J. (ed.) (1984), *Scarman and After: Essays reflecting on Lord Scarman's report, the riots and their aftermath*, London: Pergamon.

Benyon, J. and Solomos, J. (1987, eds), *The Roots of Urban Unrest*, Oxford: Pergamon Press.

Bhachu, P. (1985), *Twice Migrants: East African Sikh settlers in Britain*, London: Tavistock.

Bhat, A., Carr-Hill, R. and Ohri, S. (eds) (1988), *Britain's Black Population*, Aldershot: Gower.

Billig, M. and Bell, A. (1980), 'Fascist parties in post-war Britain', *Sage Race Relations Abstracts*, 5.1, 1–30.

Bochel, J. and Denver, D. (1983), 'Candidate selection in the Labour Party: what the selectors seek', *British Journal of Political Science*, 13.1, 45–60.

Bonham-Carter, M. (1987), 'The liberal hour and race relations law', *New Community*, 14, 1–8.

Booth, H. (1988), 'Identifying ethnic origin: the past, present and future of official data production', in Bhat A. *et al.* (eds), *Britain's Black Population*, Aldershot: Gower.

Brierley, P. (1988), 'Religion', in Halsey A. (ed.), *British Social Trends since 1900*, London: Macmillan.

Brown, C. (1984), *Black and White Britain*, London: Policy Studies Institute.

Bulmer, M. (1986), 'A controversial census topic: race and ethnicity in the British Census', *Journal of Official Statistics*, 2.4.

Bulpitt, J. (1986), 'Continuity, autonomy and peripheralisation: the anatomy of the centre's race statecraft in England', in Layton-Henry, Z. and Rich, P. (eds), *Race, Government and Politics in Britain*, London: Macmillan.

Butler, Lord (1971), *The Art of the Possible*, Harmondsworth: Penguin.

Butler, D. and Kavanagh, D. (1974), *The British General Election of February 1974*, London: Macmillan.

Butler, D. and Kavanagh, D. (1975), *The British General Election of October 1974*, London: Macmillan.

Butler, D. and Stokes, D. (1974), *Political Change in Britain*, 2nd edn, London: Macmillan.

Calvocoressi, P. (1968), 'The Official Structure of Conciliation', *Political Quarterly*, 39, 46–53.

Canovan, M. (1990), 'On being economical with the truth: some liberal reflections', *Political Studies*, 38.1, 5–19.

Carlyle, T., *Occasional Discourse on the Nigger Question*, London: Thames Bosworth, 1853.

Carter, R., Harris, C. & Joshi, S. (1987), 'The 1951–55 Conservative Government and the Racialisation of Black Immigration', Policy Papers in Ethnic Relations No. 11, Centre for Research in Ethnic Relations, University of Warwick.

Casey, J. (1982), 'One nation: the politics of race', *The Salisbury Review*, 1, 23–28.

Cashmore, E. and Troyna, B. (1983), *Introduction to Race Relations*, London: Routledge & Kegan Paul.

Central Statistical Office (1987), *Regional Trends*, 22, London: HMSO.

Childs, D. (1986), *Britain Since 1945: A political history*, 2nd edn, London: Routledge.

Cmnd. 2739 (1965), *Immigration from the Commonwealth*, White Paper, Prime Minister's Office, August, London: HMSO.

Community Relations Commission (1975), *Participation of Ethnic Minorities in the General Election of October 1974*, London: Community Relations Committee.

Conservative Central Office (1976), *The Right Approach*, London: Conservative Central Office.

CRE (1984), *Ethnic Minorities and the 1983 General Election: A research report*, London: Commission for Racial Equality.

Crewe, I. (1979), 'The black, brown and green votes', *New Society*, 12 April.

Crewe, I. (1983a), 'Representation and ethnic minorities in Britain', in Glazer, N. and Young, K. (eds), *Ethnic Pluralism and Public Policy: Achieving equality in the United States and Britain*, London: Heinemann.

Crewe, I. (1983b), 'How Labour was trounced all round', *The Guardian*, 14 June.

Crewe, I. (1975, ed.), *The British Political Sociology Yearbook – Volume Two: The Politics of Race*, London: Croom Helm.

Crewe, I., Fox, A. and Alt, J. (1977) 'Partisan dealignment in Britain 1964–74', *British Journal of Political Science*, 7.2, 129–90.

Crossman, R. (1977), *Diaries of a Cabinet Minister*, vol. 2, London: Hamish Hamilton and Jonathan Cape.

Curtice, J. (1983), 'Proportional representation and Britain's ethnic minorities', *Contemporary Affairs Briefing*, 6.2, 2–13.

Curtis, L. (1971), *Apes and Angels: The Irish in Victorian caricature*, Washington, DC: Smithsonian Institute Press.

Deakin, N. (1965), *Colour and the British Electorate*, London: Pall Mall.

Deakin, N. (1968), 'The politics of the Commonwealth Immigrants Bill', *Political Quarterly*, 391, 24–45.

Deakin, N. (1970), *Colour, Citizenship and British Society*, updated and abridged version of Rose 1969, London: Panther.

Deakin, N. and Bourne, J. (1970), 'The minorities and the 1970 General Election', *Race Today*, 2.7, 205–10.

Dearlove, J. and Saunders, P. (1984), *Introduction to British Politics: Analysing a capitalist democracy*, 1st edn, Cambridge: Polity.

Deedes, W. (1968), *Race Without Rancour*, London: Conservative Political Centre.

Denver, D. (1989), *Elections and Voting Behaviour in Britain*, Hemel Hempstead: Philip Allan.

Douglas, J. (1983), 'The Conservative Party: from pragmatism to ideology – and back?', *West European Politics*, 6.4, 71–73.

Downs, A. (1957), *An Economic Theory of Democracy*, New York: Harper & Row.

Dummet, A. and Dummet, M. (1982), 'The role of government in Britain's racial crisis', in Husbands, C. (ed.), *Race in Britain: Continuity and Change*, London: Hutchinson.

Dworkin, R. (1985), *A Matter of Principle*, Cambridge, Mass.: Harvard University Press.

Edwards, J. and Batley, R. (1978), *The Politics of Positive Discrimination: An evaluation of the Urban Programme, 1967–77*, London: Tavistock.

Elton, Lord (1965), *The Unarmed Invasion: A survey of Afro-Asian immigration*, London: Geoffrey Bles Publishers.

Employment Gazette (1991), 'Ethnic origins and the labour market', February.

Ermisch, J. (1990), *Fewer Babies, Longer Lives: Policy implications of current demographic trends*, York: Joseph Rowntree Foundation.

Fielding, N. (1981), *The National Front*, London: Routledge & Kegan Paul.

Finer, S. *et al.* (1961), *Backbench Opinion in the House of Commons 1955–59*, London: Pergamon.

Finnigan, F. (1985), 'The Irish in York', in Swift, R. and Gilley, S. (eds), *The Irish in the Victorian City*, London: Croom Helm.

FitzGerald, M. (1983), 'Are blacks an electoral liability?', *New Society*, 8 December.

FitzGerald, M. (1987), *Political Parties and Black People: representation, participation and exploitation*, 2nd edn, London: Runnymede Trust.

FitzGerald, M. (1988), 'There is no alternative . . . black people and the Labour Party', *Social Studies Review*, 4.1, 20–23.

Foot, P. (1965), *Race and Immigration in British Politics*, London: Penguin.

Freeman, G. (1979), *Immigrant Labor and Racial Conflict in Industrial Societies*, Princeton, NJ: Princeton University Press.

Fryer, P. (1984), *Staying Power: The History of Black People in Britain*, London: Pluto Press.

Gamble, A. (1986), 'The political economy of freedom', in Levitas, R. (ed.), *The Ideology of the New Right*, Cambridge: Polity Press.

Gamble, A. (1988), *The Free Economy and the Strong State: The politics of Thatcherism*, London: Macmillan.

Gartner, L. (1973), *The Jewish Immigrant in England 1870–1914*, London: Simon Publications.

Gilley, S. (1978), 'English attitudes to the Irish in England 1789–1900', in Holmes, C. (ed.), *Immigrants and Minorities in British Society*, London: Allen and Unwin.

Gilroy, P. (1987), *There Ain't No Black in the Union Jack: The cultural politics of race and nation*, London: Hutchinson.

Glazer, N. and Young, K. (eds) (1983), *Ethnic Pluralism and Public Policy: Achieving equality in the United States and Britain*, London: Heinemann.

Gouldbourne, H. (ed.) (1990), *Black Politics in Britain*, Aldershot: Avebury.

Gordon, P. (1990), 'A Dirty War: The New Right and Local Authority Anti-Racism', in Ball, W. and Solomos, J. *Race and Local Politics*, London: Macmillan.

Gordon, P. and Klug, F. (1986), *New Right, New Racism*, London: Searchlight Publications.

Granada Television (1978), Interview with Margaret Thatcher by Gordon Burns, *World in Action*, broadcast 30 January.

Greenleaf, W. (1983), *The British Political Tradition. Volume One: The Rise of Collectivism*, London: Routledge.

Grimsley, M. and Bhat, A. (1988), 'Health', in Bhat A. *et al.* (eds), *Britain's Black Population*, Aldershot: Gower.

Günther, H. (1970), *The Racial Elements of European History*, New York: Kennikat Press.

Hall, S., Critcher, C., Jefferson, T., Clarke, J. and Roberts, B. (1978), *Policing the Crisis: Mugging, the state, and law and order*, London: Macmillan.

Harris Research Centre (1983), 'National election issues – Asians and Afro-Caribbeans', conducted for *London Weekend Television*/'Eastern Eye' and 'Black-on-Black', unpublished data set JN49913, Richmond: The Harris Research Centre.

Harris Research Centre (1987), 'Political attitudes among ethnic minorities', conducted for *The Caribbean/African/Asian Times*, unpublished data set JN98746, Richmond: The Harris Research Centre.

Harris Research Centre (1991), 'Asian poll 1991', conducted for *BBC Pebble Mill*/'East', unpublished data set JN99245, Richmond: The Harris Research Centre.

Harrop, M. and Zimmerman, G. (1977), 'The anatomy of the National Front', *Patterns of Prejudice*, 11, 12.

Harrop, M., England, J. and Husbands, C. (1980), 'The bases of National Front support', *Political Studies*, 28.2, 271–83.

Haskey, J. (1990), 'The ethnic minority population of Great Britain: estimates by ethnic group and country of birth', *Population Trends*, 60, 35–38.

Heath, A. *et al.* (1991), *Understanding Political Change: The British voter 1964–87*, Oxford: Pergamon Press.

Heinemann, B. (1972), *The Politics of the Powerless: A study of the Campaign Against Racial Discrimination*, London: Oxford University Press for the Institute of Race Relations.

Hill, M. and Issacharoff, R. (1971), *Community Action and Race Relations: A study of community relations councils in Britain*, London: Oxford University Press for the Institute of Race Relations.

Hindell, K. (1965), 'The genesis of the Race Relations Bill', *Political Quarterly*, 36, 390–406.

Hiro, D. (1971), *Black British, White British*, London: Eyre and Spottiswoode.

Holmes, C. (1979), *Anti-Semitism in British Society 1876–1939*, London: Edward Arnold.

Holmes, J. (1988), *John Bull's Island*, London: Routledge.

Honeyford, R. (1983), 'Multi-ethnic intolerance', *The Salisbury Review*, 4, 12–13.

Honeyford, R. (1984), 'Education and race – an alternative view', *The Salisbury Review*, 6, 30–32.

Husbands, C. (1979), 'The "threat" hypothesis and racist voting in England and the United States', in Miles, R. and Phizacklea, A. (eds), *Racism and Political Action in Britain*, London: Routledge & Kegan Paul.

Husbands, C. (1983), *Racial Exclusionism and the City: The urban support of the National Front*, London: Allen & Unwin.

Jackson, J. (1963), *The Irish in Britain*, London: Routledge.

James, C.L.R. (1938), *Black Jacobins*, London: Secker and Warburg.

Jenkins, R. (1966), Transcript of speech to the National Committee for Commonwealth Immigrants, 23 May, London: National Committee for Commonwealth Immigrants.

Jenkins, R. and Solomos, J. (eds) (1987), *Racism and Equal Opportunity Policies in the 1980s*, Cambridge: University Press.

Jenkins, S. (1971), *Here to Live: A study of Race Relations in an English City*, London: Runnymede Trust.

Jessop, R. *et al.* (1988), *Thatcherism: A tale of two nations*, Cambridge: Polity Press.

Jewson, N. and Mason, D. (1986), 'The theory and practice of equal opportunities policies: liberal and radical approaches', *Sociological Review*, 34.2, 307–34.

John, D. (1969), *Indian Workers Associations in Great Britain*, London: Oxford University Press for the Institute of Race Relations.

Jones, G. (1980), *Social Darwinism in English Thought: The interaction between biological and social theory*, Brighton: Harvester Press.

Jones, P. (1990), 'Respecting beliefs and rebuking Rushdie', *British Journal of Political Science*, 20.4, 415–37.

Katznelson, I. (1973), *Black Men, White Cities: Race relations and migration in the United States 1900–30 and Britain 1948–68*, London: Oxford University Press for the Institute of Race Relations.

Kavanagh, D. (1990), *British Politics: Continuities and change*, Oxford: Oxford University Press.

Kirp, D. (1979), *Doing Good by Doing Little*, London: University of California Press.

Kosmin, B. and Grizzard, N. (1975), *Geographical Distribution Estimates of Ethnically Jewish Population of the UK 1974*, London: Board of Deputies of British Jews.

Kushner, A. (1986), 'British anti-Semitism in the Second World War', unpublished PhD thesis, University of Sheffield.

Labour Party (1972), *Citizenship, Immigration and Integration: A policy for the seventies*, London: Labour Party.

Labour Party (1980), *Labour and the Black Electorate*, London: Labour Party.

Labour Party (1985), *Report of the Annual Conference of the Labour Party*, London: Labour Party.

Labour Party Race Action Group (1979), *Don't Take Black Votes for Granted*, London: Labour Party.

Lansley, S., Goss, S. and Wolmar, C. (1989), *Councils in Conflict: The rise and fall of the municipal Left*, London: Macmillan.

Lawrence, D. (1974), *Black Migrants, White Natives: A study of race relations in Nottingham*, Cambridge: Cambridge University Press.

Layton-Henry, Z. (1978), 'Race, electoral strategy and the major parties', *Parliamentary Affairs*, 31.3, 268–81.

Layton-Henry, Z. (1983), 'The importance of the black electorate', *Shakti*, 2.8, 13–16.

Layton-Henry, Z. (1984), *The Politics of Race in Britain*, London: Allen & Unwin.

Layton-Henry, Z. and Rich, P. (eds) (1986), *Race, Government and Politics in Britain*, London: Macmillan.

Layton-Henry, Z. and Studlar, D. (1985), 'The electoral participation of black and Asian Britons: integration or alienation?', *Parliamentary Affairs*, 38, 307–18.

Lees, L. (1978), *Exiles in Erin: Irish migrants in Victorian London*, Manchester: University Press.

Le Lohé, M. (1975), 'Participation in Elections by Asians in Bradford', in Crewe, I. (ed.) (1975), *The British Political Sociology Yearbook – Volume Two : The Politics of Race*, London: Croom Helm.

Le Lohé, M. (1983), 'Voter discrimination against Asian and black candidates in the 1983 General Election', *New Community*, 11.1/2, 101–84.

Le Lohé, M. (1989), 'The performance of Asian and black candidates in the British General Election of 1987', *New Community*, 15.2, 159–70

Levin, B. (1978), *The Times*, 14 February.

Levitas, R. (ed.) (1986), *The Ideology of the New Right*, Cambridge: Polity Press.

Lipsey, D. (1983), 'Why Labour lost ground', *The Sunday Times*, 12 June.

Little, A. and Robbins, D. (1983), *Loading the Law: A study of transmitted deprivation, ethnic minorities and affirmative action*, London: Commission for Racial Equality.

Little, K. (1947), *Negroes in Britain*, London: Kegan Paul.

Lúkas, G. (1980), *The Destruction of Reason*, London: The Merlin Press.

Luthera, M. (1988), 'Race, community, housing and the state – a historical overview', in Bhat, A. *et al.* (eds), *Britain's Black Population*, Aldershot: Gower.

McAllister, I. and Studlar, D. (1984), 'The electoral geography of immigrant groups in Britain', *Electoral Studies*, 3, 139–50.

Macdonald, I. (1983), *Immigration Law and Practice in the United Kingdom*, London: Butterworths.

McKay, D. and Cox, A. (1979), *The Politics of Urban Change*, London: Croom Helm.

Mackenzie, J. (1984), *Propaganda and Empire: The manipulation of British public opinion, 1880–1960*, Manchester: Manchester University Press.

McKenzie, R. and Silver, A. (1968), *Angels in Marble: Working class Conservatives in urban England*, London: Heinemann.

Macmillan, H. (1973), *At the End of the Day*, London: Macmillan.

Mendus, S. (1989), *Toleration and the Limits of Liberalism*, London: Macmillan.

Messina, A. (1985), 'Race and party competition in Britain', *Parliamentary Affairs*, 38.4, 423–36.

Messina, A. (1989), *Race and Party Competition in Britain*, Oxford: Clarendon Press.

Messina, A. (1990), 'Political impediments to the resumption of labour migration to western Europe', *West European Politics*, 13.1, 31–46.

Miles, R. (1982), *Racism and Migrant Labour*, London: Routledge & Kegan Paul.

Miles, R. (1989), *Racism*, London: Routledge.

Miles, R. (1990), 'The racialisation of British politics', *Political Studies*, 38.2, 277–85.

Miles, R. and Phizacklea, A. (1977), 'Class, race, ethnicity and political action', *Political Studies*, 25.4, 491–508.

Miles, R. and Phizacklea, A. (1984), *White Man's Country: Racism in British politics*, 1st edn, London: Pluto Press.

Mill, J.S. (1850), 'The Nigger Question', *Fraser's Magazine*, January 1850.

Miller, W. (1980), 'What was the profit in following the crowd?: aspects of Conservative and Labour strategy since 1970', *British Journal of Political Science*, 10.1, 15–38.

Modood T. (1988), ' "Black", racial equality and Asian identity', *New Community*, 14.3, 397–404.

Moran, M. (1989), *Politics and Society in Britain*, 2nd edn, Basingstoke: Macmillan.

Mosse, G. (1978), *Toward the Final Solution: A History of European Racism*, London: Dent and Sons.

Mukherjee, T. (1982), 'Sri Guru Singh Sabha: Southall', in Ohri, A. (ed.), *Community Work and Racism*, London: Routledge and Kegan Paul for the Association of Community Workers.

Myrdal, G. (1944), *An American Dilemma: The Negro problem and modern democracy*, New York: Harper.

Nandy, D. (1967), 'An illusion of competence', in Deakin, N. and Lester, A. (eds), *Policies for Racial Equality*, Fabian Research Series 262, London: Fabian Society.

Nanton, P. (1989), 'The new orthodoxy: racial categories and equal opportunity policy', *New Community*, 15.4, 549–64.

Nanton, P. and FitzGerald, M. (1990), 'Race policies in local government: boundaries or thresholds?', in Ball, W. and Solomos, J. (eds), *The Local Politics of Race*, Basingstoke: Macmillan.

Nietzsche, F. (1973), *Beyond Good and Evil*, Penguin: Harmondsworth.

NOP (1978), 'Immigration and race relations', *Political, Social and Economic Review*, No. 14.

Nugent, N. and King, R. (1977), *The British Right: Conservative and right-wing politics in Britain*, London: Saxon House.

Nugent, N. and King, R. (1979), 'Ethnic minorities, scapegoating and the extreme right', in Miles, R. and Phizacklea, A. (eds), *Racism and Political Action in Britain*, London: Routledge & Kegan Paul.

Omi, M. and Winant, H. (1986), *Racial Formation in the United States*, London: Routledge.

OPCS and Registrar General of Scotland (1983), *Census 1981: Country of Birth, Great Britain*, London: HMSO.

Parekh, B. (1986), 'The "New Right" and the politics of nationhood', in The Runnymede Trust, *The New Right: Image and reality*, London: The Runnymede Trust.

Parekh, B. (ed.) (1990), *Law, Blasphemy and the Multi-Faith Society*, London: Commission for Racial Equality.

Peach, C. (1984), 'The force of West Indian island identity in Britain', in Clarke, C. *et al.* (eds), *Geography and Ethnic Pluralism*, London: George Allen & Unwin.

Peach, C. (1986), 'Patterns of Afro-Caribbean migration and settlement in Great Britain: 1945–81', in Brock, C. (ed.), *The Caribbean in Europe*, London: Frank Cass.

PEP (1967), *Racial Discrimination*, London: Political and Economic Planning.

Phizacklea, A. and Miles, A. (1979), (eds), *Racism and Political Action in Britain*, London: Routledge & Kegan Paul.

Phizacklea, A. and Miles, A. (1980), *Labour and Racism*, London: Routledge.

Pilkington, E. (1988), *Beyond the Mother Country: West Indians and the Notting Hill white riots*, London: I.B. Tauris.

Pollins, H. (1982), *Economic History of the Jews in England*, London: Associated University Presses.

Powell, J.E. (1981), Transcript of speech delivered to the Thurrock Conservative Association on 30 October 1981.

Powell, J.E. (1969), *Freedom and Reality*, Kingswood: Elliot Right Way Books.

Ramdin, R. (1987), *The Making of the Black Working Class in Britain*, Aldershot: Gower.

Rath, J. and Saggar, S. (1990), 'Ethnicity as a political tool in Britain and the Netherlands', in Messina A. *et al.* (eds), *Ethnic and Racial Minorities in Advanced Industrial Societies*, New York: Greenwood Press.

Rex, J. (1968), 'The Race Relations Catastrophe' in Burgess, T. (ed.), *Matters of Principle: Labour's Last Chance*, Harmondsworth: Penguin.

Rex, J. (1979), 'Black militancy and class conflict', in Miles, R. and Phizacklea, A. (eds), *Racism and Political Action in Britain*, London: Routledge & Kegan Paul.

Rex, J. and Mason, D. (eds) (1986), *Theories of Race and Ethnic Relations*, Cambridge: Cambridge University Press.

Rex, J. and Moore, R. (1967), *Race, Community and Conflict: A study of Sparkbrook*, London: Oxford University Press for the Institute of Race Relations.

Rex, J. and Tomlinson, S. (1979), *Colonial Immigrants in a British City: A class analysis*, London: Routledge & Kegan Paul.

Rich, P. (1986a), 'Conservative ideology and race in modern British politics', in Layton-Henry, Z. and Rich, P. (eds), *Race, Government and Politics in Britain*, London: Macmillan.

Rich, P. (1986b), *Race and Empire in British Politics*, Cambridge: Cambridge University Press.

Roberts, H. (1984), *Black Sections and the Labour Party*, London: Ernest Bevin Society.

Robinson, C. (1983), *Black Marxism*, London: Zed Books.

Robinson, V. (1986), *Transients, Settlers and Refugees: Asians in Britain*, Oxford: Clarendon Press.

Robinson, V. (1990a), 'Roots to mobility: the social mobility of Britain's black population, 1971–87', *Ethnic and Racial Studies*, 13.2, 274–86.

Robinson, V. (1990b), 'Boom and gloom: the success and failure of Britain's South Asians', in Clarke, C. *et al.* (eds), *South Asian Communities Overseas*, Cambridge: Cambridge University Press.

Rose, E.J.B. *et al.* (1969), *Colour and Citizenship: A report on British race relations*, London: Oxford University Press for the Institute of Race Relations.

Saggar, S. (1984), 'Britain's ethnic minorities and the 1983 general election: an analysis', unpublished dissertation, Department of Government, University of Essex.

Saggar, S. (1986), 'The 1983 Labour Force Survey and Britain's "Asian" population', *New Community*, 12.3, 418–29.

Saggar, S. (1987a), 'The 1984 Labour Force Survey and Britain "Asian" population', *New Community*, 13.3, 395–411.

Saggar, S. (1987b), 'The rediscovery of race in London: developments in local government in the 1980s', unpublished paper presented to the annual conference of the Political Studies Association of the United Kingdom, University of Aberdeen, April.

Saggar, S. (1988), 'Race and politics: a critical review of the literature', *Liverpool Papers in Politics*, No. 24.

Saggar, S. (1990), 'Discovering and rediscovering race', *Parliamentary Affairs*, 43, 392–94.

Saggar, S. (1991a), *Race and Public Policy: A study of local politics and government*, Aldershot: Avebury.

Saggar, S. (1991b), 'The changing agenda of race issues in local government: the case of a London borough', *Political Studies*, 24.1, 100–21.

Saggar, S. (1991c), 'Race and politics', in Hawkesworth, M. and Kogan, M. (eds), *Routledge Encyclopaedia of Government and Politics*, London: Routledge.

Saggar, S. (1992b), 'The Multiracial City: London', in Parsons, D.W. and Cope, D., *World Cities: London*, Tokyo: National Institute for Research Advancement.

Saggar, S. and Rhodes, R.A.W. (1988), 'The ethnic minority population in Essex county: a study of quantitative data sources', *Essex Papers in Politics and Government*, No.50.

Sarlvik, B. and Crewe, I. (1983), *Decade of Dealignment*, Cambridge: Cambridge University Press.

Scharf, A. (1964), *The British Press and Jews under Nazi rule*, London: Oxford University Press for the Institute of Race Relations.

Schoen, D. (1977), *Enoch Powell and the Powellites*, London: Macmillan.

Scruton, R. (1984a), 'A socialist evil to rival racism', *The Times*, 28 February.

Scruton, R. (1984b), 'Who are the real racists?', *The Times*, 30 October.

Seidel, G. (1986), 'Culture, nation and "race" in the British and French New Right', in Levitas, R. (ed.), *The Ideology of the New Right*, Cambridge: Polity Press.

Seldon, A. (1989), 'The Churchill administration, 1951–55', in Hennessy, P. and Seldon, A. (eds), *Ruling Performance: British governments from Attlee to Thatcher*, Oxford: Blackwell.

Sherman, A. (1973), *Island Refuge: Britain and refugees from the Third Reich*, London: Paul Elek.

Shyllon, F. (1974), *Black Slaves in Britain*, London: Oxford University Press.

Smith, S. (1989), *The Politics of 'Race' and Residence: Citizenship, segregation and white supremacy in Britain*, Oxford: Polity Press.

Smithies, B. and Fiddick, P. (eds) (1969), *Enoch Powell on Immigration*, London: Sphere.

Solomos, J. (1986), 'Trends in the political analysis of racism', *Political Studies*, 34.2, 313–24.

Solomos, J. (1989), *Race and Racism in Contemporary Britain*, London: Macmillan.

Southall Rights/CARF (1981), *Southall: Birth of a black community*, London: Southall Rights and Campaign Against Racism and Fascism.

Steed, M. (1978), 'The National Front vote', *Parliamentary Affairs*, 31.3, 282–93.

Stoker, G. (1988), *The Politics of Local Government*, Basingstoke: Macmillan.

Street, H. *et al.* (1967), *Anti-Discrimination Legislation: The Street Report*, London: Political and Economic Planning.

Studlar, D. (1974), 'British public opinion, colour issues and Enoch Powell: a longitudinal analysis', *British Journal of Political Science*, 4, 371–81.

Studlar, D. (1978), 'Policy voting in Britain: the coloured immigration issue in the 1964, 1966 and 1970 general elections', *American Political Science Review*, 72, 46–72.

Studlar, D. (1983), 'The Ethnic Vote, 1983: Problems of Analysis and Interpretation', *New Community*, 11. 1–2, 92–100.

Studlar, D. (1985), ' "Waiting for the catastrophe": race and the political agenda in Britain', *Patterns of Prejudice*, 19.1, 3–15.

Studlar, D. (1986), 'Non-white policy preferences, political participation and the political agenda in Britain', in Layton-Henry, Z. and Rich, P. (eds), *Race, Government and Politics in Britain*, London: Macmillan.

Studlar, D. and Layton-Henry, Z. (1990), 'Non-white minority access to the political agenda in Britain', *Policy Studies Review*, 9.2, 273–93.

Studlar, D. and McAllister, I., 'The electoral geography of immigrant groups in Britain', *Electoral Studies*, 3, (1984), 139–50.

Sutcliffe, D. (1982), *British Black English*, Oxford: Blackwell.

Taylor, S. (1979), 'The National Front: anatomy of a politial movement', in Miles, R. and Phizacklea, A. (eds), *Racism and Political Action in Britain*, London: Routledge & Kegan Paul.

Taylor, S. (1982), *The National Front in English Politics*, London: Macmillan.

Thurlow, R. (1975), 'National Front ideology', *Patterns of Prejudice*, 9.1, 1–9.

Vaughan, D. (1950), *Negro Victory*, London: Independent Press.

Walker, M. (1977), *The National Front*, London: Fontana.

Walvin, J. (1973), *Black and White: The Negro in British Society*, London: Allen & Unwin.

Walvin, J. (1982), (ed.), *Slavery and British Society, 1776–1846*, London: Macmillan.

Walvin, J. (1984), *Passage to Britain*, Harmondsworth: Penguin.

White, P. (1990), 'A question on ethnic group for the census: findings from the 1989 census test post-enumeration survey', *Population Trends*, 59, 11–20.

Whiteley, P. (1983), *The Labour Party in Crisis*, London: Methuen.

Widgery, D. (1986), *Beating Time*, London: Chatto & Windus.

Williams, E. (1944), *Capitalism and Slavery*, Chapel Hill: University of North Carolina.

Young, G. (1969), *Who Goes Home?*, London: The Monday Club.

Young, K. (1983), 'Ethnic pluralism and the policy agenda in Britain', in Young, K. and Glazer, N. (eds), *Ethnic Pluralism and Public Policy: Achieving equality in the United States and Britain*, London: Heinemann.

Young, K. and Connelly, N. (1981), *Policy and Practice in the Multi-Racial City*, London: Policy Studies Institute.

Young, K. and Glazer, N. (eds) (1983), *Ethnic Pluralism and Public Policy: Achieving equality in the United States and Britain*, London: Heinemann.

Addendum to Chapter 3

Developments during late 1991 at the Office of Population Censuses and Surveys regarding the technical input of Census data resulted in a delay in the publication of findings. The OPCS Census Division therefore decided to announce in December 1991 that the publication of county-wide and aggregated national results had been put back. The upshot of this development was that the findings of the 1991 Census, which were originally planned to be included in this volume, will not be available until autumn 1992 at the earliest. Whilst this news comes as a disappointment particularly among close census-watchers, it need not necessarily detract from the main thrust of the empirical material and conclusions drawn in Chapter 3.

Moreover, as the findings of the 1988 and 1989 Labour Force Surveys have been recently published, it is still possible to provide a reasonably up-to-date picture of the black population in Britain. According to the December 1991 issue of the OPCS' *Census Monitor*, the 1989–90 LFS results showed there to be some 2.6 million people of ethnic minority origin resident in Britain. Ethnic minorities therefore constitute around 4.5 per cent of the national population which, if directly compared with the 1981 Census findings, shows there to have been a proportionate rise of just over a sixth (from 3.8 to 4.5 per cent of the population of Great Britain). The ethnic minority population included 0.5 million of West Indian ethnic origin and 1.3 million of South Asian ethnic origin.

Index